100 Questions and Answers

Financial Accounting

Second Edition

Prepared by

CHART FOULKS LYNCH

HOLT, RINEHART AND WINSTON
LONDON · NEW YORK · SYDNEY · TORONTO

Holt, Rinehart and Winston Ltd: 1 St Anne's Road,
Eastbourne, East Sussex BN21 3UN

British Library Cataloguing in Publication Data
Financial accounting.—2nd ed.—(100
   questions and answers)
   1. Accounting—Problems, exercises, etc.
   I. Chart Foulks Lynch   II. Series
   657'.48'076   HF5661

ISBN: 0-03-910695-0

First published 1983
Second edition 1986

Printed in Great Britain by A. Wheaton & Co. Ltd., Exeter

Copyright © 1983, 1986 by Holt, Rinehart and Winston Ltd.

All rights reserved. This book is protected by copyright. No part of it may be reproduced, stored in a retrieval system, or transmitted in any form or by any means, electronic, mechanical, photocopying or otherwise, without written permission from the publisher.

Last digit is print no: 9 8 7 6 5 4 3 2 1

FINANCIAL ACCOUNTING

ACKNOWLEDGEMENTS

We wish to thank the following bodies for permission to use questions from their examination papers:

Institute of Chartered Accountants in England and Wales
Chartered Association of Certified Accountants
Institute of Cost and Management Accountants

INTRODUCTION

A book full of questions and answers could be the single most important purchase that you as a student make in preparing for your examination.

Having experienced similar questions before sitting down to the real thing will give you a tremendous advantage. Having actually answered say, fifty questions on the same topics as those to be examined must give you a good chance of meeting the ambiguities, peculiarities of terminology and downright catches that crop up in any paper.

In this book we have drawn questions from the main accounting bodies but we have not individually identified them as to source or date. The reasons we hope are obvious. Almost all the questions could have been posed by any of the accounting bodies concerned—standards are very similar and style and emphasis vary only slightly. Also, due to changing legislation we have adapted many questions to cater for the *Finance Act 1985* and *Companies Act 1985*, for instance, and it would not be fair to attribute credit or blame in these circumstances.

Dates can be misleading as students try to discern trends. These trends can best be identified from the students' own magazines, newsletters and journals. The questions we have selected generally will be examined, albeit in some disguise, on many future occasions.

The book itself is divided into main subject areas to help you select relevant questions. If you have time, treat it as a workbook—if not, use it as a final topping-up exercise.

We hope it helps to bring you examination success.

EXAMINATION TECHNIQUE

Sensible preparation and excellent examination technique will help you succeed in (if not enjoy) your forthcoming examinations.

Contained in the following few pages are some guidelines to smooth your path through the fast approaching ordeal.

Part 1—The Build-up

This vital time must concentrate on full and structured revision. There is no escape from hard work, but for optimum benefit there are some rules:

Plan your revision time

(a) Write down your revision plan, giving yourself plenty of time to revise each subject in full.
(b) Don't concentrate so much on your weak subjects that you ignore your strong ones.
(c) Do lots of questions against the clock to build up your speed. A very large proportion of candidates who fail an exam do so because they run out of time, not because they lack the basic knowledge.

Plan your leisure also

(a) Work done after midnight or when you are tired is counterproductive. You will not be able to concentrate and you will make mistakes.
(b) If you have time off work to study, try to keep to roughly similar office hours plus say 7.00–9.00 in the evening. Work Saturdays but have a break on Sunday.

Stick to your plan

(a) Despite your plan there is a great temptation to spend too much time on one subject. Don't.
(b) Beware the dreaded tipsters. Tipsters don't know, they can only guess, and with a wide syllabus, concentrating on one or two topics is very dangerous.

The day before

(a) Relax as much as possible. If you haven't done enough work by now you won't have enough time to make up the difference. The only work you must do is ensuring you know where and when you are taking the exams and checking train and bus timetables to ensure you get there in good time.

(b) Do what you like doing—play the harp, pore over your stamp collection. If your hobby is drinking, *don't*.
(c) Overhaul your equipment. New calculator batteries and some spares, plenty of sharp pencils and full pens, are all essential.
(d) Go to bed early.

The aim is to rest so that you are on top form next morning. You will appreciate this when you turn up at the examination hall and encounter in the foyer the haggard faced and bleary eyed who are frantically borrowing pencil sharpeners. If they are tired before they start, think what they will feel like after the first two papers.

Part 2—In the Examination Room

This is the point at which you undergo a metamorphosis into a ruthless 'mark grubber'. Any examiner's report invariably will refer to at least half of the points listed below, and students, when reading of such basic errors, vow that they would never have been so stupid. This vow generally lasts until the moment they enter the examination room!

Attend to detail

'Topping and tailing' should be practised on all possible occasions. Underlining headings, using £ signs, dates and so on, all help to pick up any presentation and discretion marks available.

Don't annoy the examiner

Submit your questions in the right order. Don't use words like 'obviously' and 'of course' too often. Don't be critical of any specific question or the paper in general.

Examiners are only human (we think) and such behaviour is bound to upset them. You cannot afford to waste even half a mark when your career is at stake, so play the game by their rules and change the system afterwards if you feel strongly about it.

Workings

Refer specifically to workings and put them in order, clearly labelled. Don't allow the examiner merely to stumble on them by accident.

Remember, random jottings around a page will not attract as many marks as a carefully sequenced set of workings, even if the same information is present. You will be expected to order your thoughts and present information/reports when qualified, so the examiners have a right to expect similar treatment now.

Examination Technique

Answer the question

There are many faults under this heading:
  (i) Overkill—seeing a particular word in the question and writing all there is to know about that subject. It may have nothing much to do with the real question you have been asked.
  (ii) Woods and trees—being unable to identify the major mark-carrying areas, or possibly devoting fifteen minutes to part (c) of a question carrying only 3 marks while writing only a few lines on part (a) carrying, say, 12 marks.
  (iii) Not reading the question. A question may ask for a report or a letter, but some students nevertheless steadfastly produce essays or lists or anything but the required format.
  (iv) Rewriting the question! Many students believe (mistakenly) that they can, in effect, alter the emphasis of a question, or even change it completely. Only answer the specific question set.

What I meant to say was ...

You cannot stand at the examiner's shoulder and explain the real meaning of your script or terminology. Say what you mean and leave nothing to chance. Communication is a two way process. You have first to absorb and understand what is being asked. But having got the message you must then formulate your answer in as understandable a way as possible. Both parts are equally fundamental.

Arrange your answer in a logical sequence

Spending a few moments jotting down the main points of your answer and assembling them in a logical order will pay handsome dividends. After all, jottings on a narrative question are the equivalent of ordinary figure workings for a computational problem.

Treat the examiner as an intelligent layman

You must not assume the examiner knows certain things. He probably does, but you haven't proved to him that you do if you leave such matters out altogether.
  You will probably feel less self-conscious in explaining carefully the way in which a bad debts account works if you assume that the examiner is an intelligent layman.
  But, remember also that, since the examiner is most definitely not a layman, he will not tolerate wrong statements. Don't bluff!

Use of abbreviations

Using abbreviations like confetti can cause problems, particularly where non-standard abbreviations are thrown in for good measure. CCA,

I/REV, MCT, SSAP are acceptable (but not many people know that G.I.N. means goods inwards note).

If you do use initials, always put the full meaning in on the first occasion (followed by its abbreviation).

Check whether answer is reasonable

Whenever you produce an answer to a computational question spend a few seconds asking yourself whether the solution arrived at is sensible. It is so easy to press the wrong calculator button and you must give yourself every chance of picking up these silly errors.

Answer all questions

You have 180 minutes to try for 100 marks and therefore can allocate 1.8 minutes for each mark on the paper.

Don't overrun your time on each question as you are far more likely to pick up the first five marks of a new question than the last five marks of an earlier one.

1. Don't panic—two or three deep breaths as soon as you sit down will help calm you.

   Try to ensure you are not caught out by some unexpected event. To this end find out what types of examination paper are used and check which rates and allowances you are to be provided with.

2. You are only trying to pass the paper, not (necessarily) achieve 100%. There *will* be things you don't know so don't leave the examination room after the first exam in a black depression simply because you failed to deal fully with parts 3(a) and 4(c) of a paper.

3. Remember the three R's. Perhaps the best piece of advice we can give is to obey the three *R*'s *in the following order*:
   Read
   Reflect
   Write!

Good luck with your examinations.

CONTENTS

Questions A1–A9	*Theoretical accounting*		2–5
Answers A1–A9			104–121
Questions B1–B11	*Standard applications of accounting theory*		6–14
Answers B1–B11			122–144
Questions C1–C10	*Legislative effects on accounts*		14–22
Answers C1–C10			144–164
Questions D1–D2	*The Stock Exchange*		22
Answers D1–D2			164–166
Questions E1–E8	*Accounting standards*		23–29
Answers E1–E8			166–179
Questions F1–F4	*Company capital*		29–32
Answers F1–F4			179–187
Questions G1–G3	*Structure and reorganization*		32–37
Answers G1–G3			188–195
Questions H1–H3	*Group accounts*		37–41
Answers H1–H3			196–207
Questions J1–J12	*Group accounts*		42–52
Answers J1–J12			207–251
Questions K1–K5	*Group accounts*		53–57
Answers K1–K5			251–264
Questions L1–L4	*Partnership accounts*		57–64
Answers L1–L4			264–279
Questions M1–M3	*Joint ventures*		64–67
Answers M1–M3			279–287
Questions N1–N3	*Incomplete records*		67–71
Answers N1–N3			287–298
Questions P1–P5	*Branch accounts*		71–77
Answers P1–P5			299–312
Questions R1–R5	*Hire purchase*		77–82
Answers R1–R5			313–327

Questions S1–S3	*Miscellaneous accounts*	82–84
Answers S1–S3		328–332
Questions T1–T6	*Source and application of funds;*	84–94
Answers T1–T6	*Analysis of accounts*	333–352
Questions U1–U4	*SSAP 16: current cost accounting*	94–101
Answers U1–U4		352–367
Index		369–370

? Questions

QUESTION A1

You meet John Pound in the pub; he has a small garage business and his accountant has just finished preparing accounts for his first year of trading. He says that he cannot understand all the fuss made about balance sheets and accounts because all that really matters is how much profit you make and how much money there is in the bank.

Required:

(a) a list of those likely to use John Pound's accounts;
(5 marks)
(b) a discussion of the reasons for preparing a balance sheet;
(15 marks)
(c) a discussion of John's comments that 'all that really matters is ... how much money there is in the bank'.
(5 marks)
(Total 25 marks)

QUESTION A2

'The fault of the conventional system of accounting lies in the failure to differentiate between records of fact and assessments of value. Consequently, it is impossible to distinguish between the results of actual events and the effects of accounting procedures.'

Evaluate the proposal that the conventional financial statements should be replaced by a system of reporting past and future cash flows.
(17 marks)

QUESTION A3

(a) State, and briefly evaluate, the advantages and disadvantages of exit value accounting.
(9 marks)
(b) Explain, using a simple illustration, the effect on reported profits, and the meaning thereof, of valuing the stocks and work-in-progress of a manufacturing business at current exit values.
(8 marks)
(Total 17 marks)

QUESTION A4

Who uses accounts? Do their needs vary with the size of the concern?
(20 marks)

Financial Accounting

QUESTION A5

(a) You are required to describe your understanding of the term 'value added' as used in accounting.

(*3 marks*)

(b) Using the following summarised information prepare:
   (i) a conventional profit statement of a company, and
   (ii) a value added statement.

Summarised information for XYZ Ltd, in respect of the year ended 31 December 19–9:

	£000
Salaries and wages	200
Purchased materials used in production	300
Sales	740
Corporation tax on the profit for the year	60
Dividend proposed	24
Services purchased	60
Depreciation of fixed assets	40
Loan interest paid and payable	20

(iii) There is an alternative view on the treatment of depreciation in value added statements. What is this view and how would it affect the statement you have produced in answer to question (b) (ii)?

(*6 marks*)

(c) What advantages are claimed for including a value added statement in a company's corporate report?

(*4 marks*)

(*Total 13 marks*)

QUESTION A6

(a) What is a holding gain? Explain the appropriate accounting treatment for such a gain.

(*8 marks*)

(b) How does backlog depreciation arise?

(*5 marks*)

(c) 'Provision for depreciation of fixed assets having a finite useful life should be made by allocating the cost (or revalued amount) less estimated residual values of the assets as fairly as possible to the periods expected to benefit from their use.'

(*SSAP 12*)

To what extent do you consider that the replacement cost treatment of depreciation conforms to this intention?

(*6 marks*)

(d) The following extract is taken from the historical cost balance sheet of Rochester Enterprises Ltd:

	31 Dec. 19–8 £000	31 Dec. 19–9 £000
Plant and machinery at cost	200	300
Less aggregate depreciation	40	100
Net book value	160	200

The following facts are relevant:

(i) Plant costing £200,000 was acquired on 1 Jan. 19–8. The additional items were acquired on 1 Jan. 19–9.
(ii) No plant or machinery was sold or scrapped during 19–8 or 19–9.
(iii) Of the year's depreciation written off in the 19–9 accounts, one-third is related to the items acquired on 1 Jan. 19–9.
(iv) Price index movements were as follows:

	General price index	Index of plant costs for the type of plant owned by Rochester
1 Jan. 19–8	90	80
31 Dec. 19–8	120	100
31 Dec. 19–9	140	110

Your are required to show the entries for plant and machinery in the final accounts of Rochester Enterprises Ltd as at 31 Dec. 19–8 and 19–9, on the assumption that the company used a system of replacement cost accounting making a charge for depreciation based on the relevant index at year end.

(8 marks)
(Total 27 marks)

QUESTION A7. BURBAGE LTD

Burbage Ltd is a retailing business which sells small electric motors. 1,000 motors are purchased on 2.2.–6 at a cost of £4,000. The company sells 200 motors on 20.2.–6 for proceeds of £6 per unit. At this date the replacement cost of each motor had increased to £4.50 per unit.

The company sold a further 500 motors on 29.6.–6 for proceeds of £6.50 per unit when the replacement cost of each motor was £5.25 per unit.

You are required to:
(a) Calculate gross profit on a historical cost basis, for the six months ended 30 Jun. 19–6.
(b) Calculate the effect of adopting a replacement cost basis, distinguishing between the different types of gains.
(c) Comment on the difference between the two sets of figures.

(20 marks)

Financial Accounting

QUESTION A8

'The basic objective of current cost accounts is to provide more useful information than that available from historical cost accounts alone for the guidance of the management of the bunsiness, the shareholders and others ...'.

(SSAP 16, para. 5)

Discuss in what ways, and to what extent, you think it succeeds.

(20 marks)

QUESTION A9. SPARROW LTD

Sparrow Ltd has been approached by its bankers to ascertain the requirements for overdraft facilities during the six months to 30 Sep. 19–7. You are given the following information:

(1) Sales in Feb. and Mar. were £20,000 and £24,000 respectively and a growth of £4,000 per month is predicted for the foreseeable future.
(2) The following expenses are estimated:
Wages £3,000 per month
Administration £1,000 per month
Rent £5,000 per year to 31 Mar. 19–8 (to be paid in Apr. 19–7).
(3) On 1 Apr. 19–7 a leasehold property is to be purchased for £25,000; the lease will expire in ten years time. (You can assume that there are no other fixed assets.)
(4) The company makes an average 25% gross profit on sales before deducting wages and plans to have sufficient stock at the end of each month to cover the next two months' sales; this was the case on 31 Mar. 19–7 when the stock was £45,000.
(5) All sales are on credit and debtors take an average of two months' credit. Trade creditors are paid in the month following delivery.
(6) The bank overdraft on 31 Mar. 19–7 was £3,000 and purchases in Mar. amounted to £24,000

You are required to:

(a) *Prepare a cash budget for each of the 6 months to Sep. 19–7.*

(7 marks)
(b) *Prepare a statement of the expected net profit for the six months to 30 Sep. 19–7.*

(4 marks)
(c) *Explain the reasons for the difference between budgeted profitability and budgeted liquidity for the period.*

(7 marks)
Note: Ignore any bank interest arising on the overdraft.

(Total 18 marks)

QUESTION B1. ACCOUNTING TERMINOLOGY

Explain the meaning, and give examples of:
(a) *fundamental accounting concepts,*

(*6 marks*)

(b) *accounting bases, and*

(*3 marks*)

(c) *accounting policies.*

(*3 marks*)
(*Total 12 marks*)

QUESTION B2. KINGSWEAR LTD

The following is the consolidated profit and loss account of Kingswear Ltd for the year ended 31 Dec. 19–9:

		£
Net profit after all expenses including debenture interest		3,300,000
Less:	£	
Corporation tax on profits for the year at 40%	1,100,000	
Irrecoverable ACT	100,000	
		1,200,000
		2,100,000
Less:		
Extraordinary item after adjusting for corporation tax		80,000
		2,020,000
Less:	£	
Dividends—preference paid	120,000	
Dividends—ordinary interim paid	200,000	
Dividends—ordinary final, proposed	400,000	
		720,000
Retained profit for the year		1,300,000
Add: Balance brought forward		150,000
Retained profits carried forward		£1,450,000

On 1 Jan. 19–9, there were in issue 10 million £1 ordinary shares and 2 million 6% £1 preference shares. In addition, the company had in issue

£1,250,000 10% convertible debentures carrying conversion rights into ordinary shares as follows:

Date	Price per share
30 Jun. 19–9	£1.10
30 Jun. 19–10	£1.25
30 Jun. 19–11	£1.75
30 Jun. 19–12	£1.90

No debenture holders took up the option to convert on 30 Jun. 19–9. No debenture or share issues took place during the year ending 31 Dec. 19–9.

You are required to:

(a) *Define earnings per share as applicable to a group of companies having minority interests, either as in SSAP 3, or in your own comparable words.*

(2 marks)

(b) *Write, briefly, of your understanding of* **(i)** *the 'net' basis, and* **(ii)** *the 'nil' basis of calculating earnings per share.*

(4 marks)

(c) *Calculate and state the basic earnings per share for the year ending 31 Dec. 19–9, using* **(i)** *the 'net' basis, and* **(ii)** *the 'nil' basis.*

(4 marks)

(d) *Calculate and state the fully diluted earnings per share on the 'net' basis for the year ended 31 Dec. 19–9.*

(4 marks)
(Total 14 marks)

QUESTION B3

A friend who knows little about accounting has been looking at a set of company accounts and comes to you for enlightenment on points he does not understand.

Write a response to his queries:

(a) 'There is an item "reserves", which incidentally is greater than the share capital. Does this mean that money has been put aside for future use and why is part of it "regarded as undistributable"?'

(b) 'Is the amount shown for plant and equipment under the heading of fixed assets what the company might expect to get from the plant and equipment if it was sold on the balance sheet date?'

(c) 'Before the profit and loss account and the balance sheet there is a page headed "accounting policies". Are these the same things as accounting principles? Does every company have to show them and how are they supposed to help?'

(d) 'In the profit and loss account there is something called "extraordinary items" and the notes show that it represents a profit on property disposed of. Why call this extraordinary and why is it included in the profit calculation after tax has been deducted? Could there be other items which are extraordinary?'

(*20 marks*)

QUESTION B4. JASON

Jason, Midas and Argonaut decided to seek their fortune gold mining in Utopia and purchased a gold mine for £100,000. Mineral surveys indicated that they could work the mine for four years and extract approximately 1,000 standard nuggets. At the end of that period they planned to restore the land at a cost of £10,000 and sell it for £30,000. The following events occurred during the first year:

(1) Paid £10,000 for labour and associated expenditure of mining, refining and producing 200 standard nuggets.
(2) Sold on credit 170 standard nuggets at £200 each (the normal market price).
(3) Collected cash from debtors for 150 standard nuggets.

The three friends disagree on the basis for taking credit for profit in the annual accounts. Midas wishes to adopt the conventional approach and recognise profit when the gold is sold, Argonaut wishes to recognise profit when the cash is collected and Jason when the gold is produced.

You are required to:

(*a*) Prepare an income statement for the first year on each of the alternative bases suggested, indicating clearly the profit recognised by each.
(*b*) Recommend the basis for measuring profit which should be used in this business, giving your reasons.

(*10 marks*)

QUESTION B5. P. ERCOLATOR

The trading account of P. Ercolator, a coffee importer and distributor, for the year to 31 Dec. 19–5 was as follows:

	£	£
Sales		720,000
Opening stock	45,000	
Purchases	585,000	
	630,000	
Less: Closing stock	90,000	
		540,000
Gross profit		180,000

During 19–5 cost prices were static at £600 per tonne and P. Ercolator was able to dispose of his stock at a mark-up on cost of $33\frac{1}{3}$%.

During 19–6 there was an inflation in prices and he was able to add a markup of $33\frac{1}{3}$% to the replacement cost of his stock. His transactions were as follows:

Date	Purchases tonnes	Price per tonne £	Date	Sales tonnes	Price per tonne £
31 Mar. 19–6	300	720	1 Apr. 19–6	400	960
30 Jun. 19–6	400	900	1 Jul. 19–6	360	1,200
30 Dec. 19–6	200	1,200	31 Dec. 19–6	140	1,600

You are required to:

(a) Prepare a trading account for the year to 31 Dec. 19–6 using each of the following methods as the basis for charging out the cost of goods sold:
  (i) first in, first out, and
  (ii) last in, first out.
(b) Explain to P. Ercolator the significance of each method in measuring profit and stock valuation.

(18 marks)

QUESTION B6. CARTER ENGINEERING PLC

Carter Engineering plc undertakes a variety of manufacturing and construction work. At the end of its financial year to 30 Jun. 19–9, decisions are needed on how to deal with the following items when closing off the accounts:

(a) A contract for A plc was commenced in Feb. 19–9 and should be completed by Jul. 19–0. The contract price is £335,000, and the original estimate of total costs £245,000. Work-in-progress to date is valued at £68,000.
(b) A contract for B plc was commenced in Feb. 19–8 and should be completed by Aug. 19–9. The contract price is £480,000, and work-in-progress to date is valued at £340,000. It is estimated that a further £60,000 costs will be incurred before completion.
(c) The raw materials stock includes some items costing £12,000 which were bought for processing and assembly against a special order. Since buying these items the cost has fallen to £10,000.
(d) E plc had ordered some equipment to be designed and constructed at an agreed price of £18,000. This has recently been completed at a cost of £16,800—higher than expected, due to unforeseen problems. It has now been discovered that the design does not meet certain statutory regulations, and conversion at an estimated extra cost of £4,200 will be required. E plc has accepted partial responsibility and agreed to meet half of the extra cost.

For each of the above items, say what figures you would include in stock (or work-in-progress) at the end of the year, and give a short explanation of the principle(s) or reasoning behind your answer. If appropriate, indicate any assumptions or qualifications where additional information may be required.

(14 marks)

QUESTION B7. TECHNOLOGICAL COMPONENTS LTD

Technological Components Ltd manufactures components for sale. It uses advanced machinery with an estimated useful life of four years. As the technology is continually improving it has adopted the reducing balance method for depreciation at a rate of 50% pa.

On 1 Jan. 19–6 the company took delivery of machine K, costing £200,000, which was estimated to produce up to 500,000 components pa for four years, after which it would be sold for £10,000.

On 30 Sep. 19–8 it was announced in the trade press that a replacement for machine K was now available at a cost of £100,000, which could produce at twice the rate of the old one. The directors decided that this was a 'modern equivalent asset' and are considering revaluating the old machine, K. The new machine would last four years and be worth £5,000 at that date.

You are required to:

(a) Show the effect of the purchase price of K in the accounts for the year ended 31 Dec. 19–7.

(4 marks)

(b) Calculate the new value to be placed on the old machine for the accounts for the year ended 31 Dec. 19–8.

(5 marks)

(c) Present the asset and depreciation accounts for the year ended 31 Dec. 19–8, if the new value is used in the accounts.

(4 marks)

(d) Present the appropriate disclosure in accordance with SSAP 12, assuming the depreciation item is material.

(5 marks)
(Total 18 marks)

QUESTION B8. TRUEFIX LTD

At 1 Jul. 1985 the fixed asset balances of Truefix Ltd comprised the following:

	Original cost £	Depreciation £	Net £
Freehold land and buildings	296,000	—	296,000
Plant and equipment	395,200	238,100	157,100
Vehicles	32,000	18,400	13,600

The straightline rates of depreciation based on cost, used to that date, were 10% pa for plant and equipment and $12\frac{1}{2}$% for vehicles. It is the company's practice to make a full year's charge on new items in the year of purchase. The following additional information is relevant to the calculation of depreciation for the year to 30 Jun. 1986:

(i) An item of equipment bought in Sep. 1981 for £84,000 is now recognised to have a useful life of at least 20 years.
(ii) It has been decided to charge depreciation on the freehold buildings at 2% pa. The buildings represent £180,000 of the £296,000 shown above, and were all completed in Aug. 1972.
(iii) A vehicle purchased in Jan. 1982 for £4,000 was traded in at a value of £1,800 in part exchange for a new vehicle costing £6,400.
(iv) Included with the equipment is an item which originally cost £72,000 and which is already fully depreciated but not expected to last for very much longer. Otherwise all items of equipment are less than 10 years old, and all vehicles less than 8 years old.

(a) Prepare a schedule of fixed asset movements and balances for the year to 30 Jun. 1986. Include a clear indication of the amount to be charged against the year's profits and the balances to be shown in the balance sheet.

(12 marks)

(b) A director suggests that to make a change in the annual depreciation for item (i) is against the accounting conventions of consistency and prudence. How would you respond?

(6 marks)
(Total 18 marks)

QUESTION B9

During the course of a year New Products Ltd incurred expenditure on many research and development activities. Details of three of them are given below.

Project 3   To develop a new compound in view of the anticipated shortage of a raw material currently being used in one of the company's processes. Sufficient progress has been made to suggest that the new compound can be produced at a cost comparable to that of the existing raw material.

Project 4   To improve the yield of an important manufacturing operation of the company. At present material input with a cost of £100,000 pa becomes contaminated in the operation and half is wasted. Sufficient progress has been made for the scientists to predict an improvement so that only 20% will be wasted.

Project 5   To carry out work, as specified by a credit worthy client, in an attempt to bring a proposed aerospace product of that client into line with safety regulations.

Costs incurred during the year were:

Project	3 £	4 £	5 £
Staff salaries	5,000	10,000	20,000
Overheads	6,000	12,000	24,000
Plant at cost (life 10 yrs)	10,000	20,000	5,000

You are required to:

(a) Define the following:
  (i) *pure research expenditure,*
  (ii) *applied research expenditure, and*
  (iii) *development expenditure.*

(3 marks)

(b) State the circumstances in which it may be appropriate to carry forward research and development expenditure to future periods.

(5 marks)

(c) Show how the expenditure on projects 3, 4 and 5 would be dealt with in the balance sheet and profit and loss account in accordance with SSAP 13.

(5 marks)
(Total 13 marks)

QUESTION B10. FORSTERS LTD

It is the accounting policy of Forsters Ltd to provide for deferred taxation, in accordance with *SSAP 15*, only where there is a probability that a liability will crystallise in the foreseeable future.

The following information is given in respect of the company's year ended on 30 Jun. 19–12:

(1) The company has made a taxable profit for the year of £500,000.
(2) Its freehold property, which had cost £100,000 in 19–0, was revalued at £200,000. This revaluation was incorporated in the financial statements at 30 Jun. 19–12.
(3) The other fixed assets comprised entirely plant and machinery on which 100% capital allowances had been claimed in the year of purchase. The net book value of these assets at 30 Jun. 19–11 was £600,000.
(4) Depreciation is provided on the plant and machinery at 10% per annum on the reducing balance method and is provided for the full year in the year of purchase.
(5) During the year ended 30 Jun. 19–12 expenditure on similar plant and machinery was £100,000.
(6) The company's forecasts show that capital expenditure on similar plant and machinery, which will attract the 100% capital allowances, will be £10,000 in each of the next three years. After that it is

anticipated that substantial replacement of scrapped plant will be required and annual expenditure of approximately £75,000 will be incurred. The scrapped plant will have no disposal value.
(7) At 30 Jun. 19–11, a timing difference arose through the accrual of loan interest receivable at the year end of £50,000. Receipt of this interest was on 5 Jul. 19–11. Equal amounts of interest were also received on 5 Jan. and 5 Jul. 19–12.
(8) On 1 Apr. 19–12 £125,000 with interest at 15% per annum was borrowed from a finance company. Although accrued at 30 Jun. 19–12 no payment of interest had been made. Six months interest was paid on 1 Oct. 19–12.
(9) The company expects to be paying and receiving interest at the same time in future years.
(10) It was proposed to pay a dividend after the year end of £105,000.

Assume that the company continues to trade profitably and that there are no losses brought forward. The effective rates of corporation tax are 52% on trading profits and 30% on chargeable gains, and the rate of advance corporation tax is three-sevenths.

You are required under a SSAP 15 basis to:

(a) draft a suitable statement of accounting policy on deferred taxation for inclusion in the financial statements at 30 Jun. 19–12

(2 marks)

and

(b) draft the balance sheet note, omitting comparatives, on deferred taxation. Ignore any requirement to show the movement on the deferred tax account.

(14 marks)
(Total 16 marks)

QUESTION B11. HUCKLEBERRY LTD

Huckleberry Ltd is a manufacturing company which commenced trading 10 years ago. It has not previously maintained a deferred taxation account. Owing to the issue of *SSAP 15* the directors have decided to reconsider the accounting policy on deferred tax.

They have provided you with the following information:

(a) During the year ended 31 Dec. 19–7 the company revalued a freehold property at £950,000. The company intends to incorporate this revaluation in its final accounts, but there is no intention to dispose of the property in the foreseeable future. The property was originally acquired in 19–1 at a cost of £700,000.
(b) Additions to plant and machinery during 19–7 amounted to a cost of £196,750 but there were no disposals. Depreciation provided on

plant has been calculated at £133,000. 100% FYAs are attributable to all plant expenditure.

(c) In the three years ended 31 Dec. 19–6, the company has obtained IBAs amounting to £384,400. Writing-down allowances at 4% of the cost of the industrial buildings are available. The buildings are depreciated at 2% of cost. The cost of the buildings totals £620,000.

(d) At the end of 19–6 the book written-down value of plant and machinery amounted to £643,500 compared with a tax written-down value of £141,000. All assets in this total are entitled to a writing-down allowance of 25%.

(e) Forecasts made by the company, based upon current revenue law, show that the following changes in timing differences are expected in the next four years.

	Excess of plant allowances over depreciation £
19–8	45,000
19–9	(20,000)
19–10	(50,000)
19–11	10,000

Thereafter net originating timing differences are expected. The IBAs available are as per note (c).

(f) The company lent £1,200,000 some years ago at 10% annual interest. Interest is paid quarterly in arrear commencing 30 Apr. The last date for receipt of interest is 30 Apr. 19–10.

(g) The appropriate rate of corporation tax is 52%.

(*a*) Draft the relevant extract from accounting policies for the year ended 31 Dec. 19–7.

(*3 marks*)

(*b*) Draft the relevant balance sheet notes from the accounts relating to the taxation matters above.

(*10 marks*)
(*Total 13 marks*)

QUESTION C1

Explain and illustrate the distinguishing features of *liabilities, provisions and reserves*. To what extent does the Companies Act define the terms 'provisions' and 'reserves' or specify how they are to be included in the annual report and accounts?

(Note that you are not required to give details of the creation or use of a share premium account or a capital redemption reserve)

(*10 marks*)

QUESTION C2

The *Companies Act 1985* contains, in broad terms, the following provisions relating to restrictions on distributions by way of dividends:
For all companies: No unrealised profit can ever be distributable. Profits available for distribution consist of accumulated realised profits not previously distributed or capitalised, less accumulated realised losses.
For public companies additionally: No distribution can be made which would have the effect of reducing the company's net assets below the aggregate of its called-up share capital and its undistributable reserves.

Write a memorandum to the board of a public company explaining the reasons for, and the meaning of, these requirements in clear, precise but non-technical language. Include reference to any uncertainties that may arise. You should also include in your memorandum advice as to whether, and if so how, the following events will affect the maximum distributable profit under this Act as at the balance sheet date.

(a) The revaluation of a building during the year, resulting in a £10,000 increase above the previously recorded cost price.
(b) The sale of a building during the year at book value, the book value being the result of a revaluation, by £8,000 over cost price, in the previous year.
(c) The creation of an additional depreciation charge of £9,000 for a major item of plant, caused by a shortening of its estimated useful life.

(15 marks)

QUESTION C3. PANDELAC LTD

The following information relates to Pandelac Ltd in respect of its financial year to 30 Sep. 19–9:

	£000
Sales invoiced during year	6,120
Rents received from sub-letting part of factory	9
Dividends received from investment in quoted company	14
Interest paid on loan stock (after deduction of tax)	20
Production expenses other than those shown separately	2,030
Administrative expenses other than those shown separately	1,005
Interest paid on bank overdraft	60
Bad debts written off and provisions made for doubtful debts	2
A plot of land and warehouse has been sold during the year: it originally cost £42,000 and had been depreciated by £4,000 at 30 Sep. 19–8. Sale proceeds	58

	£000
Plant hire charges (used in production)	63
It has been decided to write off certain items of stock now thought to be obsolete—they were included in the closing stock figure	37
Repairs to factory buildings were completed just prior to the year-end but the invoice has not yet been received. Estimated charges (including VAT £1,000)	14
Auditors' remuneration (including expenses of £1,000)	6
A government regional employment subsidy has been claimed but not yet received. Estimated amount (in relation to factory staff only)	21
Payments to directors for management services	47
Payment to former director in compensation for loss of office	20
Depreciation of fixed assets (Production assets £50 Other assets £8)	58
During the year it was discovered that production equipment bought in Sep. 19–8 was charged to purchases and treated as stock at 30 Sep. 19–8 rather than being capitalised. No adjustments have been made but this amount was not included in stock at 30 Sep. 19–9. Depreciation is 10% pa straight line. Cost of equipment	10
Interim dividend on ordinary share paid	16
Final dividend on ordinary shares proposed	24
Transfer to loan stock redemption reserve	10
Balance of unappropriated profits at 30 Sep. 19–8	1,635
Distribution expenses other than those shown separately	2,500

Note: The rate of income tax can be assumed to be 30%. Figures shown for dividends received, paid or payable, do not include associated tax credits. Corporation tax at 50%.

(a) *Prepare the company's profit and loss account for the year to 30 Sep. 19–9 in a form suitable for publication, communicating the information in as clear a form as possible but omitting details which are not required by statute or which would have to be assumed because data are not given.*

(18 marks)

(b) *What additional information would have to be given in respect of the directors' emoluments? Why is so much attention given to disclosure about directors' emoluments?*

(5 marks)
(Total 23 marks)

QUESTION C4

What may the capital redemption reserve be used for? How does it arise?
(10 marks)

QUESTION C5. SAFE HAVEN LTD

Safe Haven Ltd produces accounts for the calendar year. The following information relates to directors and ex-directors.

Brown retired on 31 Dec. 19–2 and the board decided that the company would pay him a pension at the rate of £4,000 pa, being two-thirds of his final salary. He joined the company on 1 Jan. 1929 and was appointed to the board on 1 Jan. 1959. He had not joined the company's pension scheme or the 'supplementary scheme' due to unsatisfactory medical reports.

Dawson, the managing director, is entitled to a salary at the rate of £35,000 pa. Being a member of the general group scheme, he contributes 5% of his salary and the company contributes 10%. Additionally, the company paid a premium of £5,000 during 19–3 in respect of the 'supplementary scheme' for him. He has agreed to waive £5,000 of the remuneration due to him for 19–3.

Franklin, the chaiman, is not a full-time director and received £7,000 during the year. He does not belong to the company's pension scheme.

Clark, the sale director, is paid a basic salary of £19,500. In 19–3 he also received commission, based on profits, of £600. He does not belong to the company's pension scheme.

Edgar, the other director, has only recently joined the company and the board. He was paid £4,600 in 19–3 and joined the company's normal pension scheme and the 'supplementary scheme' on 1 Jan. 19–3. The payment by the company to the latter scheme was £600.

Graham, the managing director of the principal operating subsidiary, who attends the group board meetings by invitation, was paid £10,500 in 19–3. He belongs to the general group pension scheme but not the 'supplementary scheme'.

The company does not provide cars or any other benefits in kind for its directors. All payments are made under the terms of annual contracts.

You are required to present the details to be disclosed in the published group accounts for the year to 31 Dec. 19–3, and the appropriate working paper. (Corresponding figures for the previous year are not required.)

(12 marks)

QUESTION C6. NOXIOUS CHEMICAL CO LTD

Extracts from trial balance:

	31 Dec. 19-9 £	19-8 £
50p ordinary shares	100,000	90,000
Share premium account	15,000	10,000
Land and buildings, at cost	175,800	95,400
Proposed ordinary dividend	10,000	9,000
Revenue reserves	43,011	24,656
Debtors	46,974	41,239
Unlisted investments (directors' valuation £12,000)	10,000	10,000
Listed investments (market value £5,720)	3,900	3,900

Further information:
(1) The shares were issued to provide additional working capital.
(2) During the year freehold land and buildings were acquired at a cost of £82,000. Buildings are depreciated at 2% pa.
(3) The land and buildings shown in the trial balance have a current market value of £320,000.
(4) Included in this year's debtors is a loan of £1,900 to Mr Cast, the chief accountant, towards the cost of a new car. It is the practice of the company to lend money to officers for cars.
(5) Turnover during the year was £1,125,000, of which 10% was exported.
(6) The company had an average of 105 employees during the year, who were paid a total of £485,240. Employees earning over £25,000 were as follows:

	No.
£25,001–£30,000	4
£30,001–£35,000	2
£35,001–£40,000	1

10 of the employees work mainly outside the UK.

(7) Political and charitable donations were as follows:

	£
Conservative party	250
Sundry political	120
Oxfam	300
Cancer Research Fund	150
Sundry charitable	80
	900

Financial Accounting 19

(8) The company has a full-time managing director, Mr Limit, who receives a salary of £26,500. The chairman, Mr Letter, and the other two directors, Mr Times and Mr Mail, receive no salary but are paid fees of £4,000 each pa. Mr Mail retires by rotation and seeks re-election.

(9) During the year Mr Mail bought 3,000 ordinary shares. There are no other directors' shareholdings.

(10) The company has signed a contract with Timothy Times Ltd for the supply of chemicals for the next six years. Mr Times is the controlling shareholder of Timothy Times Ltd.

(11) The company supplies chemicals for use in plastics manufacturing processes. During the year the company also started supplying dry-cleaners with products to be used in the cleaning process. About 18% of the company's turnover and about 25% of its profit before tax comes from the new line of business.

(12) Profit before tax was £88,000.

You are required to prepare a directors' report in a form suitable for presentation to the members at the forthcoming annual general meeting. Information which would normally be shown elsewhere in the accounts should not be included.

(16 marks)

QUESTION C7. EXTRACTS

You are required to state where the following items would appear in a company's published accounts, together with the particulars which are to be shown in respect of each item to satisfy the requirements of the Companies Act 1985:

(a) turnover,
(b) listed investments,
(c) directors' emoluments,
(d) redeemable shares (*other than in group or associate companies or own shares*),
(e) interest payable, and
(f) land held as a fixed asset.

(20 marks)

QUESTION C8. CELLARS PLC

Cellars plc, a merchandising company, has an authorised share capital of £4,000,000 divided into 16,000,000 ordinary shares of 25p each.

You have received from the company the following draft accounts for the year ended 30 Sep. 19–7:

Profit and loss account

	£000		£000
Corporation tax @ 50% (payable 1 Jan. 19–9)	3,420	Gross profit 19–7 (from turnover of £122m)	8,451
Depreciation	574	Less:	
Market research— amount written off	976	Admin expenses	(280)
Audit fee	26	Distribution expenses	(739)
Directors' remuneration (chairman £18,000)	140	Interest on bank overdraft	(1,000)
Bad debt provision	26		
Net profit for year	1,270		
	6,432		6,432

Balance sheet

	£000		£000
Share capital (fully paid)	2,500	Fixed assets, at cost	1,640
Profit and loss account	1,978	Less: Depreciation	1,214
Corporation tax	6,946		426
Creditors	496	Balance at bank	4,907
		Stocks	2,947
		Debtors	3,640
	11,920		11,920

You also obtain the following information:

(1) In arriving at the trading profit, the directors have valued the closing stocks at selling price less 45%, as all the company's physical stock records are maintained at selling prices for control purposes. In previous years stocks have been valued for accounts purposes at cost on a FIFO basis but the directors consider the administration costs of maintaining dual records too high. The effect of the change has been to reduce the closing stock by £149,000.

Financial Accounting

(2) Depreciation on fixed assets has been charged at 35% on cost instead of the normal 25% to allow for estimated increase in replacement cost of fixed assets.
(3) In previous years market costs for new merchandise have been written off over the expected life of the line. The directors have now decided to write this cost off in the year in which it is incurred. The charge for the year includes £567,000 brought forward from previous years.
(4) There is a court case pending in which a customer is claiming damages of £246,000 for the supply of faulty goods. The directors do not consider that the claim will succeed and no provision has been made.
(5) The directors recommend payment of an ordinary dividend of 10p per share.
(6) The depreciation charge may be split: Admin £70,000, Distribution £14,000, Cost of goods sold £490,000.

You are required to prepare the company's accounts for the year ended 30 Sep. 19–7 in accordance with generally accepted accounting principles and in a form suitable for presentation to members. (Corresponding figures are not required and the information given may be taken as if it included all that is necessary to satisfy the requirements of the Companies Act 1985.)

(18 marks)

QUESTION C9. PRIOR YEAR ADJUSTMENT

Godfrey Ltd wishes to change its policy of accounting for research and development to comply with *SSAP 13*. Instead of writing off expenditure over five years, expenditure is now to be written off in the year in which it is incurred. At 31 Dec. 19–7 research and development expenditure carried forward amounted to £240,000. In that year £48,000 of expenditure was incurred; in 19–8 £36,000 was incurred.

The following information is also available:
1. Retained profits at the end of 19–6 amounted to £6,850,000.
2. The reported retained profits for 19–7 were £2,100,000 after writing off research and development of £60,000.
3. The retained profits for 19–8 are £2,360,000 after charging £36,000 for research and development incurred but before writing off the opening balance brought forward from 19–7.

You are required to show the statement of retained profits in the published accounts for 19–8, including comparative figures, and the note to the accounts describing the new policy and the adjustments made.

(14 marks)

QUESTION C10. HUMPLEDINK LTD

Humpledink Ltd, with an issued share capital of £250,000 in shares of £1 each, makes up its accounts to 31 Dec. of each year, and its corporation tax is normally payable on 1 Jan. next but one. On 1 Jan. 19–5 the liabilities for corporation tax are as follows:
  Year ended 31 Dec. 19–3 £52,000 (agreed with Inland Revenue)
  Year ended 31 Dec. 19–4 £60,000 (estimated on the profits of the year) and there is a recoverable amount of ACT of £34,541, of which £16,071 is in respect of dividends paid in the year ended 31 Dec. 19–3.
  During the year ended 31 Dec. 19–5, the liability in respect of the year ended 31 Dec. 19–3 is paid on the due date, and the liability in respect of the year ended 31 Dec. 19–4 is agreed at £57,500; the assessment notice was issued on 1 Jul. 19–5.
  An interim dividend of 5p per share is paid on 30 Jun. 19–5, and the directors propose that a final dividend of 10p per share, making 15p for the year, be paid.
  The liability for corporation tax based on the profits of the year ended 31 Dec. 19–5 is estimated to be £75,000.
  Note: ACT is to be calculated at 3/7ths.

Assuming that the profit for the year ended 31 Dec. 19–5 before taxation amounted to £150,000, and that the balance brought forward from the previous year was £120,000:

(*a*) Prepare the corporation tax accounts from the information given.
(*b*) Prepare the profit and loss account for the year ended 31 Dec. 19–5.
(*c*) Show the treatment of the appropriate items in the balance sheet prepared as at 31 Dec. 19–5.

(*16 marks*)

QUESTION D1

What information regarding the future activities of a company does the stock exchange listing agreement require that company to furnish to the Stock Exchange? (*Note:* This question is in respect of information other than that which would be required under legislation or institutional rules to be included in company accounts.)

(*15 marks*)

QUESTION D2

What additional information is required to be included in annual reports and accounts by the stock exchange listing agreement?

(*20 marks*)

QUESTION E1. HIGHRISE LTD

Highrise Ltd commenced work on the construction of a block of flats on 1 Jul. 19–4.

During the period ended 31 Mar. 19–5, contract expenditure was as follows:

	£
Materials issued from stores	13,407
Materials delivered direct to site	73,078
Wages	39,498
Site expenses	4,693
Payments on account of plant and machinery	11,159
Administration expenses	3,742

On 31 Mar. 19–5 there were outstanding amounts for wages (£396), and site expenses (£122) and the stock of materials on site amounted to £5,467.

The following information is also relevant:

(1) On 1 Jul. 19–4 plant was purchased for exclusive use on site at a cost of £15,320. The purchase was financed by a hire purchase agreement which called for a deposit of £3,824 followed by 23 monthly instalments of £575 commencing in Aug. 19–4. It was estimated that it would be used for two years after which it would have a residual value of £5,000. The balance of the plant and machinery used on site was on hire. (Take H.P. interest charges to accrue evenly.)

(2) By 31 Mar. 19–5 Highrise Ltd had received £114,580, being the amount of work certified by the architects up to 31 Mar. 19–5 less a 15% retention.

(3) The total contract price is £780,000. The company estimates that additional costs to complete the project will be £490,000. From costing records it is estimated that the costs of rectification and guarantee work will be $2\frac{1}{2}$% of the contract price.

You are required to prepare the contract account for the period and a statement showing your calculation of the profit to be taken to the company's profit and loss account on 31 Mar. 19–5, together with the balance sheet details at that date. Assume for the purpose of the question that the contract is sufficiently advanced to allow the taking of profit.

(15 marks)

QUESTION E2. MO LTD

MO Ltd is a company selling goods by mail order through agents. The following is a trial balance extracted at the end of the financial year:

Trial balance at 31 Jan. 19–7

	£000	£000
Sales (£162m less VAT £12m)		150,000
Value added tax		820
Cost of goods sold	107,800	
Stock at 31 Jan. 19–7	24,625	
Agents' commission	10,820	
Salaries and wages and administration	11,360	
Selling and delivery expenses	8,210	
Audit fees	15	
Hire and loan of equipment	92	
Directors' emoluments	143	
Interest on bank overdraft	380	
Bad debts written off	46	
Provision for doubtful debts		15
Debtors and prepaid expenses	35,328	
Creditors and accrued expenses		16,980
Unclaimed dividends		1
Fixed assets at cost, less depreciation at 1 Feb. 19–6 (see details below)	8,490	
Purchases of equipment and vehicles during the year	130	
Proceeds of disposal of vehicles during the year		25
Interim dividend paid Oct. 19–6 (1.4p per share)	1,120	
ACT on interim dividend	480	
Corporation tax account	16	
Deferred taxation account		4,600
Ordinary share capital (authorised and issued: 25p shares, fully paid)		20,000
General reserve		10,000
Profit and loss account at 1 Feb. 19–6		1,800
Bank overdraft		4,814
	209,055	209,055

Notes:

(1) The following are outstanding at the year-end:

	£
Agents' commission	380,000
Audit fees	10,000

Financial Accounting

(2) The provision for doubtful debts is to be increased to £24,000.
(3) It has been decided to transfer £60,000 to a stock replacement reserve and to make a provision for obsolete stock of £40,000.
(4) A final dividend of 2.1p per share is proposed for payment in Apr. 19–7.
(5) Corporation tax on the year's profit is estimated at £5,600,000. A transfer of £50,000 is to be made to the deferred tax account representing the excess of capital allowances over depreciation charges. Tax paid in Jan. 19–7 (based on the 19–5/19–6 profits) was £3,176,000, which was £16,000 more than originally estimated. No final dividend has been paid in respect of 19–5/19–6.
(6) The equipment and vehicles sold during the year originally cost £70,000 and had a written-down value of £40,000. The fixed asset balances at Feb. 19–6 comprised:

	Freehold property £	Equipment and vehicles £
Cost	7,910,000	2,550,000
Accumulated depreciation	810,000	1,160,000

Depreciation for the year is to be provided as follows:

	£
Freehold property	90,000
Equipment and vehicles	240,000

(7) The amount owing to the Revenue Authorities for VAT at 1 Feb. 19–6 was £690,000 and £2,440,000 had been paid over during the year.

You are required to:

(a) Show the value added tax account for the year in summary form indicating what each item represents.

(3 marks)

(b) Show the corporation tax and deferred tax accounts from 1 Feb. 19–6 to 31 Jan. 19–7.

(6 marks)

(c) Prepare a schedule suitable for appending to the published balanced sheet to summarise the changes in the fixed asset balances.

(3 marks)

(d) Prepare a profit and loss account for the year to 31 Jan. 19–7 and a balance sheet at that date in a form suitable for publication. Omit any details which are not required to be disclosed by the Companies Act unless there is good reason for including them. Notes to the accounts are not required.

(16 marks)
(Total 28 marks)

(The answer uses profit and loss account format 1.)

QUESTION E3. SSAP 2 AND SSAP 4

SSAP 2 (Disclosure of accounting policies):
(a) Define the term 'fundamental accounting concepts' and discuss briefly the four concepts described in SSAP 2.

(5 marks)

(b) Give an example of an accounting situation where a conflict arises between two of the fundamental accounting concepts.

(2 marks)

SSAP 4 (The accounting treatment of government grants):
(c) Describe the accounting treatments available for each of the following grants:
  (i) a government grant towards the cost of wages for 200 employees who would otherwise be made redundant by the company, and
  (ii) a government grant of 20% of the cost of the machinery required for the production line for a new product.

(4 marks)
(Total 11 marks)

QUESTION E4. STOCK VALUATIONS

'The amount at which stocks and work-in-progress (other than long-term contract work-in-progress) is stated in periodic financial statements should be the total of the lower of cost and net realisable value of the separate items of stock and work-in-progress or of groups of similar items'.

SSAP 9

You are required, in the context of that accounting standard, to:

(a) Define the phrase 'net realisable value'.

(3 marks)

(b) Say whether 'replacement' cost is acceptable as an alternative basis of valuation and, if so, in what circumstances.

(3 marks)

(c) Say whether overheads should be included in cost and, if so, to what extent.

(3 marks)

(d) Explain briefly the following methods of valuing stock and work-in progress:
  (i) adjusted (discounted) selling price,
  (ii) first in first out,
  (iii) last in first out,
  (iv) base stock.

(8 marks)

(*Note:* You are not required to write on references to stock valuation in standards on current cost accounting.)

(Total 17 marks)

Financial Accounting

QUESTION E5. ROLLER LTD

Roller Ltd is a substantial manufacturing company.
The draft accounts of the year ended 30 Apr. 19–9 include the following items:

(1) The company had purchased raw materials from Africa for £400,000 FOB at the port. Due to a misunderstanding Roller Ltd omitted to insure the goods and the ship transporting them sank during a storm. The amount has been written off against profits.
(2) There is a new arrangement whereby all product development expenditure is written off in the year in which it is incurred. £750,000 has been charged in the profit and loss account in respect of this item. Of this amount £389,000 represents a balance brought forward from the previous year.
(3) The directors have included an overhead charge of 25% on prime cost in valuing the work-in progress at £500,000, whereas this had previously been ignored. At the end of the previous year the work-in-progress had been included in the accounts at a valuation of £350,000.
(4) An amount of £200,000 was paid for the goodwill of another business last year. The basis of trading has now been changed and it is considered that the goodwill no longer exists. The amount has been written off against profits.

You are required to state how these items should be dealt with in the published accounts presented to members.

(14 marks)

QUESTION E6. DEPRECIATION

The following extracts are from the accounting policies of two different annual reports:

'Depreciation of fixed assets:
Fixed assets are depreciated on a straight line basis at annual rates of 2% to 20% of cost, depending on the class of asset. Expenditure on tools, dies, jigs and moulds is written off to revenue. Investment and regional grants in respect of each year's capital expenditure are included with the reserves on the balance sheet and credited to profit and loss account over a period of 12 years.'

'Depreciation:
No depreciation is provided on freehold properties or properties held on leases with fifty years and over to run at the balance sheet date. Properties held on leases of less than fifty years are amortised over the unexpired term. All other fixed assets are depreciated over their estimated useful lives.'

You are required to:
(a) Comment upon the two accounting policies quoted above.
(5 marks)
(b) Discuss the purpose(s) of the depreciation charge in the profit and loss account.
(5 marks)
(c) Explain the necessity for an accounting standard on the topic of depreciation.
(5 marks)
(d) Describe the requirements of the standard on depreciation (SSAP 12).
(5 marks)
(Total 20 marks)

QUESTION E7. POST BALANCE SHEET EVENTS AND CONTINGENCIES

SSAP 17 (Accounting for post balance sheet events):
(a) What is a post balance sheet event in the context of this statement?
(2 marks)
(b) What is the difference between an 'adjusting event' and a 'non-adjusting event'?
(3 marks)
(c) State, with reasons, whether the following are adjusting or non-adjusting events:
(i) The professional valuation of a property one month after the balance sheet date at a figure of £300,000 below the current book value. The diminution in value is considered to be permanent.
(ii) The declaration of a dividend by a subsidiary one month after the balance sheet date relating to the year ended on the balance sheet date. As a result, the holding company will receive dividends of £120,000.
(iii) The destruction of the company's warehouse in a coastal town due to a freak high tide, two weeks after the balance sheet date. The loss on the building and the stock it contained amounted to £660,000; due to an administrative error neither was insured.
(6 marks)

SSAP 18 (Accounting for contingencies):
(d) What is a 'contingency' in the context of this statement?
(2 marks)
(e) In what circumstances should contingent losses be accrued in financial statements?
(2 marks)
(f) How should contingent gains be dealt with in financial statements?
(2 marks)
(Total 17 marks)

Financial Accounting

QUESTION E8. LESSEE LTD

On 31 Dec. 19–0 a company leases a machine with an expected useful life of four years on conditions which transfer substantially all the risks and rewards of ownership to the company. The cost of the machine is £50,000 and the lease is for four years. A rental of £4,291 is payable at the end of each quarter, so that the total lease payments will be 16 × £4,291 = £68,656.

The company depreciates plant of this kind over a period of four years by a straight line method. Finance charges are to be apportioned over the four years as follows:

	£
Year to 31 Dec. 19–1	7,435
Year to 31 Dec. 19–2	5,783
Year to 31 Dec. 19–3	3,850
Year to 31 Dec. 19–4	1,588
	18,656

This allocation is based on the use of an implicit interest rate of 16% as a discounting factor.

Indicate the way in which the machine and the lease liability will appear in the company's balance sheet in the years 31 Dec. 19–0 to 31 Dec. 19–4.

(15 marks)

QUESTION F1. MUGGER JAGGER LTD

The balance sheet of Mugger Jagger Ltd at 31 Dec. 19–3 showed the following extract:

	£
Ordinary shares of £1 each:	
Authorised	200,000
Issued	80,000
7% preference shares of 50p each	60,000
Share premium account (arising on issue of 7% preference shares)	2.000
Revenue reserve	186,000

During 19–4 the following occurred:

1 Mar. (a) The preference shares were redeemed at a premium of 20p per share.
  (b) 20,000 £1 8% debentures were issued at 95, to help pay for the redemption.

(c) 40,000 ordinary shares were issued at an issue price of 140p to help pay for the redemption.

1 Jul. A bonus issue of one for every four ordinary shares held was made using the balance on the capital redemption reserve and retained profits.

You are required to prepare all the relevant ledger account entries (not cash), and the final balance sheet extract.

(16 marks)

QUESTION F2. ANGLO BAVARIA PLC

Anglo Bavaria PLC made an issue of 50,000 ordinary shares of £1 each at a premium of 25p a share. Under the terms of issue cash payments were due:

		per share p
1 Jan. 19–2	On application (inclusive of 25p premium on issue)	40
1 Feb. 19–2	On allotment	60
Unspecified date	Balance	25

The response to the issue is summarised below:

No. of applicants in categories	No. of shares applied for by each applicant	No. of shares issued to each applicant
40	1,000	500
20	10,000	1,000
1	40,000	10,000

It was a condition of the issue that amounts overpaid on application were to be retained by the company and used in reduction of further sums due on or after allotment. All surplus contributions were returned on 15 Feb. 19–2. The call for the payment of the final 25p per share was made on 1 Mar. 19–2.

Schwein, who had subscribed £400 on an application for 1,000 shares, was unable to meet the balance due on the allotment of 500 shares. On 1 Apr. 19–2 the directors forfeited the 500 shares. All other shareholders paid the sums requested on the due dates.

On 1 May 19–2, the directors reissued the 500 shares as fully paid to Goody and received his cheque for £525 in full settlement on the date of issue.

You are required to:

(a) Prepare a statement as on 1 Feb. 19–2 showing the overpayments or underpayments in respect of each category of applications.

(b) Show how the above transactions would appear in the books of the company.

The cash account is not required.

(16 marks)

QUESTION F3. ROBIN LTD

Robin issued £350,000 7% debentures 10 years ago which were redeemable at a premium of 3% on 31 Dec. 19–7.

When the debentures were issued, it was provided that annual appropriations were to be made out of profits into a sinking fund to provide for their redemption, and that the appropriations be invested outside the company annually on 31 Dec. together with the sinking fund investment income received in the year ended on that date.

During the life of the debentures, the trustees were empowered to purchase for immediate cancellation any debentures available on the open market below redemption price and to finance the purchase by selling sinking fund investments. On 1 Jan 19–7 the balance on the sinking fund account amounted to £209,650, represented by an equal amount of investment at cost. The debentures in issue at that date amounted to £220,000.

During the year ended 31 Dec. 19–7 the following transactions took place:

(1) On 2 Jan. 19–7 investments costing £19,500 were sold, realising the sum of £21,040 and on the same date £20,600 debentures were purchased at 101 (including expenses) and cancelled.
(2) The half-year's debenture interest was paid on 30 Jun. 19–7.
(3) The income on sinking fund investments received during the year amounting to £10,500 was retained in cash pending the redemption of debentures.
(4) The balance of the sinking fund investments was sold and the proceeds amounting to £215,690 were received on 14 Dec. 19–7.
(5) The debentures were repaid on 31 Dec. 19–7 together with the interest due to date.

You are required to write up the ledger accounts (excluding the cash book) necessary to record the above transactions for the year ended 31 Dec. 19–7.

(22 marks)

QUESTION F4. AMOS LTD

The summarised balance sheet of Amos Ltd as at 30 Jun. 19–2 showed:

	£
Share capital:	
8% redeemable preference shares of £1 each	100,000
Ordinary shares of £1 each	150,000
8% debentures	70,000
Revenue reserves	400,000
	720,000
Represented by:	
Net assets	720,000

The redeemable preference shares was due for redemption on 31 Aug. 19–2, and were duly paid off. The company is permitted to redeem the debentures at any time at a premium of 10% and did so on 30 Sep. 19–2.

The company was in a reasonable liquid position, but to assist in providing funds for the redemption of the redeemable preference shares, a rights issue of ordinary shares was made. 20,000 ordinary shares were issued for cash at a premium of £2 per share, £1.25 payable on application on 15 Jul. 19–2, and the balance on allotment on 31 Jul. 19–2. All cash due was received on the due dates.

During the three months ended 30 Sep. 19–2, the company traded at a profit of £25,000.

You are required to:

(a) Give the journal entries (*including cash transactions*) showing the relevant entries in respect of the above.

(b) Prepare a summarised balance sheet as at 30 Sep. 19–2.

(12 marks)

QUESTION G1. EBB PLC AND FLOW PLC

Ebb plc and Flow plc decide to amalgamate their businesses through the medium of a new company, Tide plc formed for that purpose.

Tide plc is incorporated with an authorised share capital of £250,000 divided into ordinary shares of £1 each. Ordinary shares in Tide plc are to be issued, fully paid, at par to the shareholders of Ebb plc and Flow plc in exchange for their shares in those companies.

Financial Accounting

The summarised balance sheets of the two companies, as at 31 Dec. 19–0, showed the following:

	Ebb plc £	Ebb plc £	Flow plc £	Flow plc £
Fixed assets				
Freehold property, at cost		25,000		7,000
Plant and machinery, at cost, less depreciation		42,000		14,000
Trade investment		15,000		—
Current assets				
Debtors	10,400		5,700	
Stock	40,000		16,000	
Balance at bank	4,900		3,300	
		55,300		25,000
Less: Creditors—amounts due within one year		137,300		46,000
		35,200		12,000
		102,100		34,000
Representing				
Share capital—authorised and issued ordinary shares of £1 each		40,000		16,000
General reserve		50,000		10,000
Profit and loss account		12,100		8,000
		102,100		34,000

You are also given the following information:

(1) It is agreed
   (i) that the fixed assets be revalued as follows:

	Ebb plc £	Flow plc £
Freehold property	30,000	8,000
Plant and machinery	36,440	10,570
Trade investment	20,000	—

   (ii) that a provision of 10% be made on debtors for bad and doubtful debts;
   (iii) that stocks be reduced by $12\frac{1}{2}$%, and
   (iv) that the goodwill of Ebb plc be valued at £59,500 and of Flow plc at £11,000.

(2) After the amalgamation, Tide plc immediately issued for cash additional ordinary shares by means of a rights issue in the ratio of one new share for every four held. The issue was made at £1.25 per share payable in full upon application. At the same time the company

also issued £100,000 10% debenutures at 99 payable in full upon application. Both issues were fully subscribed and all monies received.

You are required to:

(a) Calculate the number of shares in Tide plc to be issued to the shareholders of Ebb plc and Flow plc respectively, indicating the ratio thereof to the former holdings.
(b) Show the journal entries in the books of Tide plc necessary to record the rights issue of ordinary shares and the debenture issue.
(c) State what assets would appear in the balance sheet of Tide plc immediately after the above transactions.

(*20 marks*)

QUESTION G2. MIX PLC

Rich Ltd and Poor Ltd decided to amalgamate their businesses with a view to a public share issue. A holding company, Mix PLC, is to be incorporated on 31 May 19–9 with an authorised capital of 600,000 £1 ordinary shares. This company will acquire the entire ordinary share capital of Rich Ltd and of Poor Ltd in exchange for an issue of its own shares.

The consideration for the acquisitions is to be ascertained by multiplying the estimated profits available to the ordinary shareholders by agreed 'price/earnings' ratios. The following figures are relevant:

	Rich Ltd £	Poor Ltd £
Issued share capital:		
Ordinary shares of £1 each	300,000	120,000
6% cumulative preference shares of £1 each	—	100,000
5% debentures, redeemable in 1990	—	80,000
Estimated annual maintainable profits, before deduction of debenture interest and taxation	57,600	23,200
Price/earnings ratios	15	10

The shares in the holding company are to be issued to members of the subsidiaries on 1 Jun. 19–9 at a premium of 25p a share and thereafter these shares will be marketable on the Stock Exchange.

It is anticipated that the merger will achieve significant economies but will necessitate additional working capital. Accordingly, it is planned that on 31 Dec. 19–9 Mix PLC will make a further issue of 60,000 ordinary shares to the public for cash at a premium of 40p a share. These shares will not rank for dividends until 31 Dec. 19–0.

Financial Accounting

In the period ending 31 Dec. 19–9 bank overdraft facilities will provide funds for the payment by Mix PLC of preliminary expenses estimated at £5,000 and management, etc. expenses estimated at £600.

It is further assumed that interim dividends on ordinary shares, relating to the period from 1 Jun. to 31 Dec. 19–9 will be paid on 31 Dec. 19–9 by Mix PLC at $3\frac{1}{2}$%, by Rich Ltd at 5% and by Poor Ltd at 2%.

You are required to project, as at 31 Dec. 19–9, for Mix PLC:

(a) the balance sheet as it would appear immediately after the fully subscribed share issue; and
(b) the profit and loss account for the period ending 31 Dec. 19–9.

Assume the rates of corporation tax and ACT to be 50% and 3/7ths. You can make any other assumptions you consider relevant.

Marks will be awarded for clear, concise presentation of working notes.

(*21 marks*)

QUESTION G3. POOH LTD

It was agreed that, with effect from 1 Jan. 19–10, Pooh Ltd would acquire the whole of the net assets of Tiger Ltd and the fixed assets, stocks and goodwill of Kanga and Roo, a partnership, by the issue of ordinary shares of £1 each fully paid at their then market value of 125p per share.

In computing the number of shares to be issued for each business:

(1) The fixed assets were to be taken at the value placed on them by an independent valuer.
(2) Stocks were to be taken at book value subject to a deduction of £1,000 from the stocks of Kanga and Roo for obsolete stock.
(3) In the case of Tiger Ltd, debtors, creditors and balance at bank were to be taken at book value less £1,500 in respect of a bad debt.
(4) Goodwill was to be valued at two years' purchase of the average profits of the last three years subject only to the following adjustments:
   In the case of Tiger Ltd:
   (i) The directors' remuneration charged in each year was to be reduced by £2,500.
   (ii) The depreciation charged in each year on 'other fixed assets' was to be substituted with depreciation on those assets calculated at 10% of cost on a straight line basis.
   In the case of Kanga and Roo:
   (i) Notional salaries of £5,000 pa, in total, were to be charged for the partners.
   (ii) £2,000, being an exceptional item of expense, was to be added back to the profits in the year to 31 Dec. 19–9.

The goodwill is to be shown as an asset in the balance sheet on 1 Jan. 19–10.

The summarised balance sheets of the three businesses at 31 Dec. 19–10 were:

	Pooh Ltd £	Tiger Ltd £	Kanga & Roo £
Freehold premises at cost	50,000	18,000	12,000
Other fixed assets at cost less depreciation	158,000	37,000	20,000
Stocks at cost	135,000	18,000	11,000
Debtors	123,000	43,000	21,000
Balance at bank	21,000	12,000	5,500
	487,000	128,000	69,500
Ordinary shares of £ each, fully paid	300,000	50,000	
Capital account:			
Kanga			30,500
Roo			11,000
Profit and loss account	122,000	26,000	
Creditors	65,000	52,000	28,000
	487,000	128,000	69,500

You ascertain:

	Pooh Ltd £	Tiger Ltd £	Kanga & Roo £
(1) The depreciation deducted from the cost of other fixed assets at 31 Dec. 19–9	62,000	25,000	10,000
(2) The independent valuations at 31 Dec. 19–9 were:			
Freehold premises		60,000	25,000
Other fixed assets		33,000	21,000
(3) The profits for the last three years ending on:			
31 Dec. 19–7		9,000	9,000
31 Dec. 19–8		12,106	6,500
31 Dec. 19–9		13,100	9,500
after charging depreciation amounting to (for the years ending):			
31 Dec. 19–7		5,250	
31 Dec. 19–8		4,458	
31 Dec. 19–9		4,336	
(4) The other fixed assets at 31 Dec. 19–9 at cost were:			
before 31 Dec. 19–6		52,000	
purchased 1 Jan. 19–8		10,000	

Financial Accounting

(5) Tiger Ltd has disposed of 'other fixed assets' on 1 Jan. 19–9 which had cost £8,000 on 1 Jan 19–6.

You are required to prepare:

(a) a statement showing the number of shares to be issued by Pooh Ltd to pay for the acquisitions; and
(b) the balance sheet, as far as the required information is available, of Pooh Ltd on 1 Jan, 19–10 after giving effect to the issue of shares for the acquisitions.

(*22 marks*)

QUESTION H1. CUMBRIA LTD AND EASEDALE LTD

The balance sheets of Cumbria Ltd and Easedale Ltd at 30 Jun. 19–5 were as follows:

	Cumbria Ltd £	Easedale Ltd £
Ordinary shares of £1 each	240,000	75,000
Revenue reserves	98,450	52,500
8% preference shares of £1	—	48,000
Dividends payable	36,000	11,340
Sundry creditors	21,050	7,500
Depreciation on plant	23,100	7,300
	418,600	201,640
Freehold property	121,000	98,000
Plant and machinery (at cost)	62,400	31,500
Investment in subsidiary	117,500	—
Stock	68,350	42,100
Debtors	31,170	16,400
Cash at bank	18,180	13,640
	418,600	201,640

You are also supplied with the following information:

(1) Cumbria Ltd acquired 60,000 ordinary shares in Easedale Ltd on 31 Dec. 19–3 when the revenue reserves of Easedale Ltd amounted to £26,100 at a cost of £101,300.
(2) Cumbria Ltd subsequently acquired 16,000 preference shares in Easedale Ltd at a cost of £16,200. At the date of acquisition, the reserves of Easedale Ltd amounted to £30,000.
(3) The closing stock of Cumbria Ltd includes £42,200 in respect of goods invoiced by Easedale Ltd at cost plus 25%.

FA–D

(4) Dividends payable by Easedale Ltd consist of:

	£
Ordinary dividend payable	7,500
Preference dividend payable	3,840
	11,340

Cumbria Ltd has not made any entry in its books in respect of either of these dividends.

You are required to prepare the consolidated balance sheet of Cumbria Ltd as at 30 Jun. 19–5. Ignore taxation.

(*18 marks*)

QUESTION H2. SUN, SEA AND SKY

As at 30 Sep. 19–8 the balance sheets of three companies showed the following position:

	Sun Ltd £	Sun Ltd £	Sea Ltd £	Sea Ltd £	Sky Ltd £	Sky Ltd £
Fixed assets						
Tangible assets						
Equipment and fittings, at cost	146,720		79,290		220,400	
Less: Aggregate depreciation	72,490		46,230		82,360	
		74,230		33,060		138,040
Investments						
Shares in Sea Ltd, at cost	67,500					
Shares in Sky Ltd, at cost	175,000					
		242,500				
		316,730				
Current assets						
Stock on hand	49,068		88,860		76,292	
Debtors	101,558		64,275		79,758	
Bills receivable*	14,600					
Balances at bank	76,408		98,540		74,062	
		241,634		251,675		230,112
		558,364		284,735		368,152

Financial Accounting

	Sun Ltd £	£	Sea Ltd £	£	Sky Ltd £	£
Less: Creditors (amounts falling due within one year)						
Trade creditors	49,467		27,406		41,086	
Corporation tax	56,490		37,409		41,206	
Bills payable			3,900			
Proposed dividends	125,000		60,000		50,000	
		230,957		128,715		132,292
		327,407		156,020		235,860

	Sun Ltd £	£	Sea Ltd £	£	Sky Ltd £	£
Financed by:						
Share capital: Authorised and issued ordinary shares of £1 each fully paid		250,000		100,000		150,000
Share premium account		40,000				
Revenue reserves		37,407		56,020		85,860
		327,407		156,020		235,860

Note: *There is a contingent liability of £3,000 for bills receivable discounted.

You are also given the following information:

(1) Sun Ltd acquired 60,000 shares in Sea Ltd in 19–2 when there was an adverse balance on revenue reserve of £20,000. A further 25,000 shares were purchased in 19–6 when the credit balance on revenue reserve was £45,000.
(2) Sun Ltd had purchased 120,000 shares in Sky Ltd in 19–7 when there had been a credit balance on revenue reserve of £65,000.
(3) Bills receivable by Sun Ltd include £1,500 from Sea Ltd. Bills payable by Sea Ltd include £2,000 to Sun Ltd.
(4) The proposed dividends from subsidiary companies have been included in the figure for debtors in the accounts of the parent company.
(5) On 1 Oct. 19–8 Sky Ltd utilised part of its reserves to make a bonus issue of one ordinary share for every three held.
(6) Corporation tax is payable on or before 1 July 19–9.

You are required to prepare the consolidated balance sheet of Sun Ltd and its subsidiaries as at 1 Oct. 19–8, together with your consolidation schedules.
(22 marks)

QUESTION H3. H, SA, SB, SC

The balance sheets of a group of companies as at 31 Dec. 19–9 were as follows:

	H Ltd £	SA Ltd £	SB Ltd £	SC Ltd £
Freehold land and property, at cost	320,000	25,000	30,000	3,000
Plant and machinery, at cost less depreciation	180,000	35,000	9,000	8,500
Vehicles, at cost less depreciation	—	17,500	8,500	6,300
Shares in subsidiary companies (see note 1)	98,000	52,500	—	—
Stocks and work-in-progress	185,000	30,000	14,000	8,750
Sundry debtors	65,000	19,880	12,750	8,500
Current accounts (see note 3)	10,250	—	—	400
Cash at bank	12,500	1,000	1,500	750
	870,750	180,880	75,750	36,200
Share capital:				
Ordinary shares of £1, issued and fully paid	550,000	125,000	50,000	15,000
Reserves	170,000	5,280	12,000	3,600
	720,000	130,280	62,000	18,600
Creditors	150,750	45,650	10,500	17,600
Current accounts (see note 3)	—	4,950	3,250	—
	870,750	180,880	75,750	36,200

Notes

(1) H Ltd's investment in the subsidiary companies is made up as follows:

	£
In SA Ltd 75,000 shares acquired on 1 Dec. 19–1	90,000
In SC Ltd 5,000 shares acquired on 30 Jun. 19–2	8,000

H Ltd had received, as dividends, after acquisition and before 31 Dec. 19–9, the appropriate share of all the pre-acquisition reserves of SA Ltd and SC Ltd. These had been correctly accounted for in the books of H Ltd.

SA Ltd's investment in the subsidiary companies is made up as follows:

	£
In SB Ltd 30,000 shares acquired on 31 Dec. 19–3	42,000
In SC Ltd 5,000 shares acquired on 30 Jan. 19–4	10,500

The pre-acquisition reserves of SB Ltd and SC Ltd were £5,000 and £2,100 respectively. The appropriate share of these reserves had been received by SA Ltd as dividends before 31 Dec. 19–9, and correctly accounted for in its books.

(2) (a) On 31 Dec. 19–3, when SA Ltd acquired control of SB Ltd, the plant and machinery of the latter company stood in its books at a value of £9,000. For the purpose of the acquisition, it was revalued at £10,500, but no entry was made in SB Ltd's books. Based on this revaluation an additional £3,300 depreciation is required for consolidation purposes.

(b) H Ltd considers that a provision of £8,000 is required for unrealised inter-company profit on stock held at balance sheet date.

(c) Cheques in transit at 31 Dec. 19–9 relating to inter-company trading were as follows:

		£
SC Ltd	H Ltd	350
SC Ltd	SA Ltd	400
SB Ltd	H Ltd	1,000
SA Ltd	SC Ltd	700

(3) Current account details are:

	In the books of			
	H Ltd £	SA Ltd £	SB Ltd £	SC Ltd £
Current account with:				
SA Ltd	5,000 Dr.	—	750 Cr.	1,800 Dr.
SB Ltd	3,500 Dr.	750 Dr.	—	—
SC Ltd	1,750 Dr.	700 Cr.	—	—
H Ltd	—	5,000 Cr.	2,500 Cr.	1,400 Cr.
	10,250 Dr.	4,950 Cr.	3,250 Cr.	400 Dr.

Taking into account necessary adjustments arising from notes 1, 2 and 3, you are required to prepare a consolidated balance sheet of H Ltd and its subsidiaries as at 31 Dec. 19–9.

Your workings must be submitted.

(*22 marks*)

QUESTION J1. GROUP ACCOUNTS

(a) Define the relationship which exists between a holding company and a subsidiary.
(*4 marks*)

(b) What is the difference between group accounts and consolidated accounts?
(*2 marks*)

(c) In what situation may a holding company dispense with the need to prepare group accounts?
(*2 marks*)

(d) Explain the ways in which trading between companies within a group may be dealt with in the consolidated accounts, including unrealised profits.
(*8 marks*)
(*Total 16 marks*)

QUESTION J2. HSA

You are given the following information regarding three companies, H Ltd, S Ltd and A Ltd.

Profit and loss accounts—year ended 31 Dec. 19–5

	H £	S £	A £
Trading profit	500,000	60,000	30,000
Investment income	9,850	—	—
	509,850	60,000	30,000
Corporation tax	260,000	32,000	14,000
	249,850	28,000	16,000
Dividends paid	75,000	—	3,000
Dividends proposed	—	10,000	—
Retained profit	174,850	18,000	13,000
Profit b/f	661,250	60,000	45,000
Profit c/f	836,100	78,000	58,000

Financial Accounting

Balance sheets as at 31 Dec. 19–5

	H £	S £	A £
Dividends receivable	8,000	—	—
Net tangible assets	1,360,000	188,000	138,000
Investments	168,100	—	—
	1,536,100	188,000	138,000
Ordinary shares of £1	700,000	100,000	80,000
Reserves	836,100	78,000	58,000
Dividends payable	—	10,000	—
	1,536,100	188,000	138,000

The following information is also relevant:

(1) H Ltd acquired 20,000 ordinary shares in A Ltd on 30 Sep. 19–4 when the reserves of A Ltd amounted to £38,000; H Ltd acquired 80,000 ordinary shares in S Ltd on 31 Dec. 19–3 when the reserves of S Ltd amounted to £42,000.

(2) Investments of H Ltd consist of:

	£
Investment in S Ltd	118,600
Investment in A Ltd	37,500
Trade investment	12,000
	168,100

(3) Investment income of H Ltd consists of:

	£
Dividends received from A Ltd	750
Dividends receivable from S Ltd	8,000
Dividends from trade investments	1,100
	9,850

You are required to prepare the consolidated profit and loss account for the year ended 31 Dec. 19–5 and the consolidated balance sheet as at 31 Dec. 19–5. Corporation tax is 50%; income tax is 30%.

(25 marks)

QUESTION J3. APRICOT LTD AND ITS SUBSIDIARY COMPANIES

Apricot Ltd is a holding company which does not publish its own profit and loss account.

On 1 Oct. 19–2 Apricot Ltd purchased 60,000 ordinary shares in Banana Ltd, which company had a total issued share capital of 75,000 ordinary shares of £1 each. In the year ended 30 Jun. 19–3 Banana Ltd made a profit of £20,000, upon which sum the tax provision was £7,500, and declared a final (and only) dividend for the year of 10p per share.

On 1 Jan. 19–4 Apricot Ltd purchased 90,000 ordinary shares of £1 each in Cherry Ltd which represented 75% of the equity capital. On the same date it purchased 50,000 10% preference shares of £1 each in a quoted company.

The profit and loss accounts for the year ended 30 Jun. 19–4 showed:

	Apricot Ltd £	Banana Ltd £	Cherry Ltd £
Trading profits	42,000	24,000	28,000
Dividends received and receivable	16,500	750	–
	58,500	24,750	28,000
Corporation tax	18,000	10,000	12,400
	40,500	14,750	15,600
Dividends paid and proposed	30,000	10,000	12,000
	10,500	4,750	3,600
Balance b/f	84,250	36,000	24,500
Balance c/f	94,750	40,750	28,100

The following information is obtained:

(1) Trading profits accrue evenly over the year. Apricot dividend income includes £2,500 from the quoted shares. Apricot did not receive any part of Cherry's interim dividend of £4,000.
(2) The only inter-company transaction was the manufacture of a machine by Banana Ltd following an order from Apricot Ltd. This machine cost £6,000 to make and was sold to Apricot Ltd on 30 Jun. 19–4 for £7,850.
(3) A 'group election' for taxation purposes in respect of distributions was in force at all relevant times.
(4) Standard rate income tax is 30%.

You are required to prepare the consolidated profit and loss account for the year ended 30 Jun. 19–4 using only the information given.

(20 marks)

Financial Accounting

QUESTION J4. ATLANTIC AND CROSSING

The balance sheets of Atlantic Ltd and Crossing Ltd at 31 Jan. 19–6 were as follows:

	Atlantic Ltd £000	Crossing Ltd £000
Fixed assets	810	290
Shares in Crossing Ltd (90,000 shares)	300	—
Net current assets	520	50
	1,630	340
Issued share capital:		
Ordinary shares of £1	500	100
Share premium account	200	—
Revenue reserves	450	240
8% debenture stock	120	—
Disposal of shares (90,000 shares)	360	—
	1,630	340

(1) Atlantic Ltd acquired 90,000 ordinary shares in Crossing Ltd on 1 Feb. 19–2 when the reserves of Crossing Ltd amounted to £180,000. The acquisition had been financed by the issue of 10,000 shares in Atlantic Ltd valued at £3 per share.
(2) On 1 Jun. 19–5 Atlantic Ltd sold all its shares in Crossing Ltd to a merchant bank for proceeds of £360,000. The reserves of the two companies at 31 Jan. 19–5 were as follows:

	£
Atlantic Ltd	350,000
Crossing Ltd	210,000

You are required to prepare:

(a) the consolidated balance sheet at 31 Jan. 19–6; and
(b) the consolidated profit and loss account for the year ended 31 Jan. 19–6 insofar as information permits.

Assume profits accrue evenly on a time basis. Assume no dividends were paid or proposed during the year, and that Atlantic's results include those of a wholly-owned non-trading subsidiary. You may also assume that no tax liability has arisen as a result of the disposal.

(15 marks)

QUESTION J5. ATLANTIC AND CROSSING—PART 2

Assume the same situation as in J4 but Atlantic sells 10,000 shares for £40,000. Net current assets of Atlantic at the end of the year are £200,000.

(20 marks)

QUESTION J6. ATLANTIC AND CROSSING—PART 3

Assume the same situation as in J4 but that Atlantic sells 45,000 shares for £240,000. Net current assets of Atlantic at the end of the year are £400,000 and crossing is to be treated as an associated company from 1 Jun. 19–5.

(20 marks)

QUESTION J7. MOORGATE PRODUCTION LTD AND TROPICAL ISLANDS DEVELOPMENTS LTD

Summarised accounts for the year ended 31 Oct. 19–9 of Moorgate Productions Ltd and its subsidiary, Tropical Islands Developments Ltd, are given below:

	Moorgate £000	Tropical N000
Fixed assets (net)	261,287	220,000
Shares in Tropical	2,400	—
Currents assets:		
Stock	67,246	52,734
Debtors	85,173	60,596
Cash	1,711	27,830
	417,817	361,160
Share capital:		
Authorized shares of £1/N1 each	75,000	25,000
Issued ordinary	73,000	20,000
Reserves	81,734	65,230
Loans	120,236	200,000
Current liabilities:		
Trade	81,579	45,698
Taxation	48,247	20,232
Dividend	13,021	10,000
	417,817	361,160

	Moorgate £000	Tropical N000
Turnover	672,436	547,634
Cost of sales	470,705	410,857
	201,731	136,777
Administrative and distribution costs	125,956	95,017
Profit before taxation	75,775	41,760
Taxation	40,000	20,232
Dividends payable	13,021	10,000
Retained profit	22,754	11,528

The subsidiary was formed by Moorgate Productions in 19–1 when the rate of exchange was N5 = £1.

The local loan was obtained when the rate of exchange was N4 = £1.

In 19–2, when the net book value per ordinary shares was N2.50, 40% of the ordinary share capital was sold to local residents at N3.00 per share and the resulting surplus included in the reserves of Moorgate.

Fixed assets totalling n440^m were acquired eight years ago when the exchange rate was N3.00 to the £1, and a further N440^m seven years ago when the rate was N2.20 to the £1.

The rate at 31 Oct. 19–9 was N2.00 to the £1, and at 31 Oct. 19–8 was n2.10 to the £.

The accounting policies of the group follows *SSAP 20* (using average rate to translate the profit and loss account).

You are required to prepare consolidated accounts for the group for the year ended 31 Oct. 19–9 on the usual basis in a form consistent with best practice as far as the given information permits.

(20 marks)

QUESTION J8. UK DEVELOPMENTS LTD

The following summarised accounts have been prepared for UK Developments Ltd and its subsidiary Emerging Country Inc for the year ended 30 Apr. 19–8.

Summarised Balance Sheets as on 30 Apr. 19–8:

	UK Developments £000	£000	Emerging Country Inc Kru 000	Kru 000
Fixed assets:				
Plant and machinery		2,000		1,600
Interest in subsidiary		750		—
Current assets:				
Stock	1,186		200	
Debtors	60		800	
Cash	2		400	
		1,248		1,400
		3,998		3,000
Less: Current liabilities				
Creditors	140		200	
Current tax	99		100	
Proposed dividend	100		200	
		339		500
		3,659		2,500
Capital and reserves				
Issued share capital		1,850		1,000
Reserves		809		500
Debentures		1,000		1,000
		3,659		2,500

Summarised Profit & Loss Accounts for the year ended 30 Apr. 19–8

	£000	Kru 000
Profit before tax	400	600
Tax	99	100
Dividend	100	200
Retained earnings	201	300

The amount of £750,000 'interest in subsidiary' represents the cost of 750,000 ordinary shares of Kru 1 acquired three years ago when the subsidiary was incorporated and £1 = Kru 1. There have been no changes in the share capital since that time. The debenture was issued at the same time and the proceeds of both issues was used to buy plant and machinery costing Kru 2,000,000. No profits have yet been distributed and the exchange rate did not change until 30 Apr. 19–8 when it was altered by Governmental decree to £1 = Kru 1.25.

You are required to (following the requirements of SSAP 20):

(a) prepare a consolidated balance sheet as on 30 Apr. 19–8 for the group using the temporal method in as much conformity with best practice as the information given will permit;
(b) calculate the consolidated profit before tax for the year ended 30 Apr. 19–8 using:
  (i) closing rate method (using average rate);
  (ii) temporal method;
(c) prepare a statement of group reserves under the temporal method.

(25 marks)

QUESTION J9. GRIP AND HAND

Grip Ltd, which has an authorised and issued share capital of 100,000 ordinary shares of £1 each fully paid, had a balance on revenue reserve of £16,200 on 31 Dec. 19–3 after paying a dividend for the year ended on that date.

You are also given the following information:
(1) On 31 Oct. 19–4 Grip Ltd purchased 9,000 of the 10,000 issued ordinary shares of £1 each fully paid in Hand Ltd for £14,250. The balance on revenue reserve of Hand Ltd as at 31 Dec. 19–3 had been £3,450 after paying a dividend for the year ended on that date.
(2) For the year ended 31 Dec. 19–4 Grip Ltd made a trading profit of £18,640 and paid a dividend of 15% whilst Hand Ltd made a trading profit of £4,000 and paid a dividend of 20%.
(3) For the year ended 31 Dec. 19–5 Grip Ltd made a trading profit of £26,540 and paid a dividend of 20% whilst Hand Ltd incurred a trading loss of £4,100 and no dividend was paid.
(4) During the year ended 31 Dec. 19–5 Hand Ltd had manufactured and sold to Grip Ltd an item of plant for £8,000 which included a profit on selling price to Hand Ltd of 25%. The plant had been included in the fixed assets of Grip Ltd and a full year's depreciation had been provided thereon at 20% on cost.

You are required to show how the above items would be reflected in the consolidated balance sheet of Grip Ltd as at 31 Dec. 19–5, together with corresponding figures for the preceding year, and to provide detailed schedules showing the compilation of the figures contained therein. The profit figures of Grip Ltd given above do not include the dividends received by them from Hand Ltd.

(25 marks)

QUESTION J10. GRIP, HOLD AND VALISE

The balance sheets of three companies showed the following positions as at 31 Dec. 19–6:

	Grip Ltd £	Grip Ltd £	Hold Ltd £	Hold Ltd £	Valise Ltd £	Valise Ltd £
Fixed assets						
Land and buildings, at cost		150,000		50,000		75,000
Fixtures and fittings, at cost	160,000		56,000		49,000	
Less: Aggregate depreciation	70,000		22,000		13,000	
		90,000		34,000		36,000
		240,000		84,000		111,000
Investments						
Shares in Hold Ltd, at cost		125,000				
Shares in valise Ltd, at cost				160,000		
Current assets						
Stocks on hand	52,490		49,330		62,400	
Debtors	72,300		47,640		45,430	
Balances at bank	129,450		26,840		79,735	
		254,240		123,810		187,565
		619,240		367,810		298,565
Creditors (amount falling due within one year):						
Creditors	78,324		93,920		20,100	
Corporation tax	73,420		62,470		36,040	
Proposed dividends	100,000		50,000		30,000	
		251,744		206,390		86,140
		367,496		161,420		212,425
Financed by:						
Share capital— authorised and issued ordinary shares of £1 each, fully paid		250,000		100,000		150,000
Capital reserve		40,000		—		30,000
Revenue reserve		77,496		61,420		32,425
		367,496		161,420		212,425

Financial Accounting

You also obtain the following information:
(1) Hold Ltd acquired 120,000 shares in Valise Ltd in 19-3 when the balance on capital reserve had been £20,000 and on revenue reserve £22,000.
(2) Grip Ltd purchased 75,000 shares in Hold Ltd in 19-4 when the balance on the consolidated revenue reserve had been £25,000. The balance on capital reserve in Valise Ltd at that time was £30,000.
(3) Grip Ltd purchased a further 15,000 shares in Hold Ltd in 19-5 when the balance on the consolidated revenue reserve had been £40,000.
(4) Proposed dividends from subsidiary companies have been included in the figure for debtors in the accounts of the parent companies.

You are required to prepare the consolidated balance sheet of Grip Ltd and its subsidiaries as at 31 Dec. 19-6, together with your consolidation schedules. Show goodwill on consolidation as an asset in the final balance sheet.

(26 marks)

Note: You should consolidate indirectly: i.e. first consolidate Valise into Hold to form the Hold Group and then consolidate the Hold Group into Grip to form the Grip Group.

QUESTION J11. LANCASHIRE, DERBYSHIRE, EAST AND COAST

The above companies form the LDEC Group. Their balance sheets at 31 Dec. 19-8 are as follows:

	Lancashire £	Derbyshire £	East £	Coast £
Fixed assets	490,000	215,000	86,000	70,000
Cost of investment	132,000	87,000	13,000	—
Stock	78,000	28,000	70,000	10,000
Debtors	82,000	36,000	22,000	5,000
Cash	88,000	19,000	49,000	5,000
	870,000	385,000	240,000	90,000
Ordinary shares of £1	200,000	80,000	60,000	20,000
Preference shares of £1	100,000	50,000	—	—
Profit and loss account	250,000	95,000	65,000	25,000
Debentures	50,000	—	30,000	—
Trade creditors	170,000	90,000	40,000	30,000
Taxation	60,000	40,000	25,000	10,000
Dividends proposed	40,000	30,000	20,000	5,000
	870,000	385,000	240,000	90,000

You are given the following additional information:
(1) Lancashire acquired 75% of the ordinary shares and 10% of the preference shares of Derbyshire in 19–3 when the reserves of Derbyshire were £40,000.
(2) Derbyshire acquired 80% of the ordinary shares and two-thirds of the debentures of East in 19–5 when the reserves of East were £20,000.
(3) East acquired 40% of the ordinary shares of Coast on 31 Dec. 19–8.
(4) Lancashire acquired 50% of the ordinary shares of Coast on 31 Dec. 19–8.
(5) The relevant companies have all taken account of intra-group dividends receivable by them including such dividends in debtors and in their reserves. Preference dividends and debenture interest have already been paid.
(6) The stock of Derbyshire includes goods purchased from East at an invoice price to Derbyshire of cost plus 30%. The cost of these goods to East was £10,000. They are included in the stock of Derbyshire at a value of £12,000.

You are required to:
(a) Prepare the consolidated balance sheet of Lancashire and its subsidiaries at 31 Dec. 19–8. (*Ignore ACT on proposed dividends.*)

(25 marks)
(b) Explain briefly the effect on the consolidated accounts had Lancashire held only 40% of the ordinary shares of Derbyshire rather than the 75% given in the question.

(5 marks)

(Total 30 marks)

QUESTION J12. GOODWILL

(a) What do you understand by 'goodwill on consolidation'?

(3 marks)
(b) Distinguish between acquired and self-generated goodwill.

(4 marks)
(c) Should goodwill of either sort be treated as a balance sheet asset—permanent or temporary? Give arguments to support your view.

(5 marks)
(d) What are the statutory and professional requirements concerning the treatment of goodwill? What is the present position regarding the treatment of goodwill on consolidation?

(6 marks)
(e) Construct four examples showing how the treatment of goodwill might be said to influence profits and return on capital employed for a group.

(4 marks)

(Total 22 marks)

QUESTION K1

When accounting for associates under *SSAP 1* the holding company's share of the accumulated profits of the associate are treated as being an asset of the holding company. If the holding company cannot force these profits to be paid as dividends should they be treated as profits of the holding company giving rise to the presumption that they are realised profits.

Discuss.

(*12 marks*)

QUESTION K2

(a) What is an associate company?

(*3 marks*)

(b) Why should we account for associates?

(*5 marks*)

(c) Outline possible methods of accounting for associates and briefly indicate your preference.

(*10 marks*)

(*Total 18 marks*)

QUESTION K3. KESTREL LTD

The summarised profit and loss accounts of Kestrel Ltd, Sparrow Ltd, Thrush Ltd and Osprey Ltd for the year ended 31 Mar. 19–5, and the issued share capital as at that date, were as follows:

	Kestrel Ltd £	Sparrow Ltd £	Thrush Ltd £	Osprey Ltd £
Balance b/f at 1 Apr. 19–4	45,000	30,500		
Trading profits	416,000	126,000	10,000	210,000
Interim dividend received from Sparrow Ltd	16,000			
Proposed dividend from Osprey Ltd	27,000			
Directors' fees from Thrush Ltd	6,000			
Balance c/f			29,800	
	510,000	156,500	39,800	210,000

Balance b/f at 1 Apr. 19–4			20,000	
Directors' fees	24,000	12,000	10,000	20,000
Depreciation	20,000	18,000	9,000	15,000
Audit fees	1,500	1,000	800	1,000
Provision for corporation tax	188,000	47,000		87,000
Transfer to reserve	50,000			
Written off shares in Thrush Ltd	8,000			
Proposed dividends, actual	150,000			60,000
Interim dividend paid, actual		20,000		
Balance c/f	68,500	58,500		27,000
	510,000	156,500	39,800	210,000
Issued ordinary share capital in £1 shares	250,000	100,000	80,000	120,000

You also obtain the following information:
(1) Kestrel Ltd has acquired the following shares:

    Sparrow Ltd   60,000 shares on 1 Apr. 19–2
                              20,000 shares on 1 Apr. 19–4
    Thrush Ltd   60,000 shares on 1 Apr. 19–3
    Osprey Ltd   54,000 shares on 1 Apr. 19–4

(2) Osprey Ltd commenced trading on 1 Apr. 19–4.
(3) The profit and loss account of Sparrow Ltd had a debit balance of £40,000 on 1 Apr. 19–2. On 1 Apr. 19–3 the credit balance on the profit and loss account of Thrush Ltd had been £4,000.
(4) An election has been made for dividends between subsidiary companies and the holding company to be treated as group income without the incidence of advance corporation tax.
(5) During the year Kestrel Ltd had purchased goods from Sparrow Ltd which had yielded a profit of 25% on selling price to Sparrow Ltd. Goods purchased by Kestrel Ltd from that company for £20,000 were included in the closing stock as at 31 Mar. 19–5, at a valuation of £19,000.
(6) The directors of Sparrow Ltd and Thrush Ltd are also directors of the holding company.

You are required to prepare a consolidated profit and loss account of Kestrel Ltd and its subsidiary companies, incorporating the results of its associated company for the year ended 31 Mar. 19–5, together with the consolidation schedules.

(28 marks)

QUESTION K4. SIGN LTD GROUP

The Sign Ltd group had held for many years a 25% holding of the equity shares of Post Ltd, an associated company. The following information is relevant for the year ended 31 Mar. 19–8:

	Sign Ltd group (incl. subsidiaries) £	Post Ltd (per own accounts) £
Turnover	1,500,000	45,000
Depreciation	42,000	4,100
Trading profit, after depreciation	80,000	7,000
Dividends receivable from Post Ltd	750	—
Other dividends, from non-group companies (cash amount)	2,600	—
Corporation tax @ 35%	34,000	3,000
Minority interest in profits for year	6,000	—
Loss on sale of government securities held for several years (after deducting minority interests)	13,000	—
Group share of post-acquisition profits retained by subsidiaries:		
At 1 Apr. 19–7	18,000	—
For year	4,100	—
Proposed dividends	13,000 (Sign Ltd)	3,000
Cost of shares in Post Ltd	44,000	—
Retained profits at 1 Apr. 19–7	60,000 (Sign Ltd)	10,000
Retained profits at date of purchase of shares in Post Ltd	40,000	2,000
Elimination of marketing expenditure c/f at 31 Mar. 19–7 now written off under a new accounting policy	12,000	—

You are required to prepare the consolidated profit and loss account, and extracts from the consolidated balance sheet. ACT is to be taken as 3/7ths.

(23 marks)

QUESTION K5. THE ROLLER GROUP LTD

The summarised profit and loss accounts of Roller Ltd, Grind Ltd and Sift Ltd for the year 31 Mar. 19–9, and the issued share capitals as at that date, were as follows:

	Roller Ltd £	Grind Ltd £	Sift Ltd £
Balance b/f at 1 Apr. 19–8	62,000	22,000	50,000
Trading profits	364,000	74,500	210,000
Dividends received from Grind Ltd:			
Preference shares	5,400	—	—
Ordinary shares	7,500	—	—
Proposed dividends from Sift Ltd	27,000	—	—
	465,900	96,500	260,000
Directors' fees	26,000	10,000	20,000
Depreciation	19,000	7,000	12,000
Audit fees	3,200	1,500	2,000
Provision for corporation tax	161,000	29,000	89,000
Dividends paid:			
Preference shares:			
30 Sep. 19–8	—	3,000	—
31 Mar. 19–9	—	3,000	—
Ordinary shares:			
30 Sep. 19–8	—	10,000	—
31 Mar. 19–9	—	10,000	—
Proposed dividends	200,000	—	60,000
Balance c/f	56,700	23,000	77,000
	465,900	96,500	260,000
Issued share capital:			
6% preference shares of £1 each	—	100,000	—
Ordinary shares of £1 each	450,000	200,000	120,000

You also obtain the following information:
(1) Roller Ltd had acquired the following shares:

    Grind Ltd 90,000 preference shares on 1 Apr. 19–8
                  150,000 ordinary shares on 1 Oct. 19–8
    Sift Ltd   54,000 ordinary shares on 1 Apr. 19–5

The preference shares carry no voting rights.
(2) The profits of Grind Ltd are deemed to accrue evenly throughout the year.

(3) On 1 Oct. 19–8 the directors of Grind Ltd resigned and were replaced by the directors of Roller Ltd who received remuneration of £5,000 from Grind Ltd.
(4) On 1 Apr. 19–5 the credit balance on the profit and loss account of Sift Ltd had been £30,000.

You are required to prepare a consolidated profit and loss account of Roller Ltd and its subsidiary company incorporating the results of its associated company for the year ended 31 Mar. 19–9, together with your consolidation schedules, as far as the information available permits. Ignore advance corporation tax.

(*20 marks*)

QUESTION L1. DEATH OF AN INSOLVENT PARTNER

The Growl Hairdressing Salon, a partnership containing three partners, Fozzie, Rolf and Zoot, has had several unsuccessful years of trading. Fozzie, Rolf and Zoot share profits 2:2:1 after allowing for salaries of £1,200 each to Fozzie and Rolf. Kermit, a former partner, has a loan account due for repayment in three instalments, the first payment being due on 30 Sep. 19–0. Interest is payable at 10% pa on this loan, which has been outstanding for one year.

Depreciation, which has not yet been charged, is to be provided at the following rates:

Freehold	Nil
Fixtures	12% pa
Motor van	25% pa

The year ended 30 Sep. 19–0 sees little improvement in the fortunes of the partnership. The profit being made is insufficient to support the three men and Fozzie begins to work only on a part-time basis. Unfortunately, an administrative mistake occurs resulting in the business paying a standing order to Fozzie, in respect of his salary, each week rather than each month.

Fozzie is unaware of this fact, he spends cash freely and awaits an angry letter from his bank manager which Fozzie finds surprisingly does not arrive. The partnership has changed its own bankers and is allowed overdraft facilities.

You calculate the following trial balance at 29 Sep. 19–0:

	£	£
Capital accounts:		
Fozzie		3,000
Rolf		3,000
Zoot		600
Drawings:		
Fozzie	5,200	
Rolf	1,200	
Profit for year (before interest)		3,965
Freehold	7,200	
Fixtures	2,000	
Motor van	500	
Stock	100	
Prepayments and creditors	60	590
Loan account		3,569
Bank overdraft		1,536
	16,260	16,260

On 30 Sep. 19–0, the following events occur:
(1) The partnership sells the freehold property for £6,700 to provide much needed cash resources. They lease back their property at a rental of £2,500 pa payable annually in advance.
(2) The company pays the instalment due to Kermit together with interest.
(3) Fozzie is walking by Trent Bridge, wearing his old black and white school scarf. He is seen by Animal, an ardent Nottingham Forest supporter and psychopath. Animal mistakes Fozzie for a Notts County supporter and throws a piano at him. Fozzie dies with no assets to his name. The partnership agreement is silent as regards the treatment of capital deficits.

You are required to prepare:

(a) the profit and loss appropriation account for year ended 30 Sep. 19–0;
(b) the partners' accounts for the year ended 30 Sep. 19–0 (in columnar form);
(c) the balance sheet at 30 Sep. 19–0.

(*18 marks*)

QUESTION L2. DISSOLUTION BY SALE TO A LIMITED COMPANY

The year to 30 Sep. 19–1 shows a welcome improvement in the fortunes of the Growl Hairdressing Salon. A further salon is opened in Derby and a new motor vehicle is purchased. On 30 Sep. Rolf and Zoot agree to amalgamate their business with that of Statler and Waldorf, who run a number of hairdressing salons in the East Midlands, and who trade under the name of 'Wuff Hairdressers'.

For the purpose of the amalgamation, the businesses are to be taken over by a company formed under the name of 'Growl Ltd'.

The following information is obtained to enable the amalgamation to be carried out:

(1) The balance sheets of the two partnerships at 30 Sep. 19–1 are as follows:

	Growl £	Wuff £
Freehold property	4,000	18,000
Fixtures	2,400	7,000
Motor vehicles	1,500	4,700
Stock	350	680
Prepayments	90	130
Cash at bank	310	—
	8,650	30,510
Less: Creditors	(930)	(800)
Bank overdraft	—	(2,100)
	7,720	27,610
Capital accounts:		
Rolf and Statler	2,281	14,200
Zoot and Waldorf	456	13,410
Currents accounts:		
Rolf	2,010	
Zoot	1,783	
Loan account—Kermit	1,190	
	7,720	27,610

(2) Rolf and Zoot share profits in the ratio of 2:1. Statler and Waldorf share profits evenly.

(3) Certain assets are revalued as follows:

	Growl £	Wuff £
Freehold property	5,500	20,000
Fixtures	2,500	6,500
Stock	340	570

(4) No cash will be taken over by the new company. The partnerships will transfer any necessary cash between them on 1 Oct. 19–1. Rolf agrees to take personal responsibility for the loan from Kermit.

(5) The motor vehicles shown in the balance sheets are to be taken over privately, as follows:
   (i) Rolf, one vehicle at a value of £1,200;
   (ii) Statler and Waldorf, one vehicle each at a value of £2,000 each, each from their respective businesses.
(6) The company is to issue 12,000 ordinary shares of £1 each in proportion to the profitability of the two partnerships, based upon one year's purchase of the average net profits of the last three years. These have been as follows:

	Growl £	Wuff £
Year ending 30 Sep. 19–1	8,453	8,300
Year ending 30 Sep. 19–0	2,743	14,300
Year ending 30 Sep. 19–9	1,704	16,100

(7) The company will issue 20% unsecured loan stock to the partnership at par to provide an income of 8% on capital employed as represented by the net assets introduced by each parternship.
(8) Rolf and Zoot agree that the shares received will be allocated equally between them and that Zoot will receive loan stock to make up the balance due to him.
(9) All the necessary transactions take place on 1 Oct. 19–1.

You are required to:

(*a*) *Prepare the closing entries in the books of the Growl Hairdressing Salon disclosing:*
   (i) *the realisation account;*
   (ii) *the Growl Ltd account;*
   (iii) *the partners' accounts.*
(*b*) *Draw up the opening balance sheet of the new company.*

(*20 marks*)

Financial Accounting

QUESTION L3. NORTHSOUTHS

North practised on his own account as Norths, and South and East were equal partners in Souths. On 1 Jan. 19–7 the two firms agreed to amalgamate as Northsouths, the three partners sharing profits or losses of the new firm equally.

As at 31 Dec. 19–6 the balance sheets of the old firms were:

	Norths £	Souths £		Norths £	Souths £
Capital:			Goodwill	—	3,000
North	1,000	—	Furniture	1,000	750
South	—	2,900	Cars	—	1,000
East	—	2,500	Debtors	4,250	1,050
Creditors	2,750	1,400	Bank balance	—	1,000
Bank overdraft	1,500	—			
	5,250	6,800		5,250	6,800

(1) It was agreed that the value of Norths' goodwill was £2,500 and that Souths' should be written down to the same figure. Norths' car was to be brought into the new firm at £500 and Souths' cars and all furniture at book values. The old firms were to collect debtors and pay creditors, but bank balances were to be taken over by the new firm.

(2) On 1 Apr. 19–7, Northsouths purchased the firm of Wests from West, who retired on that day and Wests' manager, Dee, was made an equal partner of the amalgamated firm, Northsouths and Wests. The only assets acquired from West were goodwill for £4,000, of which £1,000 was paid on completion and the balance payable by three annual instalments; and furniture for £800, paid on completion.

(3) On 31 Dec. 19–7, due to incompatibility, it was mutually agreed that the partnership of Northsouths and Wests should be dissolved and that three new firms under the original names of Norths, Souths, and Wests should be formed, by North (on his own account), South and East (equal partners) and Dee (on his own account) respectively. Each firm should take over the assets and liabilities applicable to it at book values, except that the goodwill of Wests should be written down to the amount still due to West, Dee taking over the whole of this liability.

(4) Separate cash books have been maintained by the constituent firms of Northsouths and Wests and the following is a summary of the entries therein at 31 Dec. 19–7. No other books were maintained and no entries relative to paras. (1), (2) and (3) above had been made, apart from the opening bank balances and payments to West.

	Debit			Credit		
	Norths £	Souths £	Wests £	Norths £	Souths £	Wests £
Bank balances:						
North	—	—	—	1,500	—	—
South and East	—	1,000	—	—	—	—
Payment to West	—	—	—	—	—	1,800
Car bought 1 Apr. 19–7	—	—	—	—	—	800
Cash introduced by Dee	—	—	3,500	—	—	—
Fees received	6,900	8,250	3,600	—	—	—
Rent and rates	—	—	—	600	1,550	450
Staff salaries	—	—	—	4,500	7,200	2,000
Sundry expenses	—	—	—	750	1,850	700
Drawings:						
North, South	—	—	—	1,500	1,100	—
East, Dee	—	—	—	—	1,200	1,000
Bank balances	1,950	3,650	—	—	—	350
	8,850	12,900	7,100	8,850	12,900	7,100

(5) At 31 Dec. 19–7 debtors of Norths, Souths and Wests were £2,900, £3,150 and £850 respectively, and creditors for revenue expenses were £400, £1,400 and £490 respectively. In addition, £600 was due in respect of legal fees and it was agreed that this amount should be borne £200 each by North and Dee, and £100 each by South and East. It was also agreed that furniture and cars should be depreciated at the rates of 10% and 25% pa respectively.

You are required to prepare:

(a) the profit and loss accounts for each of the firms in respect of the appropriate periods ending on 31 Dec. 19–7;
(b) capital accounts of North, South, East and Dee; and
(c) opening balance sheets of each of the new firms of Norths, Souths and Wests as at 1 Jan. 19–8.

(25 marks)

QUESTION L4. FAIRWAY LTD

On 31 Dec. 19–7 Fairway Ltd was incorporated with an authorised share capital of £100,000 in shares of £1 each to take over the business carried on at that date by the partnership of Par. Green and Bogey.

The balance sheet of the partnership as at 31 Dec. 19–7 showed the following position:

	Par £	Green £	Bogey £	£
Capital accounts	24,000	18,000	15,000	57,000
Current accounts:				
Balances as at 31 Dec. 19–6	11,940	8,480	6,000	
Add:				
Interest on capital accounts	720	540	450	
Share of profit for year	6,126	6,126	4,084	
	18,786	15,146	10,534	
Less: Drawings	8,926	8,726	4,064	
	9,860	6,420	6,470	22,750
				79,750

Represented by:

	Cost £	Depn. £	£
Fixed assets:			
Freehold land and buildings	26,000	—	26,000
Plant and machinery	42,000	22,000	20,000
Motor vehicles	19,700	4,700	15,000
	87,700	26,700	61,000
Current assets:			
Stocks		22,400	
Debtors		12,200	
Balance at bank		19,750	
		54,350	
Less: Creditors		35,600	
			18,750
			79,750

You are also given the following information:
(1) Freehold land and buildings are to be transferred to the limited company at a valuation of £30,000 and plant and machinery at £15,000. Stocks, debtors and creditors are to be transferred to the company at book value as at 31 Dec. 19–7.
(2) The motor vehicles are to be withdrawn from the business by the partners at the following valuations:

	£
Par	4,900
Green	3,500
Bogey	3,600

(3) It is estimated that the company will require an opening balance at bank of £15,000.
(4) Sufficient 9% unsecured loan stock is to be issued by the company to the partners so that they will receive the same interest as they received on capital in the partnership for the year ended 31 Dec. 19–7.
(5) Ordinary shares are to be issued at par to each partner in proportion to his share in the partnership profits.
(6) Any surplus or deficiency on partners' accounts on realisation after taking into account loan stock and shares issued is to be withdrawn or paid in, whichever the case may be.

You are required to prepare:

(*a*) *your computation of the shares and loan stock in Fairway Ltd to be issued to each partner;*
(*b*) *partners' accounts in columnar form, showing all the necessary entries to dissolve the partnership; and*
(*c*) *a balance sheet of the company upon completion of the above transactions.*

(*20 marks*)

QUESTION M1. DIGIT AND THUMB

Digit and Thumb entered into a joint venture to trade in electronic machines. It was agreed that Digit would be entitled to a commission of 5% on all gross sales of machines exported, and the profits and losses of the venture be shared as to Digit four-sevenths and Thumb three-sevenths.

The following transactions took place:

1 May Digit purchased machines at a cost of £19,460, paying £15,420 in cash and accepting a bill of exchange for the balance.

3 May Digit sent to Thumb machines which had cost £8,420. Thumb paid the carriage charges on the machines amounting to £126 and paid £2,055 to Digit.

Financial Accounting

10 May Thumb purchased machines at a cost of £7,671.
3 Jun. Thumb paid the bill which had been accepted by Digit.
15 Jun. Thumb paid shipping and insurance costs of export sales amounting to £426 and inland carriage charges of £304.
30 Jun. It was agreed to close down the joint venture by which time sales by Digit were £16,490, including exports of £12,400, and those of Thumb, £17,250, including exports of £4,260. Digit agreed to take over the remaining stock at cost for £540.

On 28 Jun. Digit had been notified by a customer in France that a machine he had sold for £400 was being returned as faulty and that he claimed a refund of the full price together with costs and damages of £110. It was agreed that Digit would forgo his commission on the sale but that the loss would be borne by the venture. Thumb agreed to pay £510 into a special bank account to enable Digit to settle the claim, and that this amount should be provided in the joint venture account as at 30 Jun.

The final settlement between Digit and Thumb was deferred until such time as the French claim had been settled.

On 30 Sep. Digit settled the claim for £429 and paid the money out of the special bank account. The returned machine was sold by Digit as scrap for £10 and the proceeds retained by him. The special bank account was closed by payment out to Digit and Thumb of the amounts due to them.

You are required to prepare:

(a) the joint venture account in the books of both Digit and Thumb; and
(b) the memorandum joint venture account, showing the position both at 30 Jun. and at 30 Sep.

(20 marks)

QUESTION M2. STAR LTD AND GARTER LTD

Star Ltd and Garter Ltd agree to enter into a joint venture on an equal basis for importing and selling electronic equipment. The bankers to the joint venture agree to provide overdraft facilities up to 50% of the working capital required. Star Ltd and Garter Ltd are to provide working capital in proportion to their agreed sharing basis in the venture. After an initial contribution totalling £20,000 they are to pay into the bank at the beginning of each month any additional amount required, based on the position shown at the end of the previous month, after the bank had added interest at $1\frac{1}{2}$% per month on the overdrawn balance at the month end.

The following information is available of the expected trading for the first six months of the venture:

(1) Sales in the first month are expected to reach £25,000 and in each subsequent month they are expected to increase by 10% over the previous month.
(2) Wages will be £3,000 per month until the month when anticipated turnover is in excess of £35,000, when it will be necessary to engage additional staff at an additional charge of £600 monthly from and including that month.
(3) Overhead expenses will be £1,200 per month for the first three months and £1,100 per month thereafter. Overhead expenses, which accrue evenly, are paid half a month in arrear.
(4) Sales will be effected through agents who receive a commission of $2\frac{1}{2}$% on selling price paid one month in arrear.
(5) The partnership makes a standard 25% gross profit on sales before charging any commission.
(6) Debtors are expected to pay in the month following sale.
(7) Regular monthly supplies of goods will be imported and must be paid for immediately against shipping documents. It is intended to have sufficient stock at the end of each month to cover the next month's sales.

You are required to prepare a statement showing the estimated bank balance at the end of each of the first six months, together with the amounts to be provided by the partners based thereon. Ignore all taxation.

(20 marks)

QUESTION M3. TRILBY AND BOWLER

Trilby and Bowler entered into a joint venture agreement for the purchase and sale of hats on 1 Jun. 19–1. Transactions were as follows:

19–1

1 Jun. Trilby purchased hats for £6,000. To finance the purchase he took out a loan of £2,000 with Cromby and paid the balance in cash.

15 Jun. Trilby sent to Bowler hats costing £2,400 and paid carriage charges of £280 in that connection.

25 Jul. Bowler sold all his hats for £5,000 and paid Cromby £2,030 in full settlement of the latter's loan with Trilby.

31 Jul. Trilby paid insurance of £600. Bowler paid £40 for rent of a garage for storing the hats.

3 Aug. Bowler paid £1,000 to Trilby.

6 Aug. Trilby sold part of the hats in his possession for £8,000. He agreed to take over the remaining hats personally at a cost of £1,800.

Each party is entitled to a commission of 5% on his own gross sales. The balance of profits is to be shared. Trilby seven-tenths, Bowler three-tenths. Final cash settlement between the partners was made on 31 Aug.

You are required to record the above transactions on the basis that:

(*a*) each party to the venture keeps a joint venture account in his own books; and
(*b*) all transactions are recorded in the books of Trilby.

(*15 marks*)

QUESTION N1. BERT CROOK

The Fence,
3 Bent Drive
12 Jan. 19–7

Dear Mr Goodman,

I am most relieved that you have agreed to assist me by sorting out the financial affairs of my second-hand business, which, as you know, I commenced on 1 Jan. 19–6. The only records I have kept are, unfortunately, to be found on rather scrufly scraps of paper stored in a large cardboard box. I expect you will want to examine these records for yourself, but I thought I might assist you if I were to summarise my business dealings up to 31 Dec. 19–6 as I recall them.

In Dec. 19–5 I was lucky enough to win £10,000 on the football pools, and this, together with £2,000 loaned to be be a friend—I agreed, incidentally, to pay him 10% pa interest—formed the initial capital of £12,000. I put £11,000 into the bank immediately—in a separate business account. I needed a van to enable me to collect and deliver the second-hand goods, and I am pleased to say that I made a profit of £320 here; a dealer was asking £2,000 for a secondhand van but I beat him down to £1,680. I have only paid by cheque £400 of this so far, but as I will finish paying the full amount in three years, it will be mine before it falls to pieces in another five years from now.

I rent some business premises, and, as they are fairly dilapidated, I only pay £700 a year. I have paid this year's rent by cheque and also £100 in respect of next year.

My first bit of business was to buy a job lot of 4,000 pairs of jeans for £12,000. I have paid a cheque for £8,000 so far, and my supplier is pressing me for the balance. To date, I have sold 3,000 pairs, and received £11,600, but I reckon I am still owed £1,000, most of which I should be able to collect. I promptly banked the £11,600 as it was all in cheques.

I bought 1,600 T-shirts for £2,400 out of my bank account. I have sold 1,400 of these for cash—£3,000 in all—but as the remainder have got damaged I would be lucky to get £100 for them.

I managed to get some pocket-calculators cheaply—100 of them only cost me £800, but I am glad I have not paid for them yet, as I think there is something wrong with them. The supplier has indicated that he will in fact accept £400 for them, and I intend to take up his offer, as I reckon I can repair them for £2 each and then sell them at £16 a time—a good profit.

I have not paid my cash into the bank at all, as the cash I got for the T-shirts and my initial float enabled me to pay for my petrol—£800—and odd expenses—£500. Also, it enabled me to draw £40 per week for myself. As I have done so well I also took my wife on holiday—it made a bit of a hole in the bank account but it was worth all £1,200 of it.

Perhaps, from what I have told you, you can work out what profit I have made—only keep it as small as possible as I do not want to pay too much tax!

Yours sincerely,

Bert Crook

From the data provided by Mr Crook, prepare a business trading and profit and loss account for the period ended 31 Dec. 19–6, and a balance sheet as at that date. Show clearly all your workings and assumptions as notes to the accounts.

(22 marks)

QUESTION N2. THE POT BLACK

The Pot Black is a snooker club which makes up its accounts to 31 Dec. On 31 Dec. 19–1 the barman/treasurer left the club premises and has not been seen since. Anxiety was expressed about the club funds as the books had not been written up for some considerable time, and it was decided to reconstruct the figures from 1 Jan. 19–1.

A summary of the bank account for the year showed the following:

	£		£
Balance at 1 Jan. 19–1	397	Insurance	180
Bank deposits	52,321	Rent and rates	2,960
		Light and heat	1,470
		Bar purchases	36,310
		Telephone and sundries	185
		Cash withdrawn	8,465
		Deposit on a new snooker table	260
		Balance at 31 Dec. 19–1	2,888
	52,718		52,718

Financial Accounting

The following information is also obtained:

(1) Receipts from table charges are controlled by another committee member and totalled £6,450. The receipt counterfoils for members' subscriptions total £7,300 for the year, of which £150 relates to 19–2. A further £6,000 has been donated for the building of a new clubhouse and this sum is to be credited to a separate new building reserve.

(2) The snooker tables owned by the club at 1 Jan. 19–1 had cost £18,000 some years ago and had a written down value of £9,800. The club purchased a new table which was installed on 31 Dec. 19–1 and had paid a 10% deposit on the table. The expected life of each table is six years with a negligible scrap value.

(3) A summary of expenditure for petty cash and wages was as follows:

	£
Glasses and crockery	860
Wages of barman and barmaids	3,950
Sundry bar expenses	580
Repairs to snooker equipment	1,020

(4) Outstanding amounts, stock and prepayments at 31 Dec. were:

	19–0 £	19–1 £
Rates prepaid	250	300
Electricity accrued	240	310
Bar purchases creditors	2,860	4,660
Bar stocks	3,880	5,990
Bar glasses and crockery stocks	1,370	1,100

(5) The bar is operated at an average gross profit margin of 20% on sales.
(6) The club has a fidelity insurance policy and it can be assumed that any cash deficiency to a maximum of £10,000 is recoverable under the policy.

You are required to:
(a) Prepare an income and expenditure account for the year ended 31 Dec. 19–1.

(13 marks)

(b) Prepare a balance sheet as at 31 Dec. 19–1.

(9 marks)

(Total 22 marks)

QUESTION N3. KENSINGTON WORKINGMEN'S CLUB

The Kensington Workingmen's Club prepares accounts annually to 30 Jun. Just prior to the accounts being prepared for 19–8 the club treasurer disappeared. The club committee is concerned by this and suspects that cash may have been taken. It requires detailed accounts to be prepared.

The following is a summary of the club's bank statement for the year ended 30 Jun. 19–8:

	£		£
Balance at 1 Jul. 19–7	2,119	Bar purchases	25,368
Bank deposits	40,340	Rates	2,360
		Light and heat	1,590
		Telephone	732
		Sundries	3,823
		Fruit machine rental	5,360
		Glasses and crockery	2,179
		Repairs and renewals	748
		Fixtures and fittings	1,634
Balance at 30 Jun. 19–8	1,377	Interest at 30 Jun. 19–8	42
	43,836		43,836

The following information is also obtained:

(1) The annual subscription is £4. The register of members totalled 1,360 at 30 Jun. 19–8. Of these, 25 had not paid for 19–7/–8 and 15 had already paid for 19–8/–9. At the beginning of the year 10 members had been in arrears with their subscriptions. All of these were paid during the current year. No subscriptions for 19–7/–8 were paid in advance. The club wishes to take credit for subscriptions as they become due.

(2) The club wishes to provide better facilities for entertainment. The estimated cost of this is £10,000. To provide for this an additional £1 levy is payable with all subscriptions. This levy has been in operation for the last few years and will continue for the foreseeable future. The levy is paid directly into a deposit account. The balance on the deposit account at 30 Jun. 19–7 was £4,261.

Interest was received as follows:

	£
31 Dec. 19–7	163
30 Jun. 19–8	201

The interest is retained within the fund.

(3) The following fixed assets were owned at 30 Jun. 19–7:

	Cost	Accumulated depreciation	Net book value
	£	£	£
Land and buildings	15,000	—	15,000
Fixtures and fittings	10,000	6,357	3,643

No depreciation is provided on the land and buildings. The fixtures and fittings are depreciated at 25% on the reducing balance a full year being provided in year of addition, nil in year of sale.

(4) It is estimated that the net book value at the date of sale of assets sold was £321. The proceeds were £250.
(5) Amounts outstanding, stocks and prepayments (other than subscriptions) at 30 Jun. were:

	19–8 £	19–7 £
Rates prepaid	647	539
Telephone accrued	152	136
Electricity accrued	279	251
Bar purchase creditors	1,405	1,537
Bar stocks	3,241	2,197
Fruit machine rental accrued	487	423

(6) The bar has an average gross profit of 25% on sales.
(7) Although no cash book has been written up, an analysis of the cash vouchers shows the following expenditure:

	£
Sundry expenses	593
Bar wages	2,391
Repairs and renewals	634
Bar purchases	792

A £50 float is kept in the till.
(8) From the returns to the Ringer Fruit Machine Co it is ascertained that the machine takings for the year amounted to £8,793. All takings from the fruit machine were banked during the year.

You are required to:

(a) Prepare a bar trading account for the year ended 30 Jun. 19–8.
(b) Prepare an income and expenditure account for the year ended 30 Jun. 19–8.
(c) Prepare a balance sheet as at 30 Jun. 19–8.

(23 marks)

QUESTION P1. X LTD

X Ltd opened a new branch shop on 1 Jan. All goods for sale at the shop are purchased by the head office and charged to the branch at retail selling price, which is cost plus $33\frac{1}{3}$%. The branch banks its takings, without deduction, for the credit of head office. Although it is a cash business the branch manager is allowed to give credit in a few special cases.

The following information is relevant for the first three months to 31 Mar:

	£
Purchases	27,130
Sales at head office	9,100
Goods sent by head office to the branch at selling price	28,000
Cash sales at branch	18,000
Credit sales by branch	2,000
Goods returned to head office at selling price	1,000
Cash collected from branch debtors	1,730
Branch expenses	1,000
Head office expenses	1,200
Closing stock at head office	2,650
Opening stock at head office	2,900
Authorised reduction in branch selling prices	820

Show, by means of ledger accounts, the above transactions in the head office books where all the records are kept. Prepare X Ltd's trading and profit and loss account. The cash book is not required. An adjustment account is maintained for branch stock.

(16 marks)

QUESTION P2. COLTS LTD

Colts Ltd has a head office in London, and also a branch in Liverpool where all sales are on a credit basis.

All goods are purchased by the head office and invoiced to customers at cost price plus $33\frac{1}{3}$%.

For the year ended 30 Sep. 19–4, the following particulars are available:

	£
Goods sent to Liverpool branch:	
At cost to head office	20,250
Selling price	27,000
Sales as shown by Liverpool branch reports	24,800
Goods returned to head office (at invoice price to customers)	900
Cash received from branch debtors and remitted to head office in London	22,800
Discount allowed to branch debtors	950
Debtors' balances at branch written off as bad	300
Branch debtors on 30 Sep. 19–3	1,800
Stock of goods on 30 Sep. 19–3 (at invoice price to customers)	5,400
Stock of goods on 30 Sep. 19–4 (at invoice price to customers)	6,600

You are required to record the appropriate accounts as they would appear in the head office books, showing the balances as at 30 Sep. 19–4, and the

Financial Accounting 73

branch gross profit for the year ended on that date. The company maintains a stock account with memorandum selling prices.

(*16 marks*)

QUESTION P3. HECTOR AND IVOR

Hector and Ivor are in partnership as retail grocers sharing profits and losses: Hector seven-tenths, Ivor three-tenths. Interest on fixed capital is allowed at the rate of 6% pa but no interest is charged or allowed on current accounts.

The main shop is in Guildford and there is a branch shop in Farnham. They are managed, respectively, by Hector and Ivor. Each partner is entitled to a commission of 10% of the net profits of the shop managed by him before charging such commission.

All goods are purchased by Guildford and goods sent to Farnham are charged out at cost. There are no credit sales.

The trial balance of the partnership as at 30 Sep. 19–8, was as follows:

	Guildford Dr. £	Guildford Cr. £	Farnham Dr. £	Farnham Cr. £
Capital accounts:				
Hector		6,000		
Ivor		4,000		
Current accounts:				
Hector		3,200		
Ivor	1,600			
Shop fittings at cost	3,400		2,800	
Motor van at cost	900		700	
Provision for depreciation at 30 Sep. 19–7:				
Fixtures and fittings		600		300
Motor van		180		140
Stock at 30 Sep. 19–7 at cost	4,300		2,900	
Purchases	50,200			
Goods sent to Farnham		21,900	21,600	
Sales		43,400		32,500
Inter-office current accounts	5,800			5,150
Salaries and wages	4,600		3,100	
Motor expenses	610		540	
Rent, lighting and trade expenses	1,870		1,320	
Sundry creditors and provisions		1,400		340
Commission paid to partners on account:				
Hector	200			
Ivor			100	
Balances at bank	7,200		5,370	
	80,680	80,680	38,430	38,430

You are given the following additional information:

(1) Stocks on hand and cost at 30 Sep. 19–8 were: Guildford £4,600; Farnham £2,800.
(2) Provision is to be made for depreciation on motor vans and shop fittings at 20% and 10% pa respectively, calculated on cost.
(3) Drawings of £600 by Hector and £480 by Ivor are included under salaries and wages of their respective shops.
(4) One-tenth of Guildford salaries and wages is to be charged to the Farnham shop for administrative services. No charge is to be made to the Farnham shop for Hector's services.
(5) On 30 Sep. 19–8 cash amounting to £350 in transit from Farnham to Guildford had been recorded in the Farnham books but not in those of Guildford.
(6) On the same day goods costing £300 in transit from Guildford to Farnham had been recorded in the Guildford books but not in those of Farnham.

You are required to prepare:

(*a*) *the trading, profit and loss, and appropriation account for the year ended 30 Sep. 19–8, showing the profits of the Guildford and Farnham shops and of the whole business; and*
(*b*) *the partnership balance sheet as at that date.*

(*26 marks*)

QUESTION P4. ROSE LTD

Rose Ltd is a retail trading company which sells all its goods at a single standard mark-up on purchase price.

On 1 Apr. 19–4 the company opened a branch in a nearby town, but, owing to a misunderstanding, very incomplete records were maintained in respect of the branch in the head office books of the company and at the branch, each believing the other to be maintaining the records.

The summarized trial balance of the books of Rose Ltd as at 31 Mar. 19–5 was:

	£	£
Ordinary shares of £1 each fully paid		20,000
General reserve		5,000
Profit and loss account as at 31 Mar. 19–4		5,298
Balance at bank	30,200	
Cash received from branch		67,052
Cash float paid to branch	200	
Debtors and creditors (head office)	15,400	29,700
Purchase (head office)	360,000	
Salaries and expenses:		
Head office	45,200	
Branch	5,600	
Sales (head office)		375,050
Fixtures and fittings (head office) at cost	12,200	
Depreciation to 31 Mar. 19–4 thereon		6,800
Fixtures and fittings (branch) at cost	4,500	
Stock at cost at 31 Mar. 19–4 (head office)	35,600	
	508,900	508,900

You ascertain that:
(1) With the exception of goods costing £2,400 paid by cash out of branch takings before banking, the branch received all its goods for resale direct from head office.
(2) The goods for resale sent to the branch during the year from head office, but not entered in the books of head office, amounted to £73,200 at selling price.
(3) The stock of goods unsold at the branch, at selling price, on 31 Mar. 19–5 amounted to £6,100.
(4) The stock of goods unsold at head office, at cost, on 31 Mar. 19–5 amounted to £37,000.
(5) Sundry expenses amounting to £210 had been paid out of the branch takings before banking the balance on the head office bank account.
(6) On 31 Mar. 19–5 there was cash in hand of £290 and debtors of £248 at the branch.
(7) The branch manager is entitled to a commission of 10% of the net profit of the branch, after charging such commission, depreciation on the branch fixtures and fittings and a contribution of £520 to head office salaries and expenses to cover supervision. He is to refund all stock shortages at selling price.
(8) Fixtures and fittings are to be depreciated for the year at 10% of cost.

You are required to prepare, as far as the information is available for Rose Ltd, for the year ended on 31 Mar. 19–5, in draft:

(a) the trading and profit and loss account; and
(b) the balance sheet as at that date.

Ignore taxation.

(24 marks)

QUESTION P5. COLONIA LTD

Colonia Ltd carries on a wholesale business from its head office and warehouse in London and a retail business from a branch in Escalonia.

Trial balances extracted from the company's two sets of books as at 31 Dec. 19–5 are as follows:

	London Dr. £	London Cr. £	Escalonia Dr. £	Escalonia Cr. £
Ordinary shares of £1 each issued and fully paid		80,000		
Balances at banks and cash in hand	38,530		14,399	
Escalonia branch account	18,089			18,089
Sales (including internal transfers)		798,600		275,840
Purchases (including internal transfers)	620,650		173,280	
Stocks at 1 Jan. 19–5 at invoiced prices	64,983		24,992	
Plant and vehicles at cost	54,800		13,330	
Provision for depreciation thereon at 1 Jan. 19–5		20,930		6,665
Salaries, wages, rents, rates, insurance and other working expenses	62,143		56,960	
Stock provision at 1 Jan. 19–5		460		
Debtors and creditors	88,100	40,354	30,072	12,439
Profit and loss account— balance at 1 Jan. 19–5		6,951		
	947,295	947,295	313,033	313,033

You are given the following information:

(1) During the year, the branch bought locally for cash, goods which cost £34,000, of which goods costing £4,600 were in stock on 31 Dec. 19–5.

(2) Except for the above, all purchases were made in London; those sent to the branch were consistently invoiced at cost plus 10%. This addition represented 8% for freight, insurance and other expenses and 2% profit.
(3) On 31 Dec. 19–5 stock was valued at invoiced prices as follows:

	£
London	58,320
Escalonia	22,752

(4) Provision is to be made for:
   (i) depreciation of plant and vehicles at 10% of cost; and
   (ii) a commission to the manager in Escalonia of $\frac{1}{2}$% of the cash collected from debtors during the year; the debtors in Escalonia at 1 Jan. 19–5 amounted to £25,000.

You are required to prepare:
(a) trading and profit and loss accounts for the year ended 31 Dec. 19–5, in columnar form for London, Escalonia and the entire undertaking; and
(b) balance sheets as at 31 Dec. 19–5 for London, Escalonia and the entire undertaking.

(20 marks)

QUESTION R1. LORRY LTD

Lorry Ltd was acquiring two lorries under hire purchase agreements, details of which are as follows:

Registration no.	NOL 862B	NOM 760C
Date of purchase	31 May 19–3	31 Oct. 19–3
Cash price	£1,800	£2,400
Deposit	£312	£480
Interest (deemed to accrue evenly over the period of the agreement)	£192	£240

Both agreements provided for payment to be made in 24 monthly instalments commencing on the last day of the month following purchase.

On 1 Sep. 19–4 vehicle NOL 862B became a total loss. In full settlement on 20 Sep. 19–4:

(1) an insurance company paid £1,250 under a comprehensive policy, and
(2) the hire purchase company accepted £600 for the termination of the agreement.

The firm prepared accounts annually to 31 Dec. and provided depreciation on a straight line basis at a rate of 20% pa for motor vehicles, apportioned as from the date of purchase and up to the date of disposal.

All instalments were paid on the due dates.

The balance on the hire purchase company account in respect of vehicle NOL 862B is to be written off.

You are required to record these transactions in the following accounts, carrying down the balances as at 31 Dec. 19–3 and 31 Dec. 19–4:

(a) motor vehicles;
(b) accumulated depreciation account;
(c) motor vehicle disposals;
(d) hire purchase company.

(20 marks)

QUESTION R2. EASY PAYMENTS LTD

Easy Payments Ltd commenced business on 1 Jan. 19–5 as suppliers of refrigerators. All sales were on hire purchase terms.

When the annual accounts for 19–5 were prepared it was decided to take credit for the gross profit, including interest, in proportion to the instalments collected.

Throughout 19–5 and 19–6 the total price (including interest) charged to every customer was 50% above the cost of the goods or, in the case of the repossessed goods mentioned below, 50% above the value at which those goods were taken back into stock. The hire purchase contracts did not require any deposits but provided for payment to be spread over a period of 12 months, by 12 equal instalments. The personal accounts of customers, which were treated as memorandum records, were debited with the total price and credited with instalments received.

The following trial balance was extracted on 31 Dec. 19–6:

	£	£
Authorised and issued share capital:		
35,000 shares of £1 each, fully paid		35,000
Fixed assets:		
Cost	10,000	
Depreciation to 31 Dec. 19–5		1,000
Hire purchase instalments, less provision		
for unrealised profit at 31 Dec. 19–5	28,350	
Stock at 31 Dec. 19–5 at cost	6,600	
Purchases	59,000	
Cash received from customers		80,625
Balance at bank	6,500	
Creditors		4,860
General expenses	16,150	
Profit and loss account at 31 Dec. 19–5		5,115
	126,600	126,600

Sales (total price, including interest) for 19–6 were £94,650.

In Oct. 19–6, the company took repossession of some goods which had cost £4,800 and had been sold earlier in the year. The unpaid instalments on these goods amounted to £2,400. The goods were taken back into stock at a valuation of £1,600 and were all resold before the end of the year. The total selling prices, both on the original sale and on the resale of these goods, are included in the sales for 19–6 (£94,650), stated above.

All goods unsold on 31 Dec. 19–6 are to be valued at cost. Provision for depreciation of fixed assets is to be at the rate of 10% pa on cost.

You are required to prepare:

(a) the trading and profit and loss account for 19–6;
(b) the balance sheet as at 31 Dec. 19–6; and
(c) the hire purchase debtors' account

(25 marks)

QUESTION R3. SMITH

On 1 Jan. 19–0 Smith opened a business dealing in a new type of power tool of which there was one model only.

The cost price of each tool is £40 and he deals with them in the following ways:

(1) sells for cash from the shop for £56 each;
(2) sends to an agent on a sale-or-return basis, the agent charging £56 each but deducting his commission of $12\frac{1}{2}$%;
(3) sells on hire purchase, when the HP selling price is £64, comprising a deposit of £18 and eight quarterly instalments of £6 each, credit being taken immediately for the gross profit and each instalment being regarded as containing £1 interest, earned when the instalment is paid;
(4) hires out at the rate of £2 per day; this rate has been calculated by assuming that after allowing for repairs, maintenance, and other costs, he will want to recover £80 per tool and the probable number of days of working life is 40. A deposit of £20 is charged and an adjustment made when the tool is returned.

During the first year he bought 500 tools and these can be accounted for as follows:

	£
Sold for cash from shop	188
Sold by agent	80
Held for the purposes of hire (of which all have been out at least once, and 18 are still out at year-end)	50
Sold on HP terms, the agreements still continuing	100
Repossessed from HP customers	2
In agent's hands at year-end	20
In stock at the shop at year-end	60
	500

A summary of the cash receipts during the year shows:

	£	£
Cash sales from shop		10,528
Sales by agent less commission	3,920	
Less: Amount not yet remitted	392	
		3,528
Hire charges, where accounts have been settled (400 days)		800
Deposits for tools out on hire		360
Hire purchase sales:		
40—deposit only	640	
60—deposit and two instalments due	1,680	
	2,320	
Less: Instalments outstanding	30	
		2,290
Hire purchase repossessions—two deposits and one instalment each received before repossession		44
		17,550

The two tools which have been repossessed are in quite reasonable condition, and Smith has decided to add them to the 50 available for hire at the year-end at a value of £30 each.

When the business was started, Smith brought in £20,000 cash as his capital. He has paid for all the 500 tools and also £2,500 working expenses. There are no assets or liabilities other than those arising from the above. Smith has drawn £4,000 for his own use during the year.

You are required to prepare:

(*a*) the trading and profit and loss account for the first year of business; and
(*b*) the balance sheet at the end of first year.

(*20 marks*)

QUESTION R4. MAYDAY LTD

Included in the transactions of Mayday Ltd during its financial year to 30 Jun. 19–2 were the following:

(1) A machine (cash price £8,000) was bought from CBA Ltd on hire purchase. The terms were a deposit of £800 on 1 Jul. 19–1 (the date of purchase) and four half-yearly instalments of £2,052 each on 31 Dec. 19–1, 30 Jun. and 31 Dec. 19–2 and 30 Jun. 19–3. Interest is apportioned on the basis of an equal amount in each instalment.

(2) Mayday Ltd has been given sole manufacturing and selling rights for a patented product by FED Ltd. The agreement is that 50p will be paid to FED Ltd for each unit sold during the year (1 Oct. to 30 Sep.) subject to a minimum payment of £5,000 each year. These royalty payments are to be made at the end of each quarter and any shortfall below £5,000 for the year made up to £5,000 and included with the Sep. payment. Such 'shortfall' payments cannot be recovered later.

The quantities actually sold in 19–1/–2 were:

	units
Oct. to Dec.	1,000
Jan. to Mar.	1,200
Apr. to Jun.	1,800

A market for the product is gradually being established and it is expected that about 2,400 units will be sold in the next quarter.

(3) Mayday Ltd has agreed to act as selling agent for IHG Ltd and will receive 5% commission on all goods sold. In May 19–2 goods costing £4,000 are sent to Mayday Ltd and expenses of £120 paid by that company on behalf of the principal. In Jun. 19–2 half of the goods are sold for £3,600 cash and the amount due settled between the parties.

You are required to:

(a) Show all the ledger accounts (*except cash account*) required to record the above information relating to the year ended 30 Jun. 19–2 including any transfers to the profit and loss account at the end of the year. Assume that all payments are made on due dates. Ignore taxation.

(*11 marks*)

(b) Briefly justify your calculations of the amounts to be transferred to the profit and loss account in respect of (*1*) and (*2*), indicating what alternative(s) might have been possible and any basic accounting principles involved.

(*5 marks*)

(*Total 16 marks*)

QUESTION R5. H PRICE

H Price is a retailer selling goods both for cash and on hire purchase. In accounts for previous years, credit has been taken for all the profit earned on hire purchase sales when the goods were invoiced. It is decided that in the accounts to 31 Dec. 19–6 only the profit proportionate to instalments received should be included, and adjustment should be made for the unrealised profit on transactions of previous years still uncompleted by that date. Hire purchase sales are charged out at a price 25% higher than cash sales.

The following balances were extracted from the books of H Price as at 31 Dec. 19–6:

	£	£
Capital account—H Price		22,000
Creditors		11,300
Sales:		
Hire purchase		60,000
Cash		14,250
Purchases	40,750	
General trade expenses	10,600	
Drawings—H Price	2,000	
Cash at bank	1,200	
Stock at 1 Jan. 19–6	11,000	
Hire purchase instalments receivable	42,000	
	107,550	107,550

The following information is relevant:

(1) Stock as at 31 Dec. 19–6 amounted to £14,600.
(2) Included in hire purchase instalments receivable were balances totalling £4,000 relating to hire purchase transactions from years previous to 19–6. The gross profit on hire purchase sales for previous years was 45%.
(3) During 19–6, goods sold in 19–6 were repossessed from defaulting hire purchasers, whose outstanding balances as at 31 Dec. 19–6 amounted to £2,800. These had not been written off in the books. Part of the repossessed goods were sold for cash, the proceeds of £1,050 being included in the total cash sales, and the remainder were included in the closing stock at £1,100. They were, however, considered to be worth only £600.

You are required to prepare:

(a) the trading and profit and loss accounts for the year ended 31 Dec. 19–6; and
(b) the balance sheet as at that date.

Ignore taxation.

(*25 marks*)

QUESTION S1. HOLMES LTD

Holmes Ltd is engaged in the manufacture of magnifying glasses. The company leased a machine from Watson Ltd on 1 Jan. 19–9 for this purpose.

The terms of the lease are as follows:
(a) The lessee should pay £5 for every magnifying glass produced.
(b) The minimum rent shall be £10,000 pa.
(c) The lessee may recover any shortworkings in the first year of operation out of excess workings in the next two following years. Shortworkings in the second or subsequent years may be recovered out of any excess in the year next following that in which the shortworking arose.
(d) The royalties are payable on 31 Dec. of each year. Details of magnifying glasses produced are:

Year ended 31 Dec.	units
19–9	1,600
19–10	1,900
19–11	2,460
19–12	1,840
19–13	2,720

You are required to show the accounts necessary to record the above transactions in the books of Holmes Ltd for the five years ended 31 Dec. 19–13.
Ignore taxation.

(15 marks)

QUESTION S2. FELL

On 21 Feb. 19–8 Fell consigned to his agent, Offe, 90 bicycles which cost £27 each, insurance and freight amounting to £162. Offe is entitled to a commission of 10% of gross sales.

Offe immediately returned 10 of the bicycles, which were of the wrong colour, and paid return freight and insurance of £30.

Fell, whose financial year ended on 30 Jun. 19–8, received from Offe an account of sales, made up to that date; this showed that Offe had sold 60 bicycles for £3,240 and that he had paid warehouse charges of £48 on the consignment, and carriage on the bicycles sold of £45. Offe sent a sight draft in settlement of the balance due, on which Fell incurred bank charges of £9.

Offe sold the remaining bicycles for £960, incurring expenses of £24. He sent Fell a second account of sales made up to 30 Sep. 19–8, accompanied by a sight draft for the balance due, on which Fell paid bank charges of £6.

You are required to write up (for the period ending 30 Sep. 19–8) the consignment account and consignee's account in Fell's books, carrying down any necessary balances at 30 Jun. 19–8.

(15 marks)

QUESTION S3. BOTTLES & CO

Bottles & Co supply their products in flasks which cost them 25p each and are charged out to customers at 50p each. If returned within two months a credit of 40p each is allowed and all flasks are valued for stocktaking purposes at 20p each.

On 1 Jan. 19–2 the stock in the warehouse was 15,200 flasks and there were in the hands of customers 7,000 flasks, for which the return period had not expired.

During 19–2 3,600 new flasks were purchased; 40,000 flasks were invoiced to customers; 35,000 flasks were returned within the period allowed; 1,950 flasks were broken in the warehouse and 3,000 were not returned and were duly paid for by customers.

On 31 Dec. 19–2 there were no flasks in the hands of customers not paid for, and for which the return period had expired. Stocktaking in the warehouse disclosed a shortage of 50 flasks.

You are required to show the flasks stock account, flasks suspense account and flasks profit and loss account for the year 19–2 as you think they should appear in the books of Bottles & Co.

(*15 marks*)

QUESTION T1. BIRKDALE ENTERPRISES LTD

The summarised balance sheets of Birkdale Enterprises Ltd are as follows:

	31 Dec. 19–7 £	£	31 Dec. 19–8 £	£
Freehold land and buildings (at cost)		155,300		186,700
Plant and machinery:				
Cost	47,800		61,000	
Aggregate depreciation	13,200		19,200	
		34,600		41,800
Stock		26,500		28,000
Debtors		28,400		32,800
Cash at bank		8,900		17,400
		253,700		306,700

	31 Dec. 19–7		31 Dec. 19–8	
	£	£	£	£
Share capital (issued and fully paid):				
£1 ordinary shares		100,000		150,000
£1 6% redeemable preference shares		50,000		—
Share premium account		7,000		14,500
Profit and loss account		57,500		74,400
8% unsecured loan stock		—		15,000
Sundry creditors		24,200		27,800
Proposed dividends		15,000		25,000
		253,700		306,700

You are also supplied with the following information:
(1) During the year the preference shares were redeemed at a premium of 5%. 50,000 £1 ordinary shares were issued at £1.20 per share, and £15,000 8% unsecured loan stock was issued at 98. The redeemable preference shares were originally issued at £1.10.
(2) Plant costing £12,000 was sold for proceeds of £8,000. Depreciation provided during the year amounted to £9,500.
(3) During the year the company had paid a preference dividend of £3,000 and an interim dividend for the year ended 31 Dec. 19–8 of £11,000.

You are required to prepare a statement of source and application of funds for the year ended 31 Dec. 19–8, in a form suitable for publication to the shareholders.
Ignore taxation.

(*22 marks*)

QUESTION T2. BAFFLE LTD

You are given below the balance sheets of Baffle Ltd and its subsidiary, New Ltd, at 31 Jul. 19–6 and 19–7.

	19–6	19–7
	£000	£000
Share capital (£1 ordinary)	2,000	2,700
Reserves	3,400	4,700
Debenture stock	1,200	1,700
Minority interests	—	700
Creditors	1,100	2,400
	7,700	12,200

	19–6	19–7
	£000	£000
Fixed assets	5,100	9,070
Goodwill	—	200
Stock	1,100	1,500
Debtors	900	1,700
Cash	600	(270)
	7,700	12,200

Baffle Ltd acquired 75% of the 1,000 ordinary shares of New Ltd on 17 Nov. 19–6. At that date the assets of New Ltd were:

	£000
Fixed assets	2,500
Stock	300
Debtors	400
Cash	500

Liabilities of New Ltd were:

	£000
Debenture stock	500
Creditors	800

There were no disposals of fixed assets during the year. Group depreciation charged during the year was £1,950,000. No dividends are proposed but interim dividends paid during the year were:

	£000
Baffle	450
New Ltd	200

These dividends were paid on 1 Jul. 19–7. Baffle Ltd paid £2,000,000 to acquire the shares in New Ltd. This was made up of an issue of shares valued at £1,750,000 plus £250,000 of cash. The share premium is included in reserves. All other reserves are revenue.

You are required to produce a consolidated statement of source and application of funds together with supporting notes.

(25 marks)

QUESTION T3. SPIXWORTH PLC

(1) The following information relates to Spixworth plc, a public company, for the year ended 30 Jun. 19-8:

	£000
Turnover	31,311
Purchases (stocks adjusted)	7,192
Wages	8,306
Salaries	2,941
Depreciation	1,056
Pension contributions	840
Directors' remuneration	36
Transfer to plant replacement reserve	300
Debenture interest paid (gross)	120
Dividends paid and proposed	900
Corporation tax for year ended 30 Jun. 19-8 (including associate £100,000)	2,600
Other direct overheads	3,520
Revenue reserves as at 1 Jul. 19-7	69,471
Group retained profit for year (including associate)	1,657
Indirect overheads	2,106

Included, where relevant, in the above figures are amounts relating to Spax Ltd, a subsidiary of Spixworth in which Spixworth has 60% of the ordinary share capital and 30% of the preference shares.

(2) Spax Ltd profit and loss account for the year ended 30 Jun. 19-8 was:

	£
Profit	50,000
Taxation	15,000
	35,000
Dividends paid/payable—preferential	10,000
	25,000
Ordinary dividends	15,000
Retained profit for year	10,000

(3) Pix Ltd is treated as an associated company of Spixworth plc. Spixworth has a 40% interest in the ordinary share capital.

Pix Ltd's profit and loss account for the year ended 30 Jun. 19–8 was:

	£
Trading profit	500,000
Investment income	50,000
	550,000
Taxation	100,000
	450,000
Ordinary dividends	100,000
Retained profit for year	350,000

(a) *You are required to prepare a value-added statement on the lines suggested in the Corporate Report.*

(14 marks)

(b) 'The maintenance of short-term profit is not the sole aim of modern business enterprises although by making the profit figure the keynote figure of financial reports, users are encouraged to believe that it is the sole aim.'

To what extent do you consider the above statement to be true in relation to companies and their published reports in modern times? Discuss briefly three other objectives of economic entities and how these objectives might be recognised in their published reports.

(8 marks)
(Total 22 marks)

Financial Accounting

QUESTION T4. SUNLIGHT PLC

The latest balance sheet and profit and loss account summary of Sunlight plc, a manufacturing company, is as follows:

Balance sheet at 31 Mar. 19–9

	£	£		£	£
Authorised share capital—400,000 £1 ordinary shares		400,000	Fixed assets: Freehold property (book value)		240,000
Issued and fully paid—200,000 £1 ordinary shares		200,000	Plant and machinery (cost less depreciation)		400,000
Capital reserves		100,000	Motor vehicles (cost less depreciation)		100,000
Revenue reserves		400,000			
Shareholders' funds employed		700,000	Office furniture (cost less depreciation)		100,000
Loan capital: 200,000 10% £1 debentures (secured on freehold property—repayable 19–21)		200,000			840,000
			Current assets:		
			Stocks	500,000	
			Debtors	200,000	
			Investments	60,000	
Book value of long term funds		900,000			760,000
Current liabilities:					
Trade creditors	119,200				
Bank overdraft (secured)	439,200				
Current taxation	88,000				
Dividend payable	53,600				
		700,000			
		1,600,000			1,600,000

Summary profit and loss account for year ended 31 Mar. 19–9

	£
Sales (all on credit)	2,000,000
Profit after charging all expenses except debenture interest	220,000
Less: Debenture interest (gross)	20,000
Profit before taxation	200,000
Less: Corporation tax on the taxable profit for year	88,000
Profit after taxation	112,000
Less: Ordinary dividend proposed	53,600
Retained profits transferred to revenue reserve	58,400

Notes:

(1) Purchases for the year were £1,080,000.
(2) Cost of sales for the year was £1,500,000.
(3) The market price of a Sunlight plc ordinary share at 31 Mar. 19–9 was £4.
(4) Income tax is to be taken at 30%. ACT is ignored.
(5) The company estimates the current value of its freehold property at £440,000.
(6) The managing director has suggested that a figure representing the company's goodwill be computed and included in the balance sheet under that heading with the shareholder's funds increased by its value.

You are required to:

(a) *Compute the following ratios:*
  (i) *primary ratio* (*using the* book *value of total assets as capital employed*)
  (ii) *secondary ratio—the profit margin;*
  (iii) *secondary ratio—the turnover of capital;*
  (iv) *current ratio;*
  (v) *liquid ratio;*
  (vi) *debtors' ratio;*
  (vii) *proprietary ratio, (shareholders' funds:total assets);*
  (viii) *stock turnover ratio;*
  (ix) *dividend yield;*
  (x) *price earnings ratio and its reciprocal.*
  (*7 marks*)

(b) *Write a brief comment on the* liquidity *of Sunlight plc, stating the reference points to which relevant ratios can be compared.*
  (*6 marks*)

Financial Accounting 91

(c) *Write to memorandum to the managing director explaining the nature of goodwill from an accountant's point of view, and stating,* with reasons, *whether or not you recommend the inclusion of a figure for goodwill in the balance sheet.*

(10 marks)
(Total 23 marks)

QUESTION T5. HENRY

Henry, a farmer, plans to erect additional farm buildings at a cost of £1,800, payment to be made in Nov. 19–3. He realises that he will need to apply for more bank borrowing facilities than usual, and in Dec. 19–2 makes reasonable estimates of his likely transactions during 19–3.

He makes the following assumptions:

(1) Balance at bank on 1 Jan. 19–3 will be £750.
(2) Monthly outgoings for wages and normal farm expenses will be £200.
(3) The quarterly rent of £100 will be paid on the usual quarter days.
(4) The main crop, barley, will be sold for cash in Aug. for £22.50 per ton. The estimated crop will be 200 tons. The cost of seed, fertilisers and planting is estimated at £600, payable in Apr. and, in addition, harvesting expenses of £200 will be paid in Aug.
(5) Subsidiary income is estimated at £700 from sale of fatstock in Apr. and £100 from sale of hay in Jun.
(6) The 19–2/–3 taxation liability has been agreed at £400 and will be paid on the due dates.
(7) Personal drawings are estimated at £100 per month, with an additional amount of £200 in Feb. to pay for a winter holiday.
(8) It is not proposed to incur any capital expenditure during 19–3 other than that relating to the additional farm buildings and the total provision for depreciation on all fixed assets for the year is to be £200. Sundry creditors in respect of farm expenses will be £125 more at the end of the year than at the beginning.

You are required to prepare:

(a) *a budget statement showing the anticipated bank balance at the end of each month during 19–3, for presentation to the bank; and*
(b) *a statement of the budgeted profit or loss for the year, showing how this is derived from the figures in the budget.*

(15 marks)

QUESTION T6. EXPLOITATION ASSOCIATES INC

The following are financial statements provided by Exploitation Associates Inc, an American company:

Comparative statements of profit and loss

	19–2 $	19–3 $
Gross sales	1,091,400	1,604,125
Less: Discounts	21,400	39,125
	1,070,000	1,565,000
Cost of goods sold:		
Opening inventory	50,500	65,000
Raw materials	225,000	293,000
Direct labour	485,000	795,000
Factory overhead	64,000	117,000
Depreciation	50,000	60,000
Closing inventory	(65,000)	(105,000)
	809,500	1,225,000
Gross margin	260,500	340,000
Selling expenses	(84,500)	(121,000)
General and administrative expenses	(64,930)	(73,310)
Operating profit	111,070	145,690
Other income (expenses)	(20,000)	5,675
Taxation	(40,982)	(68,114)
Net profit	50,088	83,251

Financial Accounting

Comparative balance sheet at 19–2 and 19–3

	19–2 $	19–3 $
Current assets:		
Cash	1,000	11,500
Debtors	52,500	95,000
Inventory	65,000	105,000
Prepaid expenses	4,000	6,000
	122,500	217,500
Fixed assets	485,000	544,000
Less: Depreciation	(342,000)	(402,000)
	143,000	142,000
Other assets	20,000	15,000
Goodwill	50,000	50,000
	70,000	65,000
	335,500	424,500
Current liabilities:		
Creditors	35,000	78,000
Bank overdraft	16,000	—
Accrued expenses	40,000	60,750
Dividends payable	2,000	3,000
Taxes due	1,500	6,499
	94,500	148,249
Bills of exchange	40,000	—
Provision for claims	10,000	10,000
Reserve for asset replacement	40,000	65,000
	90,000	75,000
Net worth:		
Preference shares	4,000	4,000
Ordinary shares	26,000	28,000
Capital surplus	5,000	10,000
Earned surplus	116,000	159,251
	151,000	201,251
	335,500	424,500

Reconciliation of surplus in 19–2 and 19–3

	19–2 $	19–3 $
Earned surplus	90,912	116,000
Add: Net profit	50,088	83,251
	141,000	199,251
Less:		
Dividends	5,000	15,000
Addition to reserve for asset replacement	20,000	25,000
Balance	116,000	159,251

Exploitation Associates Inc is seeking additional finance which your company is considering providing.

Your are required:

(a) using ratio analysis, to advise your company (in report format); and
(b) to state, with reasons, what additional statements you would ask for.

(*25 marks*)

QUESTION U1. UPPINGHAM LTD

Uppingham Ltd buy and sell sprocket-flanges. During the 3 months ended 31 Mar. 19–6 the company enter into the following transactions:

1 Jan. 19–6	Buy 500 units costing £750
31 Jan. 19–6	Sell 400 units for £2,000 and replace them with units costing £1,400
28 Feb. 19–6	Sell 200 units for £1,000. Buy 50 units costing £200
31 Mar. 19–6	Sell 200 units for £1,100. Buy 100 units costing £500.

The retail price index during the period was as follows:

1 Jan. 19–6	200
31 Jan. 19–6	220
28 Feb. 19–6	230
31 Mar. 19–6	240

You are required to prepare trading accounts using the following conventions:

(a) historical cost accounting (*FIFO*);
(b) current purchasing power accounting;
(c) current cost accounting.

(*17 marks*)

QUESTION U2. SOUTHPORT MANUFACTURING CO LTD

General background
Southport Manufacturing Co Ltd specialises in the manufacture of electronic components. The financial accountant has produced a draft set of accounts for the year ended 31 Dec. 19–8, prepared on the usual historical cost principles. The company has decided for the first time to prepare a summary of results and financial position using current cost accounting techniques.

Case study requirement
The accountant has asked you to prepare the necessary statements which the company intends to present to the shareholders, following the recommendations of SSAP 16. Make your workings to the nearest £1,000. Give comparative figures for the balance sheet.

(40 marks)

Information given
(a) *Trading and profit and loss account for the year ended 31 Dec. 19–8*

	£000	£000
Sales		800,000
Opening stock	52,000	
Purchases	640,000	
	692,000	
Closing stock	72,000	
		620,000
Gross profit		180,000
Depreciation	42,000	
General expenses (including interest of £15.3m)	31,800	
		73,800
Net profit before taxation		106,200
Corporation tax		51,000
Net profit after taxation		55,200
Interim dividend (paid 30.6–8)	10,000	
Final dividend (proposed)	20,000	
		30,000
		25,200

(b) Balance sheets as at 31.12.-7 and 31.12.-8

	31.12.-7 £000	31.12.-7 £000	31.12.-8 £000	31.12.-8 £000
Tangible fixed assets (note 1)		320,000		358,000
Current assets (note 2)	230,000		291,500	
Less Creditors (amounts falling due within one year) (note 3)	119,500		193,800	
		110,500		97,700
		430,500		455,700
5% Debenture stock		200,000		200,000
Ordinary shares of £1 each, authorised issued and fully paid		150,000		150,000
General revenue reserve		80,500		105,700
		430,500		455,700

(c) *Information relating to the above accounts*

1. Fixed assets—plant and machinery

	31.12.-7 £000	31.12.-8 £000
Cost	400,000	480,000
Aggregate depreciation	80,000	122,000
	320,000	358,000

The company acquired several additional items of machinery on 30.9.-8 and the assets held at 31.12.-7 were originally acquired on 1.1.-6. The company's depreciation policy is to provide for depreciation at a rate of 10% pa on a straight line basis.

2. *Current assets*

	31.12.-7 £000	31.12.-8 £000
Stock	52,000	72,000
Debtors	170,000	218,000
Cash	8,000	1,500
	230,000	291,500

3. Creditors (amounts due within one year)

	31.12.-7 £000	31.12.-8 £000
Creditors	63,500	122,800
Final dividend	15,000	20,000
Corporation tax	41,000	51,000
	119,500	193,800

4. Profit and loss account items

(i) Assume that sales, purchases and expenses have occurred at an even rate during the year.

(ii) Assume that in each of the two years, the stock held at the end of the year was originally acquired three months before the year end.

(iii) Assume that the debtors and creditors at the year end arose evenly over the last three months of the year.

(d) *Index numbers*

You are provided with the following index numbers for the company's assets and the retail price index.

	Plant and machinery	Stock	R.P.I.
31.12.-4	100 (base year)		
31.12.-5	105		
31.12.-6	110		
30. 9.-7	114	140	
1. 1.-8	115	145	178
31. 3.-8	117	150	
Average 19-8	120	160	190
30. 9.-8	122	170	195
31.12.-8.	125	180	199

QUESTION U3. REEFLY LTD

Reefly Ltd wishes to prepare current cost accounts in accordance with *SSAP 16*. The accounting year ending 31 Dec. 19–0, would be the first year in which the company prepared such inflation adjusted accounts. The company's profit and loss account and balance sheet prepared on a historical cost basis are given below:

Profit and loss account for year ending 31 Dec. 19–0

		£000
Sales		1,000
Less: Opening stock	300	
Purchases	900	
	1,200	
Closing stock	500	
		700
		300
Depreciation	90	
Interest payable	50	
		140
		160
Less: Corporation tax		80
		80
Dividend paid		40
Retained profit for the year		40

Summarised balance sheet (in £000) as at

	31.12.–9	31.12.–0
Plant and machinery:		
Cost	700	1,100
Accumulated depreciation	230	320
	470	780
Current assets:		
Stock	300	500
Debtors	150	250
Cash	200	50
	1,120	1,580

Shareholders' funds:		
Ordinary share capital	200	300
Revenue reserves	300	340
Loan stock	400	600
Taxation	100	112
Current liabilities:		
Creditors	120	228
	1,120	1,580

The following information is available:
the plant and machinery was purchased on 1.1.–5 for £300,000
on 1.1.–8 for £400,000
and on 30.6.–0 for £400,000

It is all being depreciated at the rate of 10% pa on a straight line basis. The annual depreciation charge in the profit and loss account is to be based on mid-year asset values, for current cost accounting purposes. The additional loan stock of £200,000 and equity shares of £100,000 were issued on 30 Jun. 19–0. Both issues were for cash.

The specific price indices relevant to the company are as follows:

	Plant and machinery	Stock, debtors and creditors
1. 1.–5	110	
1. 1.–8	150	
30.11.–9	195	120
31.12.–9	200	125
Average for 19–0	218	140
30.6.–0	220	142
30.11.–0	240	156
31.12.–0	242	160

The company has a seasonal stock problem. As the balance sheets show, the stock at the beginning of the year was £300,000 and at the end of the year £500,000. The stock levels did, however, rise steadily to a peak of £800,000 on 30 Jun. 19–0, and then steadily fell to the level on 31 Dec. 19–0. The company wishes to allow for this seasonal fluctuation of stock in its current cost accounts.

You can assume that price levels, both for plant and machinery and for items in stock, have risen steadily over the year. The stock in hand at the end of each year was purchased one month before the year end. You can further assume that the cash balance does not fluctuate in line with working capital items.

You are informed that the monetary working capital adjustment for 19–0 is £7,257. This amount is to be deducted from the historical cost operating profit.

Prepare the current cost profit and loss account for the year ending 31 Dec. 19–0, and the current cost balance sheet as at 31 Dec. 19–0 for Reefly Ltd. These accounts should be prepared in accordance with SSAP 16.

(40 marks)

QUESTION U4. CHELSEA RETAILERS PLC

The current assets and current liabilities of Chelsea Retailers Plc at the beginning and end of the year to 31 Dec. 19–0 are summarised below.

	Opening £000	£000	Closing £000	£000
Current assets:				
Stock	54		75	
Debtors	40		50	
Cash	21		15	
		115		140
Less Current liabilities:				
Trade creditors	50		60	
Bank overdraft	30		50	
		80		110
Net current assets		35		30

The bank overdraft is considered a permanent source of finance. Stock at the end of each year represents purchases made equally during the preceding three months. Debtors represent sales in the preceding two months.

The monthly index of stock prices and the general price index was:

		Stock price index	General price index
19–9	Oct.	115	162
	Nov.	117	164
	Dec.	118	167
19–0	Jan.	120	170
	Feb.	124	174
	Mar.	126	178
	Apr.	129	175
	May.	132	176
	Jun.	132	177
	Jul.	134	179
	Aug.	134	180
	Sep.	135	181
	Oct.	138	182
	Nov.	140	184
	Dec.	141	186
	Average for year	132	177

Financial Accounting

You are required to:
(a) Explain the purpose of the monetary working capital adjustment,
(3 marks)
(b) Calculate the monetary capital adjustment in accordance with SSAP 16 by reference to the data given above (work to the nearest £100).
(4 marks)
(c) Explain briefly why some authorities do not consider that a monetary working capital adjustment is necessary.
(3 marks)
(Total 10 marks)

Answers

ANSWER A1

(a) Those likely to use John's accounts include:
   (i) the Inland Revenue, to assess his liability to income tax;
   (ii) banks, to assess whether John's business is a good credit risk;
   (iii) other existing and prospective creditors (e.g. leasing companies), who wish to know how good their debts are and whether to make further advances;
   (iv) John himself should find the accounts of use in determining how well he is running his business and how to improve his efficiency;
   (v) any future investors (or partners) in John's business.

(b) A balance sheet is normally prepared to show the balances on the accounts in the books at the year end. The very preparation of a balance sheet which ties in with a profit and loss account gives a feeling of security that all has been done according to custom and all has been done well.

The only good reason for preparing a balance sheet is that it will be used. We must therefore consider who would use it. For this purpose we shall consider the users of the accounts enumerated in the answer to the first part of this question.

(i) An assessment to income tax by the Inland Revenue will normally be on the basis of the profit and loss account. However, they will like to see that assets claimed for capital allowances appear in the balance sheet.

(ii) A bank will have a working knowledge of how John manages his bank account but if they are considering lending to John they will want to know: (a) what proportion of the business finance is provided by themselves and what proportion is provided by John; (b) whether he is getting a good return on the capital he employs—enough to cover interest on a further loan; (c) how liquid John's business is: John may have large creditor balances which could suddenly fall to be payable, and if his assets are long-term ones (fixed assets and other long-term investments) he could find himself in difficulties—a bank might not like the idea of going down with him; (d) how well John manages the financial side to his business: does he collect debts swiftly and in full? Is he making the best of the credit available to him from suppliers? Is the stock uneconomically high?

(iii) Prospective creditors will be concerned that the business is sound and will use the balance sheet in the same way as the bank will.

(iv) By analysing the information in the balance sheet John should be able to detect weaknesses in his financial control and endeavour to correct them. In particular he should consider:
   (1) average credit given and taken.
   (2) stock levels, and
   (3) return on capital employed.

(v) Future investors and partners will be concerned, like other creditors, with the financial health of the business and may use the balance sheet to evaluate that health as noted above. They will also be concerned with the amount invested by John in the business which will be shown in John's capital account.

(c) 'All that matters is the money in the bank.': This has some truth in it but also a degree of inaccuracy:

(i) For a business to expand a principal requirement is the availability of cash. Money in the bank is one source of cash.
(ii) Money in the bank is not much good if it is not used for anything.
(iii) If there is insufficient money in the bank to pay creditors when debts fall due then it is not a good indicator of financial health.

ANSWER A2

Financial statements should be produced to fulfil the needs of their users. The needs of users of accounts may be classified under three headings:
(a) to know that the directors have properly managed the assets of the company (the stewardship function);
(b) to know the present financial position of the company—its liquidity and the distribution of its assets;
(c) to know the future prospects of the company—its ability to employ, pay dividends, repay loans,

Underlying these needs is the requirement for objectivity and consistency in financial reporting. The conventional system, if it does fail to differentiate between assessments of fact and value, may be endeavouring to meet too many of these needs at one time.

In this answer the writer submits that no one accounting system fulfils all the needs of users and that what is required, therefore, is not replacement of one system by another but the supplementing of one system with another.

CAsh flow accounting would serve needs (a) and (c)—showing how the directors had managed the medium through which the company acted and indicating the future ability of the company to continue to act. In order to give useful information to prospective and actual creditors, a future cash flow would need to be prepared. A future cash flow, however, would not be an objective statement and so, although useful, would be very difficult to audit—its only confirmation would come from comparison with the actual flow for the year which could be properly ascertained and audited at the year end. Users of accounts would begin to assess the usefulness of a future cash flow presented by the directors by reference to the track record of the company in meeting its previous predictions. The publication of variances would aid this assessment.

Cash flow accounting then, with the presentation of past and future cash flows, would aid the users of accounts and meet needs (a) and (c) in part. It would not, however, give any indication of profit nor would it on its own show the funds available to the company (creditors, loans), upon which it might draw—and which might be limited by, for example, gearing considerations—or the ways in which funds were held (debtors, fixed assets). For a complete picture of the health of the company a statement showing its other assets and liabilities is required and a balance sheet; and also, in order that something may be gleaned of the performance of the company, some statement of profit (howsoever defined) should be appended.

Current cost profit is an indicator of performance closely connected to cash: it indicates the excess funds generated by the activities of the business after maintaining its operating capacity. The inclusion of this figure, together with a balance sheet, and past and future cash flow summaries, would be the optimal solution.

There are two final points. Firstly, the usefulness of the accruals concept: this concept is profit and loss account orientated, being used to determine net revenue. Performance measured on this basis is intrinsically no better a measure than performance measured on a cash flow basis, except that the latter is more accessible to manipulation: creditor payments may be delayed and additional loans obtained, thus marring the objectivity needed by users. Secondly, the use by persons inside the company of financial statements. A figure of operating profit after maintaining capability, is essential to evaluate their own performance. However, in order to continue operation, cash must be available, so in the immediate future the cash flow forecast is of more importance to internal users, although in the long term a figure of past operating profit indicates the performance of the company and points to its future.

ANSWER A3

(a) 'Exit value accounting' involves showing assets in the balance sheet at realisable value. Profit under the system is the increase in the aggregate realisable value of the assets of the business.

(i) *Advantages*
(1) It is easily understood by the layman.
(2) It enables decisions to be taken as to whether it would be better to sell the assets and re-invest the proceeds elsewhere. These decisions may be internal management decisions or those of a prospective or present investor.
(3) It has the advantage of objectivity over 'entry value accounting'. This involves the estimation of the cost of an identical replacement asset: an asset may not be so replaced.
(4) It has an advantage over 'value to the business' valuation which requires the estimation of the present value of the future earnings of the asset. Exit value is more objective.
(5) It includes assets in the balance sheet at market values and therefore facilitates comparison between the financial data of different businesses.

(ii) Disadvantages
(1) Realisable values may prove difficult to measure in practice.
(2) The use of realisable values rests on the assumption that assets are to be immediately liquidated.
(3) Overall effectiveness is measured while the operational performance is ignored.

(iii) Evaluation
'Exit value' provides useful information about the immediate liquidation of the assets: it does not provide for the costs of liquidating the business (redundancy costs, etc.) and thus is not concerned so much with the realisable value of the business as with the management of its assets. Therefore, it does not ignore the 'going concern' nature of the business.

The advantages of objectivity are also somewhat dubious, in particular the stated advantage in (3) over entry value accounting, i.e. that entry value accounting presumes the replacement of an asset by an identical one. This is less of a criticism of entry value accounting than may at first be thought. This is because assets *are* usually replaced by businesses—if not by identical assets, then at least by assets with similar productive capacity.

In conclusion, exit value accounts provide more and useful information for the purposes of some decisions but on their own they do not provide enough indication of future prospects and of past operational effectiveness to be sufficient on their own.

(b) Using 'exit-value' principles, profit arises during the course of production rather than simply on realisation at the end of the production process. When the goods are sold these unrealised profits become realised profits. 'Profit' thus indicates the greater value of the business, rather than the effect of the activities of the selling function in the concern. Matching of costs and revenue becomes matching of activities and value.

Stage	Period 1 Raw materials	Period 2 1st stage WIP	Period 2 2nd stage WIP	Period 3 Finished goods	Period 4 Sale
	£	£	£	£	£
Cost of materials, labour and overheads	100	125	140	150	150
Exit value	100	135	145	165	165
Profit of period		10	(5)	10	0
At end of period:					
Unrealised profit		10	5	15	—
Realised profit		—	—	—	15

ANSWER A4

Several categories of users are traditionally considered as having an interest in the financial statements of a company. The importance of the financial statements to each category will vary with the nature and size of the concern and with the type of use made of the company's accounts by that category.

(a) *Equity investors*

In a small private company the financial statements will provide shareholders with confirmation of the financial position of the company. They may provide information to permit, for example, valuation for transfer of shares.

In a larger public concern and in quoted companies the financial statements will provide present and potential investors with information on the financial health of the company on which to base decisions as to whether or not to invest (or continue to invest) in the company. It is suggested that institutional investors such as pension funds, which often hold significant interests in public companies, have a moral duty to oversee its management (the case of *Prudential Insurance v Newman Industries* illustrates the assumption of this duty) and the company's financial statements may be the basis for their initial review of the stewardship exercised over the company's resources by management.

(b) *Loan creditors*

(i) *Present*

In a small company long-term loans will be from banks and individuals. In a larger company there may be debenture stock in addition to bank loans.

In general, the interests of debenture holders will be protected by a debenture trust deed. Under such deeds a trustee is appointed to safeguard the rights of the debenture holder against the actions of the company. In the performance of this duty the trustee will be interested in the company's accounts but will, in all probability, also receive certificates from the company's auditors regarding the company's compliance with the provisions of the debenture trust deed.

The information requirements of the loan creditors are similar to but narrower than those of equity investors. They are interested in the past performance of the company as an indication of the security of their investment and its future income stream. This knowledge will assist decisions as to whether and when to buy or sell debentures, or whether to extend loan facilities.

(ii) *Potential*

Potential providers of loan capital will also be interested in financial statements as indicators of the future position of a business. They will consider its return on assets and whether this will cover interest payments, and the liquidity of the concern. They will note how profits and liquidity have varied with trading conditions: a business with rapidly oscillating profits and losses does not give as solid and comfortable an appearance as one with a steady (growing) profit.

(c) *Employees*

(i) *The smaller company*
In a small company the trading position may be well known to employees: they will be able to see from day to day trading the level of sales and the associated costs. On the other hand, for a non-financially aware employee such information needs to be spelt out in formal statements.

(ii) *Larger concerns*
In a larger concern the position of the company will be far from readily apparent, and the only way for an employee to assess the financial position of the concern will be from formal financial statements (whether from internally prepared statements or from audited external statements).

(iii) *Needs*
What then are the needs of the employee? They will be the same in both the small and the large company—the need to assess their future prospects (the stability of their jobs and future promotion), and the availability of profits to finance increased salaries and wages. The disclosure of the salaries of higher paid employees and directors will indicate what may be available. More sophisticated trade unions make great use of financial information in collective bargaining.

(d) *Analysts and advisers of third parties* (e.g. journalists, credit rating agencies)

These people have a right to corporate information through the medium of those they advise who have an actual or potential interest. For larger companies such people will take a public role in giving advice; but in smaller companies and private concerns the right or ability to alienate an interest in the company might be limited so that less use may be made of such advice.

(e) *Business contacts* (e.g. creditors, potential customers, rivals)

In the case of a small company potential long-term customers may be interested in the financial position because their ability to receive a steady supply may be influenced. Suppliers and other creditors will be concerned with the continuing ability of the business to pay—with a larger concern there is a presumption that it is a good risk but without independent information it is difficult to judge the credit-worthiness of a small company.

For a larger company unhealthy financial statements may warn off possible creditors and customers but very often these people will be willing to trade on the basis of the name.

In both cases rivals and competitors will take an interest. In large groups the profitability of individual types of business may be hidden, reducing the usefulness of the accounts in this respect.

Another group wishing to use smaller companies' accounts will be those wishing to sue companies. They will wish to know whether there are sufficient assets to make such an action worthwhile.

(f) *The Government*

The Government's interest in accounts is twofold: statistical and fiscal. The statistical interest will vary according to the size of the company. The interest of the taxation authorities is in the accounts as a basis for more detailed tax computations. The use made of the accounts will be similar, therefore, for both small and large companies.

(g) *The public*

The public's interest in specific concerns will probably be in the larger companies: e.g. how much the chairman earns, what the political and charitable contributions were. In smaller companies, and to an extent with larger companies, the interest may be met via statistical digests showing how profitable companies have been, what the average political contribution has been and what the average director earns.

ANSWER A5

(a) 'Value added' is that amount by which the sales value of production has been enhanced by the efforts of the organisation and its employees.

It has been variously described, e.g.

(i) Salaries and wages, fringe benefits, interest, dividend, tax, depreciation, net profit (retained). Government consultative document (Green Paper): *The Future of Company Reports (1977)*.

(ii) Turnover less goods and services purchased from outside.

These two definitions are complementary and describe the two opposite sides of a value added statement (see (b)(ii)).

(iii) *The Corporate Report (1975)*. The Report defined value added as 'the wealth the reporting entity has been able to create by its own and its employees' efforts'.

Financial Accounting

(b) (i) XYZ Ltd. Conventional profit statement for the year ended 31 Dec. 19–9

	£000	£000
Sales (turnover)		740
Less:		
Purchased materials used in production	300	
Salaries and wages	200	
Services purchased	60	
Loan interest paid and payable	20	
Depreciation of fixed assets	40	
		620
Profit before tax		120
Less: Corporation tax		60
Profit after tax		60
Less: Dividend proposed		24
Retained profit for the year		36

(ii) XYZ Ltd. Value added statement for the year ended 31 Dec. 19–9

	£000	£000
Sales (turnover)		740
Less:		
Bought in materials and services and depreciation (see (b)(iii))		400
Value added available for sharing or retention		340
Applied as follows:		
To employees (see note)		200
To providers of capital:		
Interest	20	
Dividends	24	
		44
To government—taxation		60
Profits retained for future growth (see (b)(iii))		36
Application of value added		340

Note: This figure would usually include not only salaries and wages, but also employers' contributions towards pensions (if any) and social security payments.

(iii) An alternative view is that depreciation, an appropriation of profit rather than an expense, is an application of value added. If this view is taken, the total value added in the above statement would be £380,000 and the final application item could read 'profits retained for the replacement of assets and future growth—£76,000'.

(c) Some advantages claimed for including value added statements in a company's corporate report are:

(i) An improvement in 'team spirit'. It is hoped that reporting value added will generate some change in industrial outlook and attitudes so that employees will become more motivated to work, thus putting in more effort and performing better. Value added is (hopefully) seen as the achievement of a team: workers, management, and providers of capital.

(ii) The inclusion of a value added statement should facilitate the introduction of productivity schemes based on value added.

(iii) The value added statement is said to direct attention to the employees' share thereof and to trends in that share over time. Employees often receive 60% to 70% of the value added of their company and the wider knowledge of this should help combat the inaccurate belief of many that they are exploited and that their efforts unduly benefit the shareholders.

(iv) The statement is cheap and easy to prepare.

ANSWER A6

(a) *A holding gain*

A holding gain is the increase in value of assets (e.g. stock) arising from their retention in the business during a period of price inflation.

Normally, profit statements do not account for these unrealised holding gains, which represent the difference between the historical cost of assets and their replacement cost at the date of the statements. However, traditional historical cost principles dictate that when such assets are sold the profit taken includes the holding gain. Thus, the profit consists of two elements:

(a) that arising from the increase in the value of the assets held—the holding gain, and
(b) that arising from the buying, making and selling of the assets.

The gain arising from the appreciation in the value of the asset should not be treated as distributable since, in order to maintain the capacity of the business, it is necessary to replace, at current cost, that which has been used. In this respect the historical cost profit gives a misleading idea of the 'profit' of the business.

Holding gains arise also in the increase in value of fixed assets. This is normally recognised on a revaluation when a reserve is created which is not available for distribution. If the business ceases or if it curtails the extent of its activities, holding gains become available for distribution.

(b) *Backlog depreciation*

Backlog depreciation is the difference between the accumulated depreciation based on the 'current cost' of an asset at the end of a financial year and the accumulated depreciation provided at the end of the previous financial year plus the current year's current cost depreciation. In symbols:

$$\text{backlog depreciation} = A_{n+1} - (A_n + D_{n+1})$$

where:

A_n = accumulated depreciation based on current years replacement cost at the end of the year 'n'

D_{n+1} = depreciation charge for year $n + 1$ on a current replacement cost basis.

Backlog depreciation will normally arise because the gross replacement cost of the asset will increase over a period; thus, the depreciation provided on a previous year will not be the same proportion of the present inflated cost which it represented at the end of the previous year. Prior year backlog depreciation is that needed to bring the accumulated depreciation brought forward into line with the increased replacement cost.

Backlog depreciation will also arise because of the method of calculating the depreciation charge for the period. In order to charge against profits accruing over a period a figure fairly representing the use taken out of those assets in that period, the charge will be made based on the average replacement cost of the assets in the period. Thus is not necessarily the same as the extra depreciation provision required based on the year-end value of the asset.

(c) The principal problem that arises in attempting to answer this question is the determination of the intention of the quotation from (or the whole of) *SSAP 12*.

SSAP 12 was written in the context of historical cost accounting to outline how the matching concept of *SSAP 2* should be applied. It thus evinces no clear policy in regard to inflation accounting, and the matters discussed below arise from an endeavour to extend its ambit to such circumstances. The main intention is clear: the matching of the costs of holding an asset—its dissipation, wearing out and loss of value arising from the effluxion of time—should be set against the benefits derived from that asset.

In the context of current cost accounting we must redefine the idea of the 'cost of holding' the asset. The approach adopted has been to treat a portion of its current gross replacement cost as having been 'used' in each period: in other words, the 'cost' of the asset has been replaced by its 'present year's replacement cost' and a portion of that is allocated to each period.

So far we have not considered the problem of backlog depreciation. There are two questions to ask: firstly, is it a cost?; and secondly, to which period should we allocate it? Let us first consider the portion of backlog depreciation relating to previous periods. This amount represents depreciation on a holding gain—we do not account for the holding gain through the profit and loss account and so we have no benefit against which to match the backlog 'cost'. Therefore, it would seem reasonable to contend that the intention of *SSAP 12* would argue against the charging of such depreciation; or, to answer the two questions, it is not a cost and should not be allocated to any period but set against the holding gain. Now consider the element of backlog depreciation resulting from applying the depreciation percentage to the average replacement cost of the period rather than the period-end replacement cost. The same principles clearly apply: during the year there has been a holding gain of the portion of the asset consumed. Assuming the holding gain to accrue evenly over the year, then the cost of using the asset attributable to the profits of the whole year must be based upon the average replacement cost; the backlog depreciation element must be set against the holding gain. (If the gain does not accrue evenly, then the averaging method only approximates to the charge which should be made.)

In conclusion, inflation forces us to look uncomfortably far into the intentions of *SSAP 12*. Complications arising in the definition of cost, in profit allocation, and the treatment of backlog depreciation have to be viewed in the light of the inferred intentions and not those which are explicit.

(d) *Rochester Enterprises Ltd*

Balance sheets at:

	31 Dec. 19–8 £	31 Dec. 19–9 £
Plant and machinery replacement cost	250	385
Less: Depreciation	50	132
	200	253

Profit and loss accounts for the year's ended:

	31 Dec. 19–8 £	31 Dec. 19–9 £
Depreciation	50	77
Backlog	—	5

(Deducted from revaluation reserves (or retained profits b/f).)

Financial Accounting

Workings

Replacement cost	*Depreciation*
$200 \times \dfrac{100}{80} = \underline{\underline{250}}$	$40 \times \dfrac{100}{80} = \underline{\underline{50}}$
$200 \times \dfrac{110}{80} = 275$	$80 \times \dfrac{110}{80} = 110$
$100 \times \dfrac{110}{100} = 110$	$20 \times \dfrac{110}{100} = 22$
$\phantom{200 \times \dfrac{110}{80} =}\underline{385}$	$\phantom{80 \times \dfrac{110}{80} =}\underline{132}$

Depreciation charge   *Backlog depreciation*

$40 \times \dfrac{100}{80} = \underline{\underline{50}}$ $55 - 50 = \underline{\underline{5}}$

$40 \times \dfrac{110}{80} = 55$ or

$20 \times \dfrac{110}{100} = 22$ $40 \times \left(\dfrac{110 - 100}{80}\right) = \underline{\underline{5}}$

$\phantom{40 \times \dfrac{110}{80} =}\underline{\underline{77}}$

ANSWER A7. BURBAGE LTD

(a) *Historical cost basis*

	£	£
Sales: 200 at £6		1,200
500 at £6.50		3,250
		4,450
Purchases 1,000 at £4	4,000	
Less: Closing stock 300 at £4	1,200	
Cost of sales 700 at £4		2,800
Gross profit		1,650

(b) *Replacement cost basis*

Date of sale	Proceeds of sale £	Replacement cost at date of sale £	Historical cost of sales £	Operating profit £	Holding gain £
28 Feb. 19–6	1,200	900	800	300	100
29 Jun. 19–6	3,250	2,625	2,000	625	625
	4,450	3,525	2,800	925	725

The holding gain of £725 is a *realised* holding gain. There is, however, in addition, an *unrealised* holding gain which is not taken account of above. At the end of the year, unsold stock amounted to 300 units. The historical cost of this stock was £4 per unit but by 30 Jun. 19–6 its replacement cost had increased to £5.25. The unrealised holding gain is therefore 300 × £1.25 = £375.

Under replacement cost accounting, the total gains may be summarised as follows:

	£	£
Operating gains		925
Holding gains:		
Realised	725	
Unrealised	375	
		1,100
Total gains		2,025

(c) The historical cost profit figure of £1,650 is equivalent to the total of the operating gains (£925) and the realised holding gains (£725).

The usefulness of the replacement cost approach is that it attempts to match current sales revenue with the current value of stocks consumed in earning that revenue (or, as it is often referred to, the value to the business, at the date of sale, of the stocks consumed). It is useful to distinguish between operating gains and realised holding gains because they relate to two different activities, and users of accounts may find this distinction helpful. In this example £725 out of the historical cost profit of £1,650 relates to the fact that goods were bought in advance of requirement and, during the time the stocks were held by the company, their replacement cost increased.

The holding gain of £375 is different in that it has not yet been realised by sale to a third party. Replacement cost accounting requires the recognition of this gain, and the replacement cost balance sheet would include stock at its replacement cost at the balance sheet date.

ANSWER A8

The usefulness of the information provided by a set of accounts must be judged in relation to the needs of those who have a reasonable right to use those accounts.

Equity investors, apart from their interest in the stewardship of the assets exercised by the management, are concerned with the future of the business, i.e. its ability to continue to pay and increase the value of dividends. This is essentially an interest in the long-term future of the business. The interests of employees are similar but include an interest in the levels of remuneration paid to directors and other employees.

Creditors (both loan and trade creditors) on the other hand, have a more short-term interest in the business. They are concerned with its ability to pay its debts; this is represented by a need to know how the business will perform in the future and what its liquidity position will be. Taxation authorities, however, are the principal user whose interest is in historical information rather than in the future prospects of the enterprise.

We can now re-phrase the question: Do current cost accounts provide better information about the future (long-run and short-run) than historical cost accounts?

Historical cost accounts match actual revenue against historical costs, showing what has happened in the period but without giving any great indication as to the future ability of the business to continue operating.

Current cost accounts show what has happened but, by matching current revenues to the current cost of those revenues, show how much remains after maintaining the capacity of the business to continue operating. Thus, current cost accounts endeavour to show what has happened in a manner which will enable users to assess the future prospects of the business with more accuracy.

Both historical and current accounting methods presume that the business will continue (being based on the going-concern concept of *SSAP 2* and *para. 10 Sch. 4 CA 1985*) and, therefore, provide no information to assist in the decision as to whether or not to continue the business. Accounts prepared using realisable values ('exit value accounting') would give this information but do not assist greatly in measuring the performance of the business or its future earnings capacity.

Likewise, HCA and CCA are both inward looking: they both look at the business from inside and show how it has performed. If the business were regarded as an investment (rather than regarding the earning potential of the shares as the principal investment) then it would be important to look at how inflation has affected the real value of the business assets in terms of their purchasing power. The writer contends that this approach has little use since users are not concerned with the purchasing power of the assets in the business but with either the value of their income stream from the business or the ability of the business to pay them the amounts it owes.

It is often suggested that a cash flow form of financial statement would be of more use than the present profit concentrated statements. CCA, by showing what funds are available after maintaining the operating capacity of the business, represents a move towards this form of accounting. It is thus, perhaps, a method of accounting which involves a redefinition of profit as 'surplus funds'. This does not mean that it is any worse for that; if the idea of 'profit' which it embodies is more useful, then let us accept that definition.

From the concept of 'surplus funds', however, arises the 'gearing adjustment' and there is some controversy as to whether its inclusion usefully supplements the idea of profit. There are two ways of looking at the gearing adjustment. The first is as an indication of 'the benefit or cost to shareholders which is realised in the period, ... [of] ... the extent to which a proportion of the net operating assets are financed by borrowing'. In other words, the current cost adjustments reflect the need to maintain the operating capacity of the whole business but the only part which needs to be maintained is the equity financed portion; thus a deduction has to be made to reflect the static cost of the fixed capital. The second view (and in the writer's opinion the more logical approach) is to view the adjustment as the extra funds which will be received if the present level of gearing is maintained. Thus, if the net assets have increased by £10 and the company has 40% fixed interest capital, then it will expect to raise another £4 of fixed interest capital to maintain its gearing. This £4 represents excess funds after maintaining the operating capacity and so should be included in profit.

Set against the inclusion of the gearing adjustment is the argument that its inclusion gives the impression that these excess funds are 'realised profit' whereas they properly constitute extra borrowings. This argument has some compulsion but it is based on an idea of 'realised profit' which is taken from historical cost accounting.

Is the idea of extra funds available a useful one? Yes, if one is concerned with the future of the business.

ANSWER A9. SPARROW LTD

(a) *Cash budgets, Apr.–Sep. 19–7*

	Apr. £	May £	Jun. £	Jul. £	Aug. £	Sep. £
Cash inflows						
Receipt from debtors re sales in:						
—Feb.	20,000					
—Mar.		24,000				
—Apr.			28,000			
—May				32,000		
—Jun.					36,000	
—Jul.						40,000
Cash outflows						
Payments to creditors re purchases in:						
—Mar.	(24,000)					
—Apr.		(27,000)				
—May			(30,000)			
—Jun.				(33,000)		
—Jul.					(36,000)	
—Aug.						(39,000)
Expenses:						
Wages and admin	(4,000)	(4,000)	(4,000)	(4,000)	(4,000)	(4,000)
Rent	(5,000)					
Purchase of leasehold	(25,000)					
Net cash outflow	(38,000)	(7,000)	(6,000)	(5,000)	(4,000)	(3,000)
(Overdraft) brought forward at start of month	(3,000)	(41,000)	(48,000)	(54,000)	(59,000)	(63,000)
Overdraft carried forward at month end	(41,000)	(48,000)	(54,000)	(59,000)	(63,000)	(66,000)

(b) *Expected net profit for six months to 30 Sep. 19–7*

	£	£
Sales		228,000
Cost of sales		171,000
Gross profit on sales at 25%		57,000
Wages	18,000	
Administration	6,000	
Rent	2,500	
Depreciation	1,250	
		27,750
Expected net profit		29,250

(c) Budgeted profitability and budgeted liquidity

Budgeted net profit is determined using normal accounting concepts. The accruals (or matching) concept (*SSAP 2*) is fundamental to its determination. For example, cost of sales is matched with the sales for the period to obtain budgeted gross profit. Then the expenses related to the earnings of the sales in that period are deducted from the gross profit to arrive at the expected or budgeted net profit. It is not relevant to the determination of this that some of the purchases have not yet been paid for, or that some sales on credit terms have not been settled for by the debtor.

Budgeted liquidity involves the comparison of all cash inflows and all cash outflows occurring in the period. The budgeted overdraft at the period end is determined by adding the net cash outflow for the period to the opening bank overdraft position. The cash outflows would cover revenue and capital expenditure, but only revenue items relevant to the period would be included as expenses in arriving at net profit. The following differences relate to Sparrow Ltd for the six months ended 30 Sep. 19–7:

Sales/cost of sales
Sales, purchases and changes in stock levels are incorporated into the calculation of expected net profit. The cash budget reflects all cash inflows from debtors and all outflows to creditors, irrespective of the particular month when the sales or purchases were made.

Rent
The full annual sum in included as a cash outflow in Apr. 19–7 whereas only half of the annual rent is applicable as an expense for the six months ended 30 Sep. 19–7.

Depreciation
This does not involve a cash flow. The charge against gross profit represents the wasting attributable to half a year of a ten-year lease.

Capital expenditure
The cash outflow in Apr. 19–7 represents the purchase of leasehold property and is a component of the cash budget.

One way of formalising the difference between budgeted liquidity and budgeted profitability would be via a budgeted source and application of funds statement for the six months ended 30 Sep. 19–7:

Sources of funds

		£
Net profit		29,250
Add back: Items not involving the movement of funds		
—depreciation		1,250
Total generated from operations	c/f	30,500

Financial Accounting

		£
Applications of funds	b/f	30,500
Purchase of leasehold		25,000
		5,500
Change in working capital		
Increase in stock	36,000	
Increase in debtors	48,000	
Increase in rent-in-advance	2,500	
Increase in creditors	(18,000)	
Decrease in net liquid funds	(63,000)	
		5,500

Workings

(1) Purchases

	Apr. £	May £	Jun. £	Jul. £	Aug. £	Sep. £
Sales in month	28,000	32,000	36,000	40,000	44,000	48,000
Less: gross profit (25%)	7,000	8,000	9,000	10,000	11,000	12,000
Cost of sales	21,000	24,000	27,000	30,000	33,000	36,000
Plus increase in stock during month (see note)	6,000	6,000	6,000	6,000	6,000	6,000
Purchases in month	27,000	30,000	33,000	36,000	39,000	42,000

Note: Sales are budgeted to increase at the rate of £4,000 per month and it is company policy to hold sufficient stock at the end of each month to cover the next two months' sales. Therefore, increase in stock each month at cost value is (£8,000 × 75%) = £6,000, i.e. the extra stock to be purchased this month is to cover extra sales of the next two months. These extra sales will be valued at £8,000 in selling value terms. (The policy of stock holding adopted by the company can be seen to be extravagant!)

(2) Depreciation

This charge against gross profit related to the leasehold premises:

$$\tfrac{1}{10} \times £25,000 \times \tfrac{1}{2} \text{ year} = £1,250$$

(3) Stock, debtors, creditors

	31 Mar. 19–7 £	30 Sep. 19–7 £
Stock	45,000	81,000
Debtors	44,000	92,000
Creditors	24,000	42,000

Tutorial note: This question shows clearly how difficulties may arise through 'over-trading'.

ANSWER B1. ACCOUNTING TERMINOLOGY

(a) *Fundamental accounting concepts* are the broad general assumptions which underlie the periodic financial accounts of business enterprises. *SSAP 2* recognises four fundamental accounting concepts, which are now enacted in *Sch. 4 CA 1985* and called therein 'accounting principles'.

(i) *Going concern*
The balance sheet is prepared on the assumption that there is no necessity or intention to liquidate or curtail significantly the activities of the business within the foreseeable future. The balance sheet does not, therefore, purport to show the value of the assets were they to be suddenly realised at the balance sheet date.
(*Tutorial note:* Be quite sure you *understand* the going concern concept!)

(ii) *Accruals concept*
Income is recognised in the profit and loss account as it is earned, rather than when cash is collected. Against this income must be set the costs and expenses incurred in earning that income. If expenditure, such as fixed assets expenditure, benefits several accounting periods, this expenditure must be allocated over those years and matched against income.

(iii) *Consistency concept*
Similar items should be treated in a consistent manner within an accounting period and from one accounting period to the next so as to make financial results comparable.

(iv) *Prudence concept*
Provision should be made for all known losses and liabilities whereas income and profits should only be taken when realised.

Under *SSAP 2* and *para. 15 Sch. 4 CA 1985* any deviation from these fundamental accounting concepts should be disclosed in the published accounts of the concern, together with an explanation of the effect of the deviation.

(b) *Accounting bases* are the generally accepted methods of applying the fundamental accounting concepts to particular financial transactions. For example, a company would be expected to provide for depreciation of its fixed assets and would be expected to include a valuation for its stock and work-in-progress in its balance sheet so that, following the accruals concept, such stock items can be set off against the sale of those items in future accounting periods. There are, however, a number of alternative methods of providing for depreciation and of valuing stock and these are accounting bases.

Financial Accounting **123**

(c) *Accounting policies* are the specific accounting bases adopted by a particular business as being most suitable to show a true and fair view of its financial results and position.

In the case of depreciation, the provision in the accounts will depend upon the rates of depreciation used and the policy decided upon, e.g. straight line method, reducing balance method.

The valuation of stock will depend upon how cost is calculated, e.g. FIFO, average cost, etc., and the amount of overheads attributable to that stock.

ANSWER B2. KINGSWEAR LTD

(a) Earnings per share is the profit in pence attributable to each equity share based on the consolidated profit of the period after tax and after deducting minority interests and preference dividends, but before taking into account extraordinary items, divided by the number of equity shares in issue and ranking for dividend in respect of the period.

(b) (i) *The 'net' basis.* This basis includes in the tax charge all tax howsoever arising. It therefore includes ACT which is irrecoverable and double tax relief (DTR) which is lost because of a limitation due to the ACT set off against foreign income. It thus shows the effect of the dividend policy on earnings per share (EPS).

(ii) *The 'nil' basis.* This produces a figure for EPS which is independent of the dividend policy. Thus an element of the tax charge which is only attributable to the dividend paid (e.g. irrecoverable ACT or DTR lost) is excluded from the tax charge.

For most companies the net and nil bases will give the same result. *SSAP 3* dictates that the net basis should always be disclosed and that the nil basis may be disclosed if it gives an EPS figure which is materially different (by more than 10%) from the net basis.

(c) *'Net' basis*

	£
Net profit after tax	2,100,000
Less: Preference dividend	120,000
	1,980,000
Shares in issue and ranking for dividend	10,000,000
Earnings per share	19.8p

(ii) *'Nil'* basis

	£
Net profit after tax	2,100,000
Less: Preference dividend	120,000
	1,980,000
Add back: Irrecoverable ACT	100,000
	2,080,000
Shares in issue and ranking for dividend	10,000,000
Earnings per share	20.8p

(d) *Fully diluted earnings per share on net basis*

	£	£
Earnings after tax and preference dividend (as above)		1,980,000
Add: Debenture interest	125,000	
Tax @ 40%	50,000	
		75,000
		2,055,000
Number of ordinary shares		10,000,000
Maximum number issuable after the year end:		
$\dfrac{£1{,}250{,}000}{£1.25}$		1,000,000
		11,000,000
Fully diluted earnings per share		18.7p

ANSWER B3

(a) A company is financed by its equity investors and by loans. This capital is represented in the assets owned by the concern. The loan capital is fixed and a regular fixed interest payment will be made. The equity investors' interest varies. Initially, it is the amount of money they subscribe for shares on the founding of the company. The company then makes profits. It may distribute all or some of these profits to the equity investors. If it distributes only some of these profits, then the equity investors retain an interest in the profits which have not been distributed. Such non-distributed profits are called *reserves*. Normally, as indicated above, such reserves arise when the company makes a profit. The *Companies Act 1985* stipulates that only profits which have been realised may be distributed. Other forms of 'profit' may arise, e.g. a surplus (or 'profit') on revaluation of assets, a premium (or 'profit') on the issue of shares. All these profits are forms of reserves. Other reserves arise when profits are set aside for specific purposes, e.g. debenture redemption reserve.

There are three categories of reserves:

(i) *Reserves which are non-distributable by virtue of legislation*
These are the share premium account, the capital redemption reserve, and any revaluation reserves.

If shares are issued at a price in excess of their nominal value, the excess is called a *premium on issue*. The receipt of this excess is a form of 'capital profit' to the company. The excess is put to the share premium account.

If a company redeems redeemable shares or if a private company purchases its own shares, then the amount by which the share capital of the company is reduced must be transferred from the distributable reserves to a capital redemption reserve (*s. 170 CA 1985*).

If the assets of a company are revalued, the company makes an unrealised profit. This profit is not distributable and is, therefore, transferred to a revaluation reserve.

These reserves are non-distributable; this means that the company may not use them to pay a dividend. However, it may use them to issue bonus shares or pay up partly-paid shares.

(ii) *Reserves which are non-distributable by virtue of the company's articles of association or accounting convention*
These include the current cost reserve, debenture redemption reserves, general reserves, and fixed asset replacement reserves. In general they represent amounts set aside from distributable profits which are no longer regarded as distributable. A fixed asset replacement reserve may be set up when it is realised that the cost of replacing fixed assets will be higher than the funds currently retained in the business by way of depreciation. The setting up of the reserve recognises that it is necessary to retain more profits in order to maintain the ability of the business to continue operating. The current cost reserve is a creature of current cost accounting and contains not only amounts set aside from profit for maintaining the operating capacity but also revaluation surpluses arising on the restatement of the current cost balance sheet.

(ii) *Distributable reserves*
These are realised profits and are available for distribution by way of dividend.

(b) *Fixed assets*

Sch. 4 CA 1985 requires that fixed assets be shown in the accounts at cost less amounts provided for depreciation. The provision of depreciation is a means of writing off the cost of an asset over its useful life. The effect of inflation is normally to increase the cost of assets and hence it is probable that the amount which could be obtained if the asset were sold would be in excess of the amount shown in the accounts. The purpose of providing depreciation is not to write down the asset to its realisable value but to charge to the profit and loss account that part of the cost of the asset which has been consumed in the year and to match the benefit obtained from the use of the asset with its consumption (by way of use) in the business. The balance sheet is prepared on the basis that the business is a going concern and will not be liquidated. Therefore, assets are not shown therein at realisable value but at the value yet to be consumed by the business.

(c) *Accounting policies*

Part II Sch. 4 CA 1985 specifies a number of accounting principles. These are the presumptions:

(i) that the company will continue as a going concern;
(ii) that accounting policies will be applied consistently from year to year;
(iii) that a prudent view shall be taken; and
(iv) that all income and charges relating to the financial year shall be taken in without regard to the actual date of receipt or payment (matching).

These provisions mirror the accounting concepts of *SSAP 2*.

Several aspects of accounting could be dealt with in different ways in accordance with these principles. These different ways are called *accounting bases* and the bases actually selected by a company for the preparation of its financial statements are called its *accounting policies*.

For example, consider the depreciation of fixed assets. Accounting principles require the cost of using an asset to be allocated to the periods which benefit from its use. Possible accounting bases are:

(1) allocate the cost by equal annual instalments to the years expected to benefit;
(2) allocate the cost on a reducing balance basis.

The method chosen represents the accounting policy of the company and accounting principles require it to be applied consistently.

(d) *Extraordinary items*

Investors are concerned with the ability of the company to make profits. One indicator of its future ability is its past record. For this to be a reliable indicator it must show the ordinary profits of the company rather than the effect of one-off transactions. The profits or losses from one-off transactions are called *extraordinary items* and are separately disclosed in the profit and loss account. The conditions which a profit or loss must fulfil in order to be classed as extraordinary are closely defined. They are:

(i) that the amount of the profit or loss is material; and
(ii) that the event giving rise to the item is both out of the normal course of business and not expected to recur.

ANSWER B4. JASON

(a) *Income statement comparing recognition of revenue on an accruals basis with a cash basis*

	Basis 1 Sales (Accruals)		Basis 2 Cash	
	Units	£000	Units	£000
Income (A)	170	34	150	30
Wages and sundry expenses	200	10	200	10
Depletion of mine (workings (i))		16		16
	200	26	200	26
Closing stock	30	3.9	50	6.5
Total expenditure incurred (B)	170	22.1	150	19.5
Net profit (A) − (B)		11.9		10.5

Basis 3

	£000	£000
Net profit on a production basis		
Value of output (on basis of sales price)		40
Wages and production expenses	10	
Depletion of mine	16	
		26
Net profit		14

Workings

(i) Depletion of mine is arrived at on basis of estimated output, i.e. for current year:

$$\frac{200}{1,000} \times £(100,000 - 30,000 + 10,000)$$

$$= £16,000$$

(ii) *Closing stock*
30/200 × 26 = 3.9
50/200 × 26 = 6.5

(iii) *Profit figures* (check on calculations)

$$\text{Cost of production per unit} = \frac{£26,000}{200} = £130.$$

Profit per unit = £200 − £130 = £70
Profit figures: Basis 1   170 × £70 = £11,900
               Basis 2   150 × £70 = £10,500
               Basis 3   200 × £70 = £14,000

Assumptions
(1) It is usual to write off costs of assets such as mines and oil wells over estimated production. This is likely to match costs against revenues in a more realistic way.
(2) Closing stock in the case of the first two bases includes an element of depletion.

(b) The conventional basis, recognising profit when gold is sold, is the preferable approach as it follows both the accruals concept and the prudence concept. On this method, income is recognised as soon as it is realised, namely at the point of sale. This method follows recognised accounting practice. Revenue is allocated between accounting periods on this basis, and against this revenue is matched the costs of earning the revenue, namely depletion of the mine and mining and production costs.

The second approach is excessively prudent and is unlikely to be acceptable. The third approach ignores the prudence concept as it recognises unrealised profits. The profit on the 30 unsold nuggets should not be recognised until they have been realised by way of sale to a third party. This third approach is, therefore, unacceptable.

Tutorial note: Although the question does not refer to the respective balance sheets, it should be appreciated that the balance sheet will contain a fixed asset (the mine) and unsold stocks. It should be ensured at each balance sheet date that these are not carried at a figure in excess of their current values. This could be important, for example, if the mineral surveys turned out to be incorrect and the mine was capable only of producing an output well below 1,000 nuggets.

ANSWER B5. P. ERCOLATOR

(a) **(i)** *Trading account for year to 31 Dec. 19–6 using FIFO basis*

	Workings	£000	£000
Sales	(1)		1,040
Cost of sales:			
Opening stock		90	
Purchases	(2)	816	
		906	
Less: Closing stock	(3)	180	
			726
Gross profit			314

(ii) *Trading account for year to 31 Dec. 19–6 using LIFO basis*

	Workings	£000	£000
Sales	(1)		1,040
Cost of sales:			
Opening stock		90	
Purchases	(2)	816	
		906	
Less: Closing stock	(4)	138	
			768
Gross profit			272

Workings

(1) *Sales*

	Tonnes	Price per tonne £	£000
19–6			
1 Apr.	400	960	384
1 Jul.	360	1,200	432
31 Dec.	140	1,600	224
			1,040

(2) *Purchases*

	Tonnes	Price per tonne £	£000
19–6:			
31 Mar.	300	720	216
30 Jun.	400	900	360
30 Dec.	200	1,200	240
			816

(3) *Closing stock on a FIFO basis*

		Tonne	Price per tonne £	£000	£000
19–6					
1 Jan. Opening stock		150	600		90
31 Mar. Purchases		300	720		216
		450			306
1 Apr. Sales	(150)		(600)	(90)	
	(250)		(720)	(180)	
	—	(400)		—	(270)
		50			36
30 Jun. Purchases		400	900		360
		450			396
1 Jul. Sales	(50)		(720)	(36)	
	(310)		(900)	(279)	
	—	(360)		—	(315)
		90			81
30 Dec. Purchases		200	1,200		240
		290			321
31 Dec. Sales	(90)		(900)	(81)	
	(50)		(1,200)	(60)	
	—	(140)		—	(141)
31 Dec. Closing stock		150			180

(4) *Closing stock on a LIFO basis*

	Tonne	Price per tonne £	£000	£000
19–6				
1 Jan. Opening stock	150	600		90
31 Mar. Purchases	300	720		216
	450			306
1 Apr. Sales (300)		(720)	(216)	
(100)		(600)	(60)	
	(400)			(276)
	50			30
30 Jun. Purchases	400	900		360
	450			390
1 Jul. Sales	(360)	(900)		(324)
	90			66
30 Dec. Purchases	200	1,200		240
	290			306
31 Dec. Sales	(140)	1,200		(168)
31 Dec. Closing stock	150			138

(b) In inflationary conditions, the LIFO method will lead to lower closing stock valuations as items in stock will be valued at earlier lower prices. The effect of this is that the cost of sales will be at the latest prices, thus leading to a lower profit figure. This situation approximates to *current cost profit*.

The FIFO method leads to the reverse situation; closing stocks are valued at the latest price, and consequently cost of sales will be at lower historical cost. This leads to higher closing stock values and higher profit figures.

ANSWER B6. CARTER ENGINEERING PLC

(a) £68,000.

The contrast is insufficiently complete to judge its outcome with any certainty. No figure for present expected costs to completion is given and it is presumed that these, if known, would not indicate a future loss on the contract.

(b) Profit $\frac{34}{40} \times £(480{,}000 - 400{,}000) = £68{,}000$
∴ Work-in-progress $= £(340{,}000 + 68{,}000)$
$= £408{,}000$

The contract is well advanced. The future costs to completion estimate indicates that there is a substantial degree of certainty that the contract will be completed at a total profit of £80,000. Assuming all parts of the work to be equally profitable, the proportion of the profit taken should relate to the amount of work completed. Hence, $\frac{34}{40}$ of the profit is taken. An allowance would have to be made for any rectification or guarantee work if not included in the £60,000.

(c) Assuming that the costs for the special order are reasonably certain and that a profit should be made on the order, then the stock should be taken in at cost, £12,000.

(d) The asset should be taken into the balance sheet at net realisable value after allowing for costs to completion, i.e.

$$£(20{,}100 - 4{,}200) = £15{,}900$$

ANSWER B7. TECHNOLOGICAL COMPONENTS LTD

(a) (i) *Extract from accounting policies statement*
   Depreciation. This has been calculated in order to write off the cost of the assets over their expected lives. The following rates of depreciation were applied:

   Plant and machinery   50% reducing balance method

(ii) *Extract from balance sheet at 31 Dec. 19–7*
Included within fixed assets—plant and machinery totals:

	£
Cost	200,000
Accumulated depreciation	150,000
	50,000

(iii) *Extract from profit and loss account for the year ended 31 Dec. 19–7*
Included within total depreciation charge: £50,000.

(b) Under historical cost accounting, assets are usually stated at their original or historical cost, less accumulated depreciation. However, a modification to the historical cost convention is permitted (*s. 31(2) Part II Sch. 4 Companies Act 1985*)—audit reports often refer to the *historical cost convention as modified by the revaluation of certain assets*.

Such revaluations usually relate to freehold and leasehold properties although some companies occasionally incorporate revaluation of plant and machinery into their accounts.

For many items of plant and machinery, where there has been only gradual technological change, the use of suitable index numbers may provide an acceptable basis for a valuation.

However, there will be occasions where the application of index numbers to book figures will provide unrealistic results. This may occur, for example, where there has been rapid technological change. One solution in such cases is to adopt the concept of the modern equivalent asset.

It is assumed that the valuation required is as at 30 Sep. 19–8. *Para 20, SSAP 12 (Accounting for depreciation)* requires that where assets are revalued, depreciation after the revaluation date should be based on the revalued amount.

Calculation of valuation at 31 Dec. 19–8

The replacement for machine K has a service potential twice that of machine K:

	£	£
Current valuation of service potential of machine K if new is		
£100,000 × $\dfrac{500,000}{1,000,000}$		50,000
Allowing for 2 years 9 months expired life on a reducing balance basis at a rate of 50%		
19–6 (12 months)	25,000	
19–7 (12 months)	12,500	
19–8 (9 months)	4,687	
		42,187
Revised valuation at 30 Sep. 19–8		7,813
Continuing with same depreciation rate:		
Three months depreciation to 31 Dec. 19–8		
– 50% of £7,813 × $\frac{3}{12}$ (it is assumed that time apportionment provides a reasonably acceptable result)		977
Written down value at 31 Dec. 19–8		6,836

At the date of valuation, 30 Sep. 19–8, it is important to ensure that £7,813 reflects a realistic value of the remaining service potential of the asset.

Tutorial note: Strictly speaking, part (b) requires only a calculation. The explanations above are included because of the unusual nature of the situation.

(c) *Fixed asset—cost or valuation account*

	£		£
19–8			
Jan. 1 Balance b/f	200,000	Sep. 30 P & L a/c	
		(revaluation)	192,187
		Dec. 31 Balance c/f	7,813
	200,000		200,000

Accumulated depreciation account

	£		£
		19–8	
Sep. 30 P & L a/c		Jan. 1 Balance b/f	150,000
(revaluation)	168,750	Sep. 30 P & L a/c	
Dec. 31 Balance c/f	977	(depreciation)	18,750
		Dec. 31 P & L a/c	
		(depreciation)	977
	169,727		169,727

Working
Depreciation, nine months to 30 Sep. 19–8 = 50% × £50,000 × $\frac{9}{12}$
= £18,750

Notes
(1) Depreciation after 30 Sep. 19–8 is based on the revalued amount of £7,813.
(2) Deficit on revaluation of £23,437 (192,187 − 168,750) should be debited to profit and loss account.

(d) *Extract from statement of accounting policies*

Depreciation
The same note would relevant as for part (a).

Profit and loss account

	£
Depreciation charge:	
Based on cost	18,750
Based on revalued amount	977
	19,727
Exceptional items:	
Deficit on revaluation of plant and machinery (working 1)	23,437

Note to accounts
The effect of the revaluation of plant and machinery during the year is to reduce the depreciation charge by £5,272 (working 2).

Assumption
It is assumed that revaluation of plant occurs frequently and the deficit on revaluation is ordinary rather than extraordinary.

Workings
(1) Deficit on revaluation of plant, £192,187 − £168,750 = 23,437
(2)   £
Depreciation charged assuming no revaluation:
50% × £50,000   25,000
Less: Depreciation actually charged   19,727

  5,273

Balance sheet
Fixed assets—see note.

Note on fixed assets (comparatives ignored)

	Plant and machinery £
Cost and valuation:	
Cost at 1 Jan. 19–8	200,000
Revaluation during year	192,187
Revaluation at 31 Dec. 19–8	7,813
Depreciation:	
Balance at 1 Jan. 19–8	150,000
Amount provided during year	19,727
Adjustment on revaluation during year	(168,750)
Balance at 31 Dec. 19–8	977
Valuations have been incorporated in fixed assets as follows:	
Directors' valuations, 19–8	7,813

ANSWER B8. TRUEFIX LTD

(a) Schedule of fixed assets—year to 30 Jun. 1986

	Freehold land and buildings £	Plant and equipment £	Vehicles (working 3) £	Total £
Cost:				
At 1 Jul. 1985	296,000	395,200	32,000	723,200
Additions	—	—	6,400	6,400
Disposals	—	—	(4,000)	(4,000)
	296,000	395,200	34,400	725,600
Depreciation:				
At 1 Jul. 1985	—	238,100	18,400	256,500
Charge for year	3,600	27,070	4,500	35,170
Prior year adjustment (working 1)	46,800	(working 2)		46,800
Disposals	—	—	(2,200)	(2,200)
	50,400	265,170	20,700	336,270
Balance at 30 Jun. 1986	245,600	130,030	13,700	389,330

Workings

(1) *Land and buildings*
    13 years' prior year adjustment (1972–3 to 1984–5) at £3,600 pa = £46,800.

(2) *Plant and equipment*
    £(395,200 − 84,000 − 72,000) at 10% = £23,920
    Opening book value of item (i) is £50,400 and this will now last 16 years = £3,150 pa.

    Total = £(23,920 + 3,150)
         = £27,070.

(3) *Vehicles*

    Book value of vehicle sold (at 1 Jul. 1985) = £2,000, i.e. loss of £200. Balance of £34,400 cost is all subject to $12\frac{1}{2}\%$ = £4,300. Note that charge for year could have been shown as £4,300 and disposal of £2,000 with the adjustment for the loss being charged separately to the profit and loss account. The above method recognises that the £200 represents an earlier under-provision of depreciation.

(b) The overall aim of the depreciation charge is to match revenue with expense. This means apportioning the cost less any residual value over the life of the assets as fairly as possible.

The accounting policy adopted is to depreciate on a straight line basis over the useful life of the asset. To change the period over which an asset is depreciated (because it is recognised that its useful life is greater than hitherto thought) does not constitute a change of that accounting policy, but only a change in the estimate of the useful life. Hence, merely by changing the estimate, the company is still consistently applying its accounting policy. If the change made a significant difference to the company's results, it should be referred to in a note.

The doctrine of prudence should only be applied where it is uncertain what the outcome of a set of circumstances will be. In this case there is little uncertainty and the usual overriding of the matching concept by the prudence concept will not apply.

ANSWER B9

(a) *SSAP 13* ('Accounting for research and development') provides the following definitions.

(1) *Pure research expenditure*
This is expenditure on original investigation undertaken in order to gain new scientific or technical knowledge and understanding. Pure research is not primarily directed towards any specific practical aim or application.

(2) *Applied research expenditure*
This is expenditure on original investigation undertaken in order to gain new scientific or technical knowledge and directed towards a specific practial aim or objective.

(3) *Development expenditure*
This is expenditure on the use of scientific or technical knowledge in order to produce new or substantially improved material, devices, products, processes, systems or services prior to the commencement of commercial production.

(b) Research and development expenditure may be carried forward in the following circumstances:

(1) The cost of fixed assets used for research and development activities should be capitalised and written off over the useful life of the asset: *para, 19, SSAP 13*.
(2) Where companies enter into a firm contract to carry out development work on behalf of a third party and the expenditure incurred is, thus, recoverable: *para. 14, SSAP 13*.

(3) Development expenditure may be deferred to future periods if the following circumstances apply:

(i) there is a clearly defined project;
(ii) the related expenditure is separately identifiable;
(iii) the outcome of such a project has been assessed with reasonable certainty as to (a) its technical feasibility and (b) its ultimate commercial viability considered in the light of factors such as likely market conditions (including competing products), public opinion, consumer and environmental legislation;
(iv) if further development costs are to be incurred on the same project, the aggregate of such costs together with related production selling and administration costs are reasonably expected to be more than covered by related future revenues; and
(v) adequate resources exist, or are reasonably expected to be available, to enable the project to be completed and to provide any consequential increase in working capital: *para. 21, SSAP 13.*

(c)

New Products Ltd
Balance sheet as at . . .

Fixed assets

	£
At cost	30,000
Less: Depreciation	3,000
	27,000

Current assets
Work-in-progress 49,000

Deferred asset
Research and development expenditure 22,000

	£
Depreciation	x

(This figure would include the £3,000 of depreciation on the research of development assets, required to be included to conform with *para. 14(1)(a) Sch. 9 CA 1985*.)

Notes to the accounts
1. *Movements on deferred development expenditure*

	£
b/f at 1 Jan.	x
Expenditure incurred during the year and deferred at the balance sheet date	22,000
c/f at 31 Dec.	x

2. Work-in-progress represents research and development expenditure incurred in respect of contracts entered into between your company and its clients and recoverable at the balance sheet date.
3. Development expenditure on projects carried on by the company has been written off as incurred except to the extent that such expenditure can be regarded with reasonable assurance to be recoverable in the future.

Workings

	Project 3 £	Project 4 £	Project 5 £	Total £
Staff salaries	5,000	10,000	20,000	35,000
Overheads	6,000	12,000	24,000	42,000
	11,000	22,000	44,000	77,000
Plant at cost	10,000	20,000	5,000	35,000
	21,000	42,000	49,000	112,000
Fixed assets c/f	9,000	18,000	—	27,000
	12,000	24,000	49,000	85,000
Work-in-progress	—	—	49,000	49,000
	12,000	24,000	—	36,000
Research and development expenditure c/f	—	22,000	—	22,000
Research and development expenditure charged to profit and loss account	12,000	2,000	—	14,000

Notes and assumptions

(1) *Project 3*

The expenditure has been written off on the basis that its recovery is not assured: *para. 22, SSAP 13*. It is considered that the costs incurred in developing the new compound will not necessarily lead to lower future costs of production. Although a shortage in the raw material currently being used is possible, the actual shortage involved cannot be estimated with reasonable certainty.

(2) *Project 4*

The expenditure has been carried forward with the exception £2,000 depreciation on the plant used in the project. The savings from this project appear to be £30,000 ((50% − 20%) × £100,000). This more than covers the salaries and overheads incurred.

(3) *Project 5*
The expenditure has been carried forward as work-in-progress. This includes the plant cost. It is assumed that the contract with the creditworthy client covers the cost of such fixed assets as well as the revenue items.

ANSWER B10.   FORSTERS LTD

(a) *Accounting policies*
Deferred tax is provided in respect of the tax effects arising from all timing differences of material amount to the extent that it is probable that a liability will crystallise. Deferred tax is not provided to the extent that it is probable that a liability will not crystallise.

(b) *Note to the accounts*
  (i)

	£
Deferred taxation	76,097
less: ACT	45,000
	31,097

The liability is estimated to crystallise in approximately equal amounts over the next three years.

  (ii) Potential liability at 30 Jun. 19–12:

	£
Accelerated capital allowances (W2/W1)	327,600
Short-term timing differences (W3)	23,562
Revaluation surpluses (W4)	30,000
Advance corporation tax (W5)	(45,000)
	336,162

Workings

1. Accelerated capital allowances at 30 Jun. 19–12—full potential liability.

	£
NBV of plant and machinery at 30 Jun. 19–11	600,000
Additions	100,000
	700,000
Depreciation (10%)	(70,000)
NBV of plant and machinery at 30 Jun. 19–12	630,000
Tax WDV of plant and machinery at 30 Jun. 19–12	£ Nil
Deferred tax on £630,000 at 52% (full potential liability)	£327,600

Financial Accounting

2. Short-term timing differences:

	£
Interest payable accrued £125,000 @ 15% × 3/12	(4,688)
Interest receivable accrued	50,000
Net timing difference	45,312
Potential deferred tax on £45,312 @ 52%	23,562

3. *Reversal of timing differences*
   As the payment and receipt dates of interest will be the same in future periods any reversal of differences at 30 Jun. 19–12 will be compensated by originating timing differences at 30 Jun. 19–13 and so on for future periods.

   Reversal of accelerated capital allowances over next three years:

	£
NBV of plant and machinery @ 30 Jun. 19–12	630,000
Additions during 19–13	10,000
	640,000
Depreciation for 19–13 (10%)	(64,000)
NBV @ 30 Jun. 19–13	576,000
Additions during 19–14	10,000
	586,000
Depreciation for 19–14 (10%)	(58,600)
NBV @ 30 Jun. 19–14	527,400
Additions during 19–15	10,000
	537,400
Depreciation for 19–15	(53,740)
NBV @ 30 Jun. 19–15	483,660

Year to 30 Jun.	Capital allowances £	Depreciation £	Reversal of timing differences £
19–13	10,000	64,000	54,000
19–14	10,000	58,600	48,600
19–15	10,000	53,740	43,740
	30,000	176,340	146,340

Deferred tax on £146,340 at 52% (*SSAP 15* partial provision) £76,097

4. Revaluation surplus

   £100,000 at 30%   £30,000

No provision has been made for the tax on the revaluation surplus since it has been assumed that the company has no intention of selling the property.

5. Advance Corporation Tax

   £105,000 × 3/7   £45,000

The maximum amount of ACT that can be deducted from deferred taxation without regard to its 'recoverability' per *SSAP 8* is 30/52 × £76,097 = £43,902.

As however the company is anticipated to continue to trade profitably, it is likely that the ACT can be offset against corporation tax for the year ended 30 Jun. 19–13 and thus the balance of £1,098 £(45,000 − 43,902) can either:

(i) also be deducted from deferred tax; or
(ii) be shown as a deferred asset.

Option (i) has been taken in the suggested solution.

ANSWER B11. HUCKLEBERRY LTD

(a) *Accounting policies*

Deferred tax, computed under the liability method, is provided in respect of the tax effects arising from all timing differences of material amount to the extent that it is probable that a liability will crystallise.

Deferred tax is not provided to the extent that it is probable that a liability will not crystallise.

(b) *Note to the accounts*

(i)

	31.12.–7	31.12.–6
Deferred taxation (working 2) comprising accelerated capital allowances and interest receivable	£4,056	Nil

(ii) Potential liability (working 1):

	31.12.–7	31.12.–6
	£	£
Accelerated capital allowances	499,772	441,844
Short-term timing differences	10,400	10,400
Revaluation surpluses	75,000	—

Financial Accounting

(iii) Movement in deferred taxation account:

	£
Balance 1.1.–7	Nil
Transfer from profit and loss account	4,056
Balance 31.12.–7	4,056

Tutorial Note: SSAP 15 requires the unprovided liability not the potential liability to be disclosed, analysed into its major components. In this example it is not possible to state whether the £4,056 provided relates to capital allowances or interest.

Working 1—Calculation of contingent liability in respect of deferred taxation

Deferred tax account

	At 1.1.–7 Timing differences Gross £	Opening balance £	Movements during year Gross		Net £	At 31.12.–7 Closing balance
Plant						
A/cs NBV	643,500		CAs	232,000*		
Tax WDV	141,000		Depcn	133,000		
	502,500 × 52%	261,300		99,000 × 52%	51,480	312,780
IBAs						
A/c NBV	(620,000					
	−37,200) 582,800		CAs	24,800		
Tax WDV	(620,000					
	−384,400) 235,600		Depcn	12,400		
	347,200 × 52%	180,544		12,400 × 52%	6,448	186.992
		441,844			57,928	499.772
Interest received						
Debtor						
(1,200,000 × 10% × 2/12)	20,000 × 52%	10,400			Nil	10,400
		451,944			57,928	510,172
Property revaluation		Nil			75,000	75,000

*Capital allowances in year:

100% FYA	= £196,750
WDA £141,000 × 25%	= £ 35,250
	£232,000

Working 2—Provision required 31.12.–7

	Interest £	IBAs £	Plant allowances £	Net £	Cumulative £
19–8	—	12,400	45,000	57,400	57,400
19–9	—	12,400	(20,000)	(7,600)	49,800
19–10	(20,000)	12,400	(50,000)	(57,600)	(7,800)
19–11	—	12,400	10,000	22,400	14,600

Required = £7,800 × 52%
= £4,056

On LIFO basis the reversal of £57,600 will be met out of net positive timing differences arising in 19–8 and 19–7. Provision required at 31.12.–6 is therefore Nil.

ANSWER C1

Liabilities are precise amounts which the company is contractually bound to pay and so include items such as trade creditors, wages owing to employees and borrowings. Provisions are amounts provided in the financial statements for estimated losses or liabilities rather than a specific amount for a known liability. For instance, provisions for the reduction in value of stock, debtors or fixed assets and for liabilities which may arise in an uncertain amount in respect of claims against the company are all provisions. Both liabilities and provisions are connected with the measurement of profit: recognising one of these must reduce the profit in a year. Reserves, however, are not to do with the measurement of profit but with its appropriation. They are appropriated from profits having regard to the future requirements of the company. They may also arise from capital transactions. When fixed assets are revalued upwards the amount of the revaluation is not a realised profit and so is not shown in the profit and loss account, but is taken to a revaluation reserve. When shares are insured at a premium, the premium is again not strictly a profit and is taken to a reserve called the share premium account.

The *Companies Act 1985* distinguishes between liabilities, provisions, and reserves for the purpose of their balance sheet presentation but does not define these terms other than by indicating which specific items should be shown under each heading.

The balance sheet formats require 'Provisions for liabilities and charges' to be divided where appropriate into (1) pensions and similar obligations, (2) taxation including deferred taxation, and (3) other provisions. Reserves are required to be split between revaluation reserve and other reserves, i.e. (1) capital redemption reserve, (2) reserve for own shares, (3) reserves provided for by the articles of association, and (4) other reserves. The profit and loss account balance is also to be shown. Liabilities are to be shown divided into (1) debenture loans, (2) bank loans and overdrafts (3) payments received on account, (4) trade creditors, (5) bills of exchange payable, (6) amounts owed to group companies, (7) amounts owed to related companies, (8) other creditors including taxation and social security, and (9) accounts and deferred income. The liabilities are again to be divided into two categories—those falling due within one year and those falling due after more than one year. Provisions for depreciation, reduction in value of stock and debtors are to be made by showing those items at the reduced amount in the balance sheet.

Material amounts transferred to and from reserves and provisions are required to be disclosed.

ANSWER C2

Memorandum to the board of A. Pubco Ltd

From: A Certacc

Re: The provisions of the *Companies Act 1985* relating to the payment of dividends

The substance of the requirements of the *Companies Act 1985* is to allow distributions to be made only from positive retained profits. For this purpose 'retained profits' are 'accumulated uncapitalised and undistributed realised profits less accumulated realised losses', in other words the amount standing to the credit of the retained profit and loss reserves account if normal accounting procedures are followed.

The Act does not define the term 'realised' and so its interpretation is left to accountants and the UK and Irish accountancy bodies have jointly issued a statement giving guidance on this point. *SSAP 2* indicates that a profit is made on a transaction when the result of the transaction is in the form either of cash or assets, the ultimate cash realisation of which may be assessed with reasonable certainty. An unrealised profit is thus an expected profit rather than one which has clearly crystallised. The guidance statement requires that a profit which is required by statements of accounting practice to be recognised in the profit and loss account should normally be treated as a realised profit unless the *SSAP* specifically states that it should be treated as unrealised.

A realised loss is more difficult to define and *CA 1985 Sch. 4* indicates that all liabilities and losses which have arisen or are likely to arise in respect of a financial year shall be taken into account in determining profit. *S. 275 CA 1985* requires that provisions for loss in value and depreciation, and estimated future losses should be treated as realised losses.

For public companies the additional requirement means that unrealised profits and losses must not be taken into account. (Unrealised losses may arise (The 1985 Act declares) when it is uncertain whether previous losses were realised or unrealised.) Thus any excess of unrealised losses over unrealised profits (e.g. revaluation reserves) must be deducted from realised profits less realised losses in order to obtain the maximum distributable amount.

The effect of the requirements introduced by the 1980 Act, now consolidated into the 1985 Act, was to reverse earlier case law. Prior to the Act *Ammonia Soda Co v Chamberlain* and *Dimbula Valley Ceylon Tea Co v Laurie* had established that dividends could be paid out of profits made in a year whether or not there were accumulated deficits on the reserves. The requirements for public companies now require that the maximum dividend payable at any time is the difference between all accumulated profits and all accumulated losses according to the latest annual or 'properly prepared' accounts.

The specified events will affect the maximum distributable profit in the following ways:

(a) The revaluation results in an unrealised surplus which will not affect the amount available for distribution in a private company but in a public company where any unrealised deficits exist may make a larger distribution possible.
(b) The sale represents the conversion of an unrealised surplus into a realised one and thus increases the accumulated realised profits and diminishes the unrealised profits. Therefore the maximum distribution may increase even though for a public company there will be a corresponding reduction in any surplus of unrealised profits over unrealised losses, which may result in the second restriction limiting the maximum dividend.
(c) Provisions are specifically included in the term 'realised losses' so there is a reduction in distributable profit. There is also a compulsory reduction in the net assets of the company.

ANSWER C3. PANDELAC LTD

Profit and loss account for the year ended 30 Sep. 19–9

(a)

	Notes		£
		Turnover	6,120
	1	Cost of sales (working 1)	2,163
		Gross profit	3,957
		Distribution expenses	(2,500)
	2	Administrative expenses (working 2)	(1,088)
	3	Other operating income (working 3)	29
	4	Income from fixed asset investments (working 4)	20
	5	Interest payable	(80)
		Profit before tax	338
	6	Tax on profit on ordinary activities (working 5)	(160)
		profit on ordinary activities after taxation being the profit for the year	178

Appropriations

Dividends proposed:

Interim paid	16	
Final proposed	26	
		(40)
Transfer loan stock redemption reserve		(10)
Retained profits for year		128
Retained profits at 30 Sep. 19–8		1,635
Retained profits at 30 Sep. 19–9		1,763

Notes to the accounts

1. Included in the cost of sales are charges for

	£000
Depreciation	51
Hire of plant	63
Obsolute stock written off	37

2. Included in the charge for administrative expenses are:

	£000
Auditors' remuneration	6
Depreciation	8
Directors' emoluments	47
Directors compensation for loss of office	20

3. Other operating income includes the profit in the sale of a factory of £20,000.

   (*Tutorial note:* This item is treated as being exceptional rather than extraordinary, since insufficient information is given about the possible recurrence of such an item. If it was clearly non-recurring it would be an extraordinary item.)

4. The income receivable from fixed asset investments all relates to quoted investments.

5. Interest payable comprises:

	£
Interest on loan stock	20
Interest on bank overdraft	60
	80

6. *The tax charge*

	£
UK corporation tax on profits for the year (including tax on capital gain on sale of warehouse £5,000)	154
Tax on dividends received	6
	160

Workings

1. *Cost of sales*

	£
Production expenses	2,030
Plant hire	63
Obsolete stock	37
Factory repairs (14 − 1)	13
Depreciation (50 + 1)	51
Equipment correction	(10)
Government subsidy	(21)
	2,163

2. Administrative expenses

	£
As shown	1,005
Bad debts	2
Auditors	6
Directors (47 + 20)	67
Depreciation	8
	1,088

3. Other operating income

	£
Profit on sale of warehouse 58 − 38 =	20
Rental income	9
	29

4. Dividends received

$$14 \times \tfrac{10}{7} = £20$$

5. Taxation

	£		
Profits	338		
Less: Warehouse sale	(20)		
Investment income	(20)		
	298	@ 50% =	149
CGT on warehouse 58 − 42 × 30%			5
Tax on dividends 20 − 14			6
			160

It is assumed that:
(a) There is no deferred tax write back or charge,
(b) there is no irrecoverable ACT,
(c) there are no brought-forward losses,
(d) no balancing charge for IBA purposes arises on the warehouse sale, and
(e) the government subsidy is taxable.

(b) Additional information would need to be given about the number of directors whose emoluments (excluding pension contributions) were less than £5,000, those who were within each multiple of £5,000, and those who received no emoluments. The chairman's emoluments (again excluding pension contributions) must also be shown separately, as must those of the highest-paid director if his emoluments were in excess of the chairman's.

The number of directors (if any) who waived rights to receive emoluments and the aggregate amount involved must be disclosed.

The board of directors has the authority to fix directors' emoluments, and the disclosure requirements aim to provide maximum information (short of giving actual emoluments for named directors) so that shareholders can judge whether the powers are being abused.

ANSWER C4

The capital redemption reserve arises when redeemable shares are redeemed and where that redemption is such that the nominal value of the shares redeemed exceeds the *aggregate* proceeds of any fresh issue made to finance that redemption. The amount to be transferred to the capital redemption reserve is the amount of that excess (*s. 170 CA 1985*).

The capital redemption reserve may only be used:
(i) to pay up unissued shares and issue them as fully paid bonus shares to the members (*s. 170 CA 1985*), or
(ii) in a scheme of capital reduction under *ss. 135, 427 & 582 CA 1985*.

ANSWER C5. SAFE HAVEN LTD

Disclosure of directors' remuneration in consolidated profit and loss account for the year ended 31 Dec. 19–3

	£	£
Directors' emoluments:		
Fees	7,000	
Salaries	64,260	
Pension to former director	4,000	
		75,260
One director waived emoluments amounting to £5,000		
Emoluments (excluding pension contributions) of:		
Chairman		7,000
Highest paid director		30,000

Other directors were paid emoluments (excluding pension contributions) within the ranges:

£ £	No.
0–5,000	1
20,001–25,000	1

Financial Accounting

Working paper

Summary of emoluments, pension and compensation receivable or waived by directors and past directors:

(1) Receivable for the year ended 31 Dec. 19–3:

	Dawson (Managing director) £	Franklin (Chairman) £	Clark (Sales director) £	Edgar (Director) £	Total £
Fees	—	7,000	—	—	7,000
Salaries	30,000	—	19,500	4,600	54,100
Commission	—	—	600	—	600
Gross emoluments	30,000	7,000	20,100	4,600	
Pension contributions:					
General scheme (10% of entitled salary)	3,500	—	—	460	3,960
Supplementary scheme	5,000	—	—	600	5,600
					64,260
Pension to former director (Brown)					4,000

(2) Adjustments in respect of previous years: Nil

Notes:
It is assumed that:
(i) Pension contributions were made both by the company and Dawson in respect of remuneration waived.
(ii) The amount paid to the chairman represents merely fees for attending board meetings, and not a salary for part-time services.

(3) Pension scheme contributions:

	£
Dawson:	
General scheme (10% × £35,000)	3,500
Supplementary scheme	5,000
Edgar:	
General scheme (10% × £4,600)	460
Supplementary scheme	600
	9,560

ANSWER C6. NOXIOUS CHEMICAL CO LTD

Report of the directors

The directors submit their annual report and audited accounts of the company for the year ended 31 Dec. 19–9.

Principal activities
The principal activity of the company continues to be the supply of chemicals to the plastics manufacturing industry. The company also supplies dry-cleaning products.

Review of the financial year
During the year the company started supplying dry-cleaning products and 18% of its business and 25% of its profit tax arise from this new field. It is envisaged that this diversification will continue. In order to provide additional working capital for this expansion 20,000 50p ordinary shares were issued.

Results of the year
The company's profit before tax was £88,000. Contributions to turnover and profit before tax from the company's activities were as follows:

Activity	Proportion of turnover %	Contribution to profit before tax £
Supply of chemicals to plastics industry	82	66,000
Dry-cleaning products	18	22,000
	100	88,000

Dividends
We recommend that a dividend of 10% amounting to £10,000 be paid on the ordinary shares.

Transfer to reserves
After payment of dividends, the amount transferred to reserves is £18,355.

Land and buildings
The only significant change in the company's fixed assets during the year was the acquisition of further freehold land and buildings at a cost of £82,000.
The land and buildings shown in the balance sheet at £175,800 have a current market value of £320,000.

Political and charitable contributions

	£
Charitable contributions in year	530
Political contributions in year (Including £250 to the Conservative party)	370

Share issue

Class	No.	Consideration	Reason for issue
50p ordinary	20,000	£15,000	For increased working capital

Directors

Directors who have served during the year:
Messrs Limit, Letter, Times and Mail

Mr Mail retires from the board and, being eligible, offers himself for re-election.

Directors' interests in the company's shares and debentures are as follows:

Director	Class	31 Dec. 19–8	31 Dec. 19–9
Mr Mail	50p ordinary	Nil	3,000

ANSWER C7. EXTRACTS

The following are the requirements of the *Companies Act* and exclude exemptions on account of the size of the company or the nature of its business:

(a) *Turnover*

In any profit and loss account format the turnover must be separately disclosed.

In addition, by way of note or otherwise, an analysis of its turnover into class of business and by geographical market should be made. The directors' opinion of the profits deriving from each class of business must be shown. The *Companies Act 1985* does not define 'class of business' other than to say that where classes do not differ substantially they shall not be treated as separate. It would be sensible to regard different product divisions within a company as giving rise to separate classes of business.

The method of calculation of turnover should be disclosed under the accounting policy note.

(b) *Listed investments*

These must be shown at cost less any amounts written off or at market value and must be divided between those which are fixed assets in which case they must be disclosed in the balance sheet under the heading 'Fixed assets—Investments—Other investments other than loans'; and those which are current assets in which case they must be disclosed under the heading 'Current assets—Investments—Other investments'.

In either case the following additional information is required: The aggregate market value of the investments where it differs from the stated value; and
Both the market value and the stock exchange value where the market value is higher than the stock exchange value. (This may happen if the market is temporarily disposed or there has been little trading in the securities concerned.)

The aggregate book value has to be subdivided between investments granted a listing on a recognised stock exchange in Great Britain and those listed elsewhere.

(c) *Directors' emoluments*

It is necessary to distinguish between:
(1) amounts receivable in respect of services as directors, and
(2) amounts in respect of other offices for the following:

    (i) fees and other emoluments, which include expense allowances charged to UK tax, pension contributions paid by the company on behalf of directors, salaries, bonuses and the estimated monetary value of benefits-in-kind.

Emoluments, received by directors of the holding company from subsidiaries, must also be shown under (1) and (2) above.

    (ii) directors' and past directors' pensions.

    (iii) compensation paid to directors or past directors for loss of office: *s. 29 Sch. V CA 1985.*

The number of directors whose fees and emoluments, excluding pension contributions, fall within successive ranges of £5,000 must also be shown: *s. 25 Sch. V 1985.*
e.g.

£	No. of directors
1– 5,000	X
5,001–10,000	X
10,001–15,000	X
15,001–20,000	X

Additional information is required in respect of the chairman's emoluments and those of the highest paid director if they exceed those of the chairman: *ss. 24–25 Sch. V CA 1985.*

Where the director performs his duties wholly or mainly outside the UK, the last two items above (i.e. those required under *s. 25 Sch V CA 1985*) do not apply.

The number of directors who have waived rights to receive emoluments during the year, and the aggregate amount of the sums involved must be given: *s. 27 Sch. V CA 1985*.

The requirements of *ss. 24–27 Sch. V CA 1985* in respect of the three items mentioned above do not apply where the company is neither a holding company nor a subsidiary company and the aggregate of the directors' emoluments as required by *s. 22 Sch. V CA 1985* (see above) do not exceed £60,000.

(d) *Redeemable shares*

The following details must be disclosed in respect of any part of the capital which consists of redeemable shares:
 (a) the earliest and latest dates on which the company has the power to redeem those shares;
 (b) whether the shares must be redeemed in any event or are liable to be redeemed at the option of the company;
 (c) whether any (and if so, what) premium is payable on redemption: *para. 38 (2) Sch. 4 CA 85*.

(e) *Interest payable*

This must be shown separately in aggregate on the face of the profit and loss account in accordance with the statutory profit and loss account formats. In addition the amount of interest payable in the following classes should be declared:
 (a) on bank loans and overdrafts, and loans made to the company which
  (i) are repayable otherwise than by instalments and fall due within five years of the balance sheet date, or
  (ii) are repayable by instalments the last of which falls due within five years;
 (b) on any other kind of loan (whether secured or not): *para. s. 53 (2) Sch. 4 CA 1985*.

(f) *Land held as a fixed asset*

For all fixed assets there are requirements to show:
 (1) cost or subsequent valuation (see (6) below),
 (2) accumulated depreciation,
 (3) provisions for diminution in value,
 (4) net book value ((1) minus (2)),
 (5) the aggregate amounts of assets acquired and disposed of or scrapped during the period,
 (6) where there has been a valuation:
  (i) for each separate valuation, the year and amount of the valuation,
  (ii) if the valuation has occurred during the current year, the name (or qualification) of the valuer and the basis of the valuation applied,

(iii) the amount it would be shown at if strict historical accounting rules applied: *paras. 17 et seq Sch. 4 CA 1985*.

Specifically for land held as a fixed asset, it is necessary to distinguish between:
—freehold land,
—land held on long lease (at least 50 years to run from the balance sheet date),
—land held on short lease (less than 50 years to run from the balance sheet date): *para. 44 Sch. 4 CA 1985*.

ANSWER C8. CELLARS PLC

Profit and loss account for the year ended 30 Sep. 19–7

Notes		£000
1	Turnover	122,000
	Cost of sales (working 1)	113,899
	Gross profit	8,101
2	Distribution costs (working 2)	(749)
2	Administrative expenses (working 3)	(931)
3	Interest payable (bank overdraft)	(1,000)
	Profit on ordinary activities	5,421
3	Tax on profit on ordinary activities	(3,420)
	Profit on ordinary activities after taxation being the profit for the financial year	2,001
	Appropriations	
4	Proposed dividends	(1,000)
7	Transfer to fixed asset replacement reserve	(164)
	Retained profit	837

		£000	
6	*Statement of retained profits/reserves*		
	Retained profits at the beginning of the year		
	As previously stated	708	
	Prior year adjustment	(567)	
	As restated		141
	Retained profits at end of year		978
	Earnings per share (note 14)		20p per share

Financial Accounting

Balance sheet as at 30 Sep. 19–7

Notes		£000	£000
	Fixed assets		
	Tangible assets		
9	Plant and machinery		590
	Current assets		
10	Stocks	2,947	
10	Debtors	3,640	
10	Cash at bank and in hand	4,907	
	Deferred asset: ACT recoverable	429	
		11,923	
	Creditors: Amount falling due within one year		
	Trade creditors	496	
11	Other creditors including taxation and social security	3,955	
	Proposed dividend	1,000	
	Net current assets	5,451	
			6,472
	Total assets less current liabilities		7,062
	Creditors: amounts falling due after more than one year		
8	Other creditors including taxation and social security		3,420
			3,642
	Capital and reserves		
5	Called up share capital		2,500
6	Other reserves		164
6	Profit and loss account		978
			3,642

Notes to the accounts

1. *Accounting policies*
   (a) *Basis of preparation*
       These accounts have been prepared under the historical cost convention.
   (b) *Turnover*
       Turnover is based upon the invoiced value of sales less creditors thereon. Value added tax is excluded.

(c) *Depreciation*
Depreciation has been charged in the profit and loss account in order to allocate the cost of the fixed assets over their expected useful lives of four years, in equal instalments. In addition in the current year a reserve has been made to allow for the increase in the replacement cost of these assets. This has been based upon 10% of the cost of the fixed assets.

(d) *Stocks*
Stock has been consistently valued at the lower of cost or net realisable value. The basis for arriving at cost for stock evaluation has been refined in 19–7. The former use of a FIFO basis has been replaced by taking stock at prices less a standard gross margin. The effect of this change in 19–7 was an estimated reduction to the year-end stock valuation of £149,000.

(e) *Market research costs*
Market research costs were previously written off over the expected useful life of the product line. In order to comply with *SSAP 13*, the company has altered its policy regarding such costs. In future these costs will be written off as incurred. The effect of this change is to reduce opening reserves by £567,000 as outlined in note 6 to the accounts.

2. *Trading profit before taxation*
The trading profit is arrived at after charging the following items:

	£000	£000
Depreciation of fixed assets		
—cost of sales	350	
—charged to distribution costs	10	
—charged to administration expenses	50	
		410
Market research expenditure		409
Audit fee		26
Directors' remuneration (including amounts paid to the chairman of £18,000)		140

3. *Taxation*
This represents a provision for UK corporation tax on the profit of the current year at a rate of 50%. This tax becomes payable on 1 Jan. 19–9.

4. *Dividends*
This represents a final proposed dividend of 10p on each ordinary share in issue. No interim dividend was paid during the year.

5. *Share capital*
Authorised
    16,000,000 ordinary shares of 25p each
Issued and fully paid
    10,000,000 ordinary shares of 25p each.

6. Reserves

	Total £000	Profit & Loss account £000	Fixed asset replacement reserve £000
Bal. b/f at 1 Oct. 19–6			
As originally reported	708	708	
Prior year adjustment	(567)	(567)	
As restated	141	141	
Retained this year	1,001	1,001	
Transfer to replacement reserve (note 7)	—	(164)	164
Bal. c/f at 30 Sep. 19–7	1,142	978	164

The prior year adjustment arises in respect of a change in accounting policy in relation to market research expenditure. The sum involved represents expenditure incurred to 1 Oct. 19–6 previously carried forward and charged against the expected life of the product line. The expenditure has now been written off in order to comply with *SSAP 13*.

7. Transfer to fixed asset replacement reserve

An appropriation has been made based on 10% of the cost of fixed assets being used by the company. Your directors consider that such an appropriation is needed so as to provide for the increased costs to replace the fixed assets of the company. It is not intended that these sums shall be made available to appropriate dividends.

8. Future taxation

	£000
UK corporation tax payable on 1 Jan. 19–9	3,420

9. Fixed assets

	£000	£000
Plant and machinery:		
Cost		1,640
Depreciation—at 1 Oct. 19–6	640	
—charged this year	410	
	—	1,050
Book value at 30 Sep. 19–7		590

10. Current assets

Stock
Debtors
Cash at bank

This note would show a breakdown of these items under the relevant headings

11. *Other creditors* including taxation and social security

	£000
Corporation tax payable 1 Jan. 19–8	3,526
ACT payable on dividend (working 4)	429
	3,955

12. *Contingent liability*
    There is a court case pending against the company regarding an alleged supply of faulty goods. The claim is for £246,000. Your directors do not consider it likely that the claim will succeed and hence no provision has been made in these accounts.

13. *Earnings per share*
    The earnings on each ordinary share is 20 pence. This is calculated by dividing the net profit after tax of £2,001,000 by the 10 million ordinary shares in issue ranking for dividend.

Workings

1. Cost of sales

	£000
Turnover	122,000
given G.P.	(8,451)
	113,549
Depreciation	
£490,000 × $\frac{25}{35}$ =	350
	113,899

2. *Distribution costs*

	£000
As stated	739
Depreciation £14,000 × $\frac{25}{35}$	10
	749

3. *Administrative expenses*

	£000
As stated	280
Depreciation £70,000 × $\frac{25}{35}$	50
Audit fee	26
Directors' remuneration	140
Bad debt provision	26
Market research £(976,000 − 567,000)	409
	931

Financial Accounting

4. *ACT on proposed dividend*
   $\frac{3}{7} \times £1,000,000$ £429,000

5. *Prior year adjustment*
   It is assumed that the market research costs were allowed for taxation purposes when they were incurred. As there is no deferred taxation account the prior year adjustment is shown at its gross cost. It has been assumed that the corporation tax charge for the current year (as per draft profit and loss account) has been computed correctly with regard to the market research costs.

ANSWER C9. PRIOR YEAR ADJUSTMENT

Statement of retained profits

Workings		19–8 £000	19–7 £000
(1)	Opening balance as previously reported	8,950	6,850
	Prior year adjustment (see note)	240	252
		8,710	6,598
(2)	Retained profit for year	2,360	2,112
	Balance at end of year	11,070	8,710

Note: The policy followed in accounting for research and development expenditure, which was written off over five years, was changed during the year ended 31 Dec. 19–8 to comply with *SSAP13*, and such expenditure is now written off in the year in which it is incurred. Research and development expenditure carried forward at 31 Dec. 19–7 amounted to £240,000. In restating the results for 19–7 on the basis of the new policy, the charge for research and development in that year has been decreased by £12,000 and added to the balance of expenditure not written off. The resulting total of £252,000 relates to 19–6 and earlier years and has been charged against retained profits at the beginning of 19–7.

Workings:

		£000
(1)	Balances previously reported:	
	At beginning of 19–7	6,850
	Retained for 19–7	2,100
	At beginning of 19–8	8,950

(2) Retained profits per accounts for 19–7   2,100
    Add: Research and development written off   60

      2,160
    Less: Research and development incurred   48

      2,112

(3) Research and development reconciliation:
    Balance at end of 19–7   240
    Add: Research and development written off in 19–7   60

      300
    Less: Research and development incurred in 19–7   48

    Balance at beginning of 19–7   252

ANSWER C10. HUMPLEDINK LTD

(a) Corporation tax account—liability year ended 31 Dec. 19–3

	£		£
Cash	35,929	Balance b/f	
		52,000 − 16,071	35,929
	35,929		35,929

Corporation tax account—liability year ended 31 Dec. 19–4

	£		£
Profit and loss account:		Balance b/f	
Over provision		60,000 − 18,470	41,530
60,000 − 57,500	2,500		
Balance c/f	39,030		
	41,530		41,530

Corporation tax account—liability year ended 31 Dec. 19–5

	£		£
ACT on dividend paid	5,357*	Profit and loss account	75,000
Balance c/f	69,643		
	75,000		75,000

*Dividend on 250,000 shares @ 5p = £12,500
ACT @ $\frac{3}{7}$ = 5,357

ACT payable account

	£		£
		*ACT on proposed dividend	10,714
		Dr. Deferred asset.	

*ACT at $\frac{3}{7}$ on proposed dividend of 25,000 = £10,714.

(b) *Profit and loss account for year ended 31 Dec. 19–5*

	£	£
Profit for year before taxation		150,000
Corporation tax based on the profit for year	75,000	
Corporation tax provisions for previous year, no longer required	(2,500)	
		72,500
Profit for year available for appropriation		77,500
Less: Appropriations:		
dividends paid and proposed		(37,500)
Retained profit for financial year		40,000
Retained earnings b/f		120,000
Retained earnings c/f		160,000

(c) *Balance sheet at 31 Dec. 19–5*

	£
Creditors: amounts falling due after more than one year	
Other creditors including taxation and social security	
Future taxation:	
Corporation tax payable 1 Jan. 19–7	69,643
Deferred asset:	
ACT recoverable	10,714
Creditors: amounts due within one year	
Other creditors including taxation and social security	
Current taxation	
£(39,030 + 10,714)	49,744
Accruals and deferred income	
Proposed dividend	25,000

ANSWER D1

The stock exchange listing agreement requires that the company:

(1) Notify to the stock exchange any information necessary to avoid the establishment of a false market and apprise investors of the position of the company.
(2) Notify the date of any board meeting at which the declaration or payment of a dividend is expected or at which profits or losses of a period will be approved for publication.

(3) Announce at the earliest opportunity:
   (i) a decision to pay a dividend,
   (ii) profits for full or half year,
   (iii) any proposed change in capital structure.
   This is to prevent too many people having private knowledge of privileged information. Information is made available generally as soon as possible: so a profit figure is announced as soon as it is agreed with the auditors but well before the date of preparation of formal accounts.
(4) Notify the press any details of offers.
(5) Notify any:
   (i) mergers and take-over decisions,
   (ii) changes in directors,
   (iii) changes in tax status,
   (iv) changes in share structure,
   (v) changes in character of group or business.
(6) Forward for approval copies of all circulars before sending out.
(7) Forward circulars when sent out.
(8) Issue half yearly accounts.
(9) Include additional details in yearly accounts.
(10) Make directors' service contracts available for inspection.
(11) Send out proxy forms for any shareholders meeting.
(12) Obtain consent of a general meeting for any issue.
(13) Register share transfers and issue share certificates quickly and free of charge.
(14) Adopt certain rules regarding meetings of the directors.

ANSWER D2

The following information is required in the annual report and accounts under the terms of section 10 of the stock exchange listing agreement:

(a) A statement by directors as to the reasons for any significant departure from a SSAP.
(b) An explanation if trading results for the period differ significantly from any published forecast.
(c) A geographical analysis of turnover and of contribution for trading results.
(d) The name of the principal country in which each subsidiary operates.
(e) For each investment which is not a subsidiary but where group interest exceeds 20% of equity capital (i.e. normally an associate under *SSAP 1*), the
   (i) country of operation,
   (ii) issued capital and reserves,
   (iii) percentage interest of holding company in each class of capital or loan stock.

(f) An analysis of loans into bank loans and overdrafts and other borrowings broken down according as the amounts are payable
  (i) in one year or less,
  (ii) between one and two years,
  (iii) between two and five years,
  (iv) in five years or more.
(g) A statement showing interest capitalised.
(h) A statement showing the interest of each director in the share capital of the company or its subsidiaries noting changes in interest during the year and distinguishing between beneficial and non-beneficial interest.
(i) A statement of the interest of any person in any substantial part of the share capital.
(g) A statement of whether or not the company is a close company for tax purposes.
(h) Particulars of any significant contract with a director or in which any director had an interest.
(i) Emoluments received by directors.
(j) Dividends waived by any particular shareholder.

ANSWER E1. HIGHRISE LTD

Contract account

	£		£	£
Materials:		Stock of materials		
Ex stores	13,407	on site at		
Direct to site	73,078	31 Mar. 19–3		5,467
Wages £(39,498 + 396)	39,894	Plant—WDV		11,450
Site expenses £(4,693 + 122)	4,815			
Administration	3,742			16,917
Plant—at cost	15,320	Work-in-progress		
Hire of plant	2,735	c/d:		
HP interest	648	Cost	136,722	
		Profit to date	23,120	
	153,639			159,842
P & L account	23,120			
	176,759			176,759

Financial Accounting

Calculation of profit to date

	£	£
Contract price		780,000
Costs:		
To date	136,722	
To complete	490,000	
Guarantee £($2\frac{1}{2}\% \times 780{,}000$)	19,500	
		646,222
Estimated profit on whole contract		133,778

Value of work to date $= £114{,}580 \times \frac{100}{85}$
$= £134{,}800$

Profit to date $= £\dfrac{134{,}800}{780{,}000} \times 133{,}778$

$= £23{,}120$

Balance sheet details

	£
Long-term contract work-in-progress:	
At cost plus attributable profit	159,842
Less: Progress payments	134,800
	25,042
Debtors:	
Progress payments receivable £(134,800 − 114,580)	20,220

Notes:

(1) It is assumed that the work certified is invoiced immediately by Highrise Ltd and that the 15% retention is payable to Highrise within 12 months of the balance sheet date.

(2) In the solution the proportion of profit taken to date is based upon the certified value of work to date as a proportion of the total contract value. An alternative approach which would be acceptable would be to compare the costs to date as a proportion of total estimated costs on the contract, i.e.

$$£\dfrac{136{,}722}{646{,}222} \times 133{,}778 = £28{,}304$$

It would not appear to be acceptable to compare the invoiced amount (£114,580) to the total contract value (£780,000) since the calculation of profit on the whole contract (£133,778) allows for costs of rectification and guarantee. The 15% retention by the customer affects cash flow but not directly the profit on the contract.

It should also be pointed out that since the contract is only approximately 20% complete, it is unlikely at such an early stage that any profit at all would be taken into account since the outcome of the contract is unlikely to be reasonably foreseeable.

Other workings

Hire of plant

	£
Paid for plant on H.P.:	
Deposit	3,824
Instalments 8 × £551	4,408
	8,232
Total paid for plant	10,967
Hire charges	2,735

H.P. interest

	£
Total H.P. cost:	
Deposit	3,824
Instalments 23 × £575	13,225
	17,049
Cost	15,320
H.P. interest	1,729

Taken evenly: $\frac{9}{24} \times £1,729 = £648$

ANSWER E2. MO LTD

(a) Value added tax account

	£000		£000
19–7		19–6	
31 Jan. Input tax		1 Feb. Balance b/d	690
(on purchases)	9,430		
Payment to		19–7	
revenue		31 Jan. Output tax	
authorities	2,440	(on sale)	12,000
Balance c/d	820		
	12,690		12,690

(b) Corporation tax account

	£000		£000
19–7		19–6	
Jan. Cash	3,176	1 Feb. Balance b/d	3,160
Cash (ACT on interim dividend)	480	19–7	
		31 Jan. Profit and loss account —under-provision	16
Balance c/d CT	5,120	Profit and loss account on the year's profits	5,600
	8,776		8,776

Deferred tax account

	£000		£000
19–7		19–6	
31 Jan. Balance c/d	4,650	1 Feb. Balance b/d	4,600
		19–7	
		31 Jan. Profit and loss account	50
	4,650		4,650

Deferred asset—ACT recoverable

	£000
19–7	
31 Jan. ACT payable (the liability being shown under Creditors: amounts due within one year).	720

(c) Fixed assets

	Freehold property £000	Equipment and vehicles £000	Total £000
Cost 1 Feb. 19–6	7,910	2,550	10,460
Additions during year	—	130	130
	7,910	2,680	10,590
Cost of disposals	—	70	70
	7,910	2,610	10,520
Depreciation			
Balance 1 Feb. 19–6	810	1,160	1,970
Disposals during year	—	30	30
	810	1,130	1,940
Charge for year	90	240	330
	900	1,370	2,270
Book value at 31 Jan. 19–7	7,010	1,240	8,250

(d) *Profit and loss account for year ended 31 Jan. 19–7*

	£000	£000
Turnover		150,000
Cost of sales (107,800 + 92 + 15 + 40 + 330)		(108,277)
Gross profit		41,723
Distribution costs £(380 + 10,820 + 8,210)	19,410	
Administrative expenses (working 1)	11,583	
Interest payable	380	
		(31,373)
Profit before tax		10,350
Tax on profit before ordinary activities		(5,666)
Profit for financial year		4,684
Appropriations:		
Transfer to stock replacement reserve	60	
Dividends paid and proposed	2,800	
		(2,860)
Retained profit for year		1,824
Retained profit b/f		1,800
Retained profit c/f		3,624

Financial Accounting

Balance sheet at 31 Jan. 19–7

	£000	£000
Fixed assets		
Tangible assets:		
Land and buildings (see (c))	7,010	
Equipment (see (c))	1,240	
		8,250
Current assets		
Stock	24,585	
Debtors	35,304	
	59,889	
Creditors (amounts falling due within one year):		
Bank overdraft	4,814	
Trade creditors (working 2)	16,980	
Other creditors (working 2)	6,331	
Accruals (working 2)	2,400	
	30,525	
Net current assets		29,364
Total assets less current liabilities		37,614
Provisions for liabilities and charges		
Deferred taxation £000 (4,650 − 720)		3,930
Capital and reserves:		
Called-up share capital		20,000
General reserve	10,000	
Stock replacement reserve	60	
		10,060
Profit and loss account		3,624
		37,614

Workings

(1)

	£000
Salaries and wages	11,360
Audit fees £000 (15 + 10)	25
Directors' emoluments	143
Bad debts written off	46
Increase in bad debt provision	9
	11,583

(2)

	£000	£000
Trade creditors:		
Creditors and accruals* per trial balance		16,980
Other creditors:		
Agents' commission	380	
Audit fee	10	
VAT	820	
Corporation tax	5,120	
Unclaimed dividend	1	
	6,331	
Accruals:		
Proposed dividend	1,680	
ACT $\frac{3}{7} \times$ £1,680,000	720	
	2,400	

*This item would normally be disclosed under accruals if separate information were available.

ANSWER E3. SSAP 2 AND SSAP 4

(a) Fundamental accounting concepts are the broad basic assumptions which underlie the periodic financial accounts of business enterprises.

The four concepts described in *SSAP 2* are:

(i) The 'going concern' concept: the enterprise will continue operating for the foreseeable future, in particular that there is no need to include in the accounts provisions for liquidating or significantly curtailing the business.

(ii) The 'accruals' concept: revenue and costs are recognised when earned or incurred, not when received or paid, and are 'matched' against each other as closely as possible.

(iii) The 'consistency' concept: there is consistency of accounting treatment of like items both within each accounting period and from one period to the next.

(iv) The 'prudence' concept: unrealised revenue and profits are not anticipated, but provision is made for all liabilities or losses as soon as these are foreseen.

(b) An example of a conflict between the prudence concept and the accruals concept arises in *SSAP 9* (*Stocks and work-in-progress*). When considering the valuation of long-term contract work-in-progress, the prudence concept would dictate that no profit be taken until the contract is complete and the actual profit that has been made is known. The accruals concept would require profit to be taken according to the proportion of the contract which has been completed, provided that the outcome of the project can be assessed with reasonable certainty. *SSAP 9* requires the latter course to be adopted. Unless a separate standard indicates to the contrary *SSAP 2* requires prudence to override the other concepts in the case of conflict.

(c) (i) A grant towards the cost of employees' wages in a revenue-based grant, i.e. it relates to a specific category of revenue expenditure. Such a grant should be credited to profit and loss account in the same period as the expenditure to which it relates is charged.
(ii) A grant towards purchase of machinery is a capital-based grant. There are two acceptable accounting treatments. The grant can be deduced from the cost of the machinery, and depreciation charged to profit and loss account over the life of the asset on the net amount. Alternatively, the grant can be treated as a deferred credit, which is transferred to profit and loss account over the life of the asset, while depreciation is charged on the full cost of the asset. The overall profit and loss effect of the two methods is identical. The second approach accords with the requirements of *Companies Act 1985* which prohibits the netting off of assets and liabilities.

ANSWER E4. STOCK VALUATIONS

(a) *SSAP 9* defines 'net realisable value' as the actual or estimated selling price (net of trade but before settlement discounts) less:
(i) all further costs to completion; and
(ii) all costs to be incurred in marketing, selling and distributing.

(b) Generally *SSAP 9* does not regard replacement cost as a correct basis for valuing stock. However, where the value of the raw material content forms a high proportion of the total value of stock in process of production and the price of the raw material is liable to considerable fluctuation, it is common practice to make rapid changes in selling prices to accord with the changes in the price of the raw material. In cases of this kind the replacement cost basis may be extended to cover stock in process of production and finished stock as well as the stocks of raw material.

(c) Appendix of *SSAP 9* states that production overheads are to be included in cost of conversion together with direct labour, direct expenses and subcontracted work. This inclusion is a necessary corollary of the principle that expenditure should be included to the extent to which it has been incurred in bringing the product to its present location and condition. All abnormal conversion costs, however (such as exceptional spoilage, idle capacity, and other losses) which are available under normal operating conditions, need, for the same reason, to be excluded.

Where firm sales contracts have been entered into for the provision of goods or services to customer's specification, overheads relating to design, and marketing and selling costs incurred before manufacture, may be included in arriving at cost.

The costs of general management, as distinct from functional management, are not directly related to current production, and are, therefore, excluded from cost of conversion, and hence from the cost of stocks and work-in-progress.

(d) (i) *Adjusted (discounted) selling price*
In the case of retail stores holding a large number of rapidly changing individual items, stocks on the shelves have often been stated at current selling prices less the normal gross profit margin. In these particular circumstances this may be acceptable as being the only practical method of arriving at a figure which approximates to cost, but only if it can be demonstrated that the method gives a reasonable approximation of the actual cost. The selling price used for the purpose of discounting should normally be the original price fixed for the article.

(ii) *First in first out*
The calculation of the cost of stocks and work-in-progress is on the basis that the quantities in hand represent the latest purchases or production.

(iii) *Last in first out*
The calculation of the cost of stocks and work-in-progress is on the basis that the quantities in hand represent the earliest purchases or production.

(iv) *Base stock*
The calculation of the cost of stocks and work-in-progress is on the basis that a fixed unit value is ascribed to a predetermined number of units in stock, any excess over this number being valued on the basis of some other method. If the number of units in stock is less than the predetermined minimum, the fixed unit value is applied to the number in stock.

ANSWER E5. ROLLER LTD

(1) This loss should be treated as an exceptional item because it is exceptional on account of size and incidence and derives from the ordinary activities of the business (*para. 11. SSAP 6*). Losing £400,000 of stock at sea is (or should be) a rare occurrence and yet purchasing and transporting raw materials is an ordinary activity of the business.

SSAP 6 requires that such items should be included in arriving at the profit before taxation and their nature and size disclosed separately within the accounts (*para. 14*).

(2) The company is changing its accounting policy with regard to the charging of product development expenditure, probably to comply with the requirements of *SSAP 13*. This requires companies to write off their development expenditure in the year in which it is incurred unless that expenditure fulfils a set of clearly defined circumstances (*para. 21*).

This change of policy means that certain expenditure incurred in previous years is now to be written off. *SSAP 6* requires that alterations to previous years' profits resulting from a change in accounting policy should be treated as prior year adjustments (*para. 12*). Such adjustments, less attributable taxation, should be accounted for by restating the balance of profits brought forward (*para. 16*).

Roller Ltd should only charge the current year's product development expenditure (£361,000) in the profit and loss account and this would be treated as an exceptional item if it is an abnormally large charge. The writing-off of the balance from previous years (£389,000) should be treated as a prior year adjustment.

(3) *SSAP 9* requires that stocks and work-in-progress should be valued at the lower of cost and net realisable value (*para 1*). 'Cost' is defined as including the cost of purchase and the cost of conversion which includes attributable overheads (*paras. 17, 18 & 19*).

Roller Ltd is changing the basis of valuation of work-in-progress, probably to comply with *SSAP 9*. This is a change in accounting policy. Opening and closing stock in the trading account should be valued on the same basis so that a meaningful gross profit figure is obtained. This means that last year's closing stock should be revalued on the new basis. The difference between the old and new figures will be a change in the previous year's profits and should be accounted for as a prior year adjustment.

The closing work-in-progress valuation of the previous year (£350,000) is at prime cost. An overhead loading of 25% is required to bring this valuation into line with the current year. The valuation should be increased by £87,500 (25% × £350,000). The effect on the profit figure for the year should be shown.

(4) This should be treated as an extraordinary item because it is both material and not expected to recur frequently, and derives from a transaction outside the ordinary course of business (*para. 11, SSAP 6*). Extraordinary items, net of attributable taxation, should be separately disclosed in the profit and loss account below the tax charge (*para. 15, SSAP 6*).

ANSWER E6. DEPRECIATION

(a) (i) Neither statement of depreciation policy gives meaningful information as to the actual rates of depreciation used. A range of 2% to 20% (policy 1) is sufficiently wide to encompass most commonly used rates, and different rates should, therefore, be related to different assets. If fixed assets were not depreciated over their estimated lives (policy 2), the accounts would not comply with fundamental accounting principles (*SSAP 2*).
(ii) Policy 2 does not state what method of depreciation is used.
(iii) Policy 1 does not comply with *SSAP 4*, which specifically requires grants treated as deferred credits not to be shown as part of shareholders' funds. The credit should be taken to the profit and loss account on the same basis as that on which the fixed asset purchased is amortised, and in particular over the useful life of the asset.
(iv) Depreciation should be allocated to accounting periods so as to charge a fair proportion to each accounting period during the expected useful life of the asset. Policy 1 may not ensure this for tools, dies, jigs and moulds.
(v) Buildings have a limited life and should be depreciated having regard to the same criteria as in the case of other fixed assets. Freehold land will not normally require a provision for depreciation. The cost or valuation figures for freehold property, therefore, need analysing between the land and building elements so that the latter may be depreciated. This does not appear to have been done by either company, although the first company may have no freehold, with long leaseholds accounting for the 2% rate.

(b) Depreciation is a measure of the wearing out, consumption or other loss of value on a fixed asset whether arising from use, effluxion of time or obsolescence through technology and market changes. The main purpose of the depreciation charge in the profit and loss account is, therefore, to allocate this depreciation as fairly as possible to the periods expected to benefit from the use of the asset. The charge is, therefore, made in accordance with the accrual (or matching) concept under which revenue realised in an accounting period is compared with the costs or expenses of earning that revenue.

(c) Financial statements are normally intended to be as helpful as possible to a wide audience, who require as much consistency and comparability as is practicable between the financial statements of all enterprises. As soon as consistency or comparability is required between the financial statements of two or more enterprises, reasonable consistency of accounting treatment is also needed, e.g. in the depreciation of land and buildings.

The trend away from strict historical cost accounting (with, for example, the revaluation of certain assets becoming permissible) and the development of more complex corporate structures have resulted in an increase in the number of different accounting practices available to the extent that reasonable comparability has often

Financial Accounting

become ineffective or impossible. It is in this context that accounting standards are required, not necessarily imposing uniformity but at least narrowing the choices, so as to make financial statements more helpful to users. In particular, depreciation is an important charge in most accounts and there is a need to ensure adequate disclosure of the relevant accounting policies.

Finally, there was a requirement to cover *IAS 4* with a UK accounting standard.

(d) The requirements of the standard on depreciation are as follows:

(i) Provision for depreciation of fixed assets having a finite useful life should be made by allocating the cost (or revalued amount) less estimated residual value of the assets as fairly as possible to the periods expected to benefit from their use.

(ii) Where there is a revision of the estimated useful life of an asset, the unamortised cost should be charged over the revised remaining useful life.

(iii) If at any time the unamortised cost of an asset is seen to be irrecoverable in full, it should be written down immediately to the estimated recoverable amount, which should be charged over the remaining useful life.

(iv) Where there is a change from one method of depreciation to another, the unamortised cost of the asset should be written off over the remaining useful life on the new basis commencing with the period in which the change is made. The effect, if material, should be disclosed in the year of change.

(v) Where assets are revalued in the financial statements, the provision for depreciation should be based on the revalued amount and current estimate of remaining useful life, with disclosure in the year of change of the effect of revaluation, if material.

(vi) The following should be disclosed in the financial statements for each major class of depreciable asset:

(1) the depreciation methods used;
(2) the useful lives or the depreciation rates used;
(3) total depreciation allocated for the period;
(4) the gross amount of depreciable assets and the related accumulated depreciation.

ANSWER E7. POST BALANCE SHEET EVENTS AND CONTINGENCIES

(a) A post balance sheet event is an event, favourable or unfavourable, which occurs between the balance sheet date and the date on which the financial statements are approved by the board of directors.

(b) An adjusting event is a post balance sheet event which provides additional evidence of a condition existing at the balance sheet date, and should be reflected in the financial statements.

A non-adjusting event is a post balance sheet event which concerns a condition which did not exist at the balance sheet date. It does not result in changes to the figures in the financial statements, but should be disclosed in the notes to the financial statements if it is so material that its non-disclosure would affect the ability of users of the statements properly to assess the financial position.

(c) (i) This is an adjusting event, since the valuation provides information about a condition existing at the balance sheet date. It would become a non-adjusting event only if it could be demonstrated that the decline in value occurred after the year-end.
(ii) This is an adjusting event, since the dividend relates to the period up to the balance sheet date.
(iii) This is a non-adjusting event: catastrophes such as fire or flood fall into this category. Although the loss would not be accrued, the amount may well be sufficiently material to require disclosure by way of note.

(d) A contingency is a condition which exists at the balance sheet date where the outcome will be confirmed only on the occurrence or non-occurrence of one or more uncertain events. A contingent gain or loss is a gain or loss dependent on a contingency.

(e) A material contingent loss should be accrued in financial statements where it is probable that a future event will confirm a loss which can be estimated with reasonable accuracy on the date on which the financial statements are approved by the board of directors. A material contingent loss not so accrued should be disclosed except where the possibility of loss is remote.

(f) Contingent gains should not be accrued in financial statements. A material contingent gain should be disclosed in financial statements only if it is probable that the gain will be realised.

ANSWER E8. LESSEE LTD

(a) The machine will be included in leased plant and be shown as follows:

In accounts for year ended 31 Dec.

	19–0 £	19–1 £	19–2 £	19–3 £	19–4 £
Cost	50,000	50,000	50,000	50,000	50,000
Depreciation	—	12,500	25,000	37,500	50,000
Written down value	50,000	37,500	25,000	12,500	—

Financial Accounting

(b) The liability would be shown as follows (with appropriate division between the relevant balance sheet headings):

In accounts for year ended 31 Dec.

	19–0 £	19–1 £	19–2 £	19–3 £	19–4 £
Minimum lease payments	68,656	51,492	34,328	17,164	—
Future finance charges	18,656	11,221	5,438	1,588	—
Net liability	50,000	40,271	28,890	15,576	—

(c) A note to the accounts would disclose the following:
Future minimum lease rentals to which the company is committed are:

In accounts for year ended 31 Dec.

	19–0 £	19–1 £	19–2 £	19–3 £	19–4 £
Year ending:					
31 Dec. 19–1	17,164	—	—	—	—
31 Dec. 19–2	17,164	17,164	—	—	—
31 Dec. 19–3	17,164	17,164	17,164	—	—
31 Dec. 19–4	17,164	17,164	17,164	17,164	—
	68,656	51,492	34,328	17,164	—
Less: Financial charges allocated to future periods	18,656	11,221	5,438	1,588	—
	50,000	40,271	28,890	15,576	—

ANSWER F1. MUGGER JAGGER LTD

Ordinary share capital account

	£			£
		19–4		
		1 Mar.	Balance b/d	80,000
			Application and allotment account	40,000
		1 Jul.	Bonus issue 1:4	
			CRR	4,000
			Revenue reserves	26,000
				150,000

Share premium account

	£		£
19–4		19–4	
1 Mar. Redemption of preference shares account	2,000	1 Mar. Balance b/d	2,000
Debenture discount	1,000	Application and allotment account	16,000
Balance c/d	15,000		
	18,000		18,000

8% £1 debenture account

	£		£
19–4		19–4	
		1 Mar. Cash	19,000
		Debenture discount	1,000
			20,000

Debenture discount account

	£		£
19–4		19–4	
1 Mar. 8% debentures	1,000	1 Mar. Share premium account	1,000

Redemption of preference shares account

	£		£
19–4		19–4	
1 Mar. Cash	84,000	1 Mar. Preference shares	60,000
		Premium on redemption:	
		Share premium	2,000
		Revenue reserves	22,000
	84,000		84,000

Revenue reserves

19–4		£	19–4	£
1 Mar.	Redemption of:		1 Mar. Balance b/d	186,000
	Preference shares	22,000		
	CRR	4,000		
1 Jul.	Ordinary share			
	capital	26,000		
	Balance c/d	134,000		
		186,000		186,000

Capital redemption reserve

19–4		£	19–4	£
1 Jul.	Ordinary share capital	4,000	1 Mar. Revenue reserves	4,000

Balance sheet (extract) at 1 Jul. 19–4

Creditors: amounts falling due in more than one year:
  8% £1 debentures   £20,000

Captial and reserves

	£
Ordinary shares of £1 each:	
Authorised	200,000
Issued	150,000
Share premium account	15,000
Revenue reserves	134,000
Share capital and reserves	299,000

Working

	£
Transfer to capital redemption reserve	
Proceeds of fresh issue: 40,000 × 140p	56,000
Nominal value redeemed	60,000
To CRR	4,000

ANSWER F2. ANGLO BAVARIA PLC

No of applicants in categories	Application — No. of shares per applicant	Application — Total shares	Application moneys	Allotment — Issued to each applicant	Allotment — Total shares	Total due on application and allotment	Over-payments	Under-payments
			£			£	£	£
40	1,000	40,000	16,000	500	20,000	20,000	—	4,000
20	10,000	200,000	80,000	1,000	20,000	20,000	60,000	—
1	40,000	40,000	16,000	10,000	10,000	10,000	6,000	—
		280,000	112,000		50,000	50,000	66,000	4,000

(b)

Application and allotment account

	£		£
19–2		19–2	
1 Feb. Ordinary share capital account	37,500	1 Jan. Bank—application moneys on 280,000 shares @ 40p per share	112,000
Share premium account	12,500	1 Feb. Bank	3,900
15 Feb. Bank—excess application moneys returned	66,000	1 Apr. Forfeited shares account	100
	116,000		116,000

Ordinary share capital

	£		£
19–2		19–2	
1 Apr. Forfeited shares account	500	1 Feb. Application and allotment account	37,500
1 May Balance c/f	50,000	1 Mar. Call account	12,500
		1 May Forfeited shares account	500
	50,500		50,500

Share premium account

	£		£
19–2		19–2	
1 May Balance c/f	12,800	1 Feb. Application and allotment account	12,500
		1 May Forfeited shares account	300
	12,800		12,800

Call account

	£		£
19–2		19–2	
1 Mar. Ordinary share capital account	12,500	1 Mar. Bank	12,375
		1 Apr. Forfeited shares account	125
	12,500		12,500

Forfeited shares account

	£		£
19–2		19–2	
1 Apr. Application and allotment account	100	1 Apr. Ordinary share capital account	500
Call account	125	1 May Bank (Goody)	525
1 May Ordinary share capital account	500		
Share premium account	300		
	1,025		1,025

ANSWER F3. ROBIN LTD

7% debentures account

	Interest £	Capital £		Interest £	Capital £
19–7			19–7		
2 Jan. Debenture redemption account—nominal value		20,600	1 Jan. Balance b/f		220,000
30 Jun. Interest—7% on £199,400 for six months	6,979		31 Dec. P & L account	13,958	
31 Dec. Debenture redemption account—nominal value		199,400			
Interest	6,979				
	13,958	220,000		13,958	220,000

Sinking fund account

	£		£
19–7		19–7	
2 Jan. Debenture redemption account—premium	206	1 Jan. Balance b/f	209,650
31 Dec. Debenture redemption account—premium	5,982	14 Dec. Profit on sale of investments	27,080
Voluntary capital reserve	220,000	32 Dec Income on investments	10,500
P & L account—excess fund no longer required	21,042		
	247,230		247,230

Sinking fund investments account

	£		£
19–7		19–7	
1 Jan. Balance b/f	209,650	2 Jan. Sale of investments	21,040
14 Dec. Sinking fund account—profit on sale of investments	27,080	14 Dec. Sale of investments	215,690
	236,730		236,730

Debenture redemption account

	£		£
19–7		19–7	
2 Jan. Cash—cost of debentures purchased at 101	20,806	2 Jan. Debentures account—nominal value	20,600
		Sinking fund account—premium on purchase	206
	20,806		20,806
19–7		19–7	
31 Dec. Cash—debentures redeemed at 103	205,382	31 Dec. Debenture account	199,400
		Sinking fund account—premium on redemption	5,982
	205,382		205,382

Workings

Sinking fund cash account

19–7	£	19–7	£
2 Jan. Sale of investments	21,040	2 Jan. Purchase of debentures	20,806
14 Dec. Sale of investments	215,690	31 Dec. Redemption of debentures	205,382
31 Dec. Income from investments	10,500	Balance transferred to general cash	21,042
	247,230		247,230

ANSWER F4. AMOS LTD

(a) *Journal*

		£	£
19–2			
15 Jul.	Cash	25,000	
	Share premium		25,000
	Rights issue of 20,000 £1 ordinary shares @ £3 per share; receipt of application money @ £1.25 per share		
31 Jul	Cash	35,000	
	Share capital		20,000
	Share premium		15,000
	Receipt of call money @ £1.75 per share		
31 Aug.	8% redeemable preference shares	100,000	
	Cash		100,000
	Redemption of 8% redeemable preference shares at par		
	Revenue reserves	40,000	
	Capital redemption reserve		40,000
	Transfer out of distributable reserves in accordance with *s. 170 CA 1985* an amount equal to the difference between:		
	(i) the nominal value of preference shares redeemed (100,000); and		
	(ii) the aggregate proceeds of new share capital issued (60,000)		

		£	£
30 Sep.	8% debentures	70,000	
	Share premium	7,000	
	Cash		77,000
	Redemption of debentures at a premium of 10% and writing off that premium in accordance with s. 130 CA 1985		
	Revenue reserves	70,000	
	Reserve arising on redemption of debentures		70,000
	Transfer to a voluntary non-distributable reserve of an amount equal to the nominal value of debentures redeemed other than out of the proceeds of a fresh issue (not statutorily necessary, but good accounting practice)		

(b) *Summarised balance sheet as at 30 Sep. 19–2*

	£	£
Net assets		628,000
Capital and reserves		
Called up share capital		
Ordinary shares of £1 each		170,000
Share premium account		33,000
Other reserves:		
Capital redemption reserve	40,000	
Arising on redemption of debentures	70,000	
		110,000
Profit and loss account		315,000
		628,000

ANSWER G1. EBB PLC AND FLOW PLC

(a) *Calculation of shares to be issued by Tide plc to shareholders of Ebb plc and Flow plc*

	Ebb plc £	Flow plc £
Freehold	30,000	8,000
Plant and machinery	36,440	10,570
Trade investment	20,000	—
Goodwill	59,500	11,000
Current assets		
Stock	35,000	14,000
Debtors (less provision)	9,360	5,130
Bank	4,900	3,300
	195,200	52,000
Less: Creditors (amounts due within one year)	35,200	12,000
Total consideration to be settled by issue of £1 shares at par	160,000	40,000
Issued share capital	£40,000	£16,000
Shares to be issued on exchange	160,000	40,000
Basis of allotment	4 for 1	5 for 2

(b) *Journal*

	£	£
Cash	62,500	
Ordinary share capital		50,000
Share premium		12,500
Rights issue of £1 ordinary shares @ £1.25 on basis of 1 for every 4 held, payable in full on application		
Cash	99,000	
Debenture discount	1,000	
10% debentures		100,000
Issue of debentures at 99, payable in full on application		
Share premium	1,000	
Debenture discount		1,000
Writing off debenture discount in accordance with *s. 130 CA 1985*		

(c) **Balance sheet extracts** (*immediately after acquisition and share and debenture issues*)

The assets would be disclosed as follows:

	£
Fixed assets—investments	
Shares in group companies (at cost)	200,000
Current assets:	
Cash at bank and in hand	161,500

In addition a note would be appended to the balance sheet, setting out details of the number, description and amount of shares owned in and name and country of incorporation of, each subsidiary company.

ANSWER G2. MIX PLC

Balance sheet at 31 Dec. 19–9
(*immediately after issue of shares to public*)

Workings

		£
(1)	*Fixed assets*	
	Investment: shares in group companies (at cost)	468,000
	Current assets	
	Cash at bank and in hand	82,696
		550,696
	Capital and reserves	
(2)	Called up share capital	
	Ordinary shares of £1 each	434,000
(5)	Share premium account	112,600
	Profit and loss account	3,696
		550,696

Profit and loss account for the period of seven months ended 31 Dec. 19–9

Workings

		£
(3)	Administrative expenses	(600)
	Income from shares in group companies	24,858
		24,258
	Tax on profit on ordinary activities (being tax credit on dividends received)	(7,458)
	Profit on ordinary activities after taxation	16,800
(4)	Appropriation:	
	Interim dividend of 3½p per share paid	(13,104)
	Retained profit	3,696

Workings

(1) *Investments in subsidiaries*
Computation of consideration for acquisition:

	Rich Ltd £	Poor Ltd £	Total £
Estimated profits	57,600	23,200	
Less: Debenture interest	—	4,000	
		19,200	
Less: Corporation tax @ 50%	28,800	9,600	
	28,800	9,600	
Less: Preference dividend	—	6,000	
(a) Profits for ordinary shares	28,800	3,600	
(b) Price/earnings ratio	15	10	
(c) Consideration ((a) × (b))	£432,000	£36,000	468,000

Financial Accounting

(2) *Ordinary share capital*
Shares in Mix PLC issued to members of subsidiaries:

	Rich Ltd £	Poor Ltd £	Total £
Nominal ($\frac{100}{125}$ × consideration)	345,600	28,800	374,400
Premium ($\frac{25}{125}$ × consideration)	86,400	7,200	93,600

Public issue:
  Nominal (60,000 × £1)
  Premium (60,000 × 40p)   24,000

Total premium   117,600

Total nominal value of shares issued:
  To members of subsidiaries   374,400
  To public   60,000

Total issued capital   434,400

(3) *Investment income*

	Actual £	Tax credit 3/7ths £	Actual plus credit £
Dividends from:			
Rich Ltd—5% × £300,000	15,000	6,429	21,429
Poor Ltd—2% × £120,000	2,400	1,029	3,429
	17,400	7,458	24,858

(4) *Cash at bank*

	£	£
Issue of shares to public:		
Nominal		60,000
Premium		24,000
		84,000
Dividends from subsidiaries (actual)		17,400
		101,400
Less:		
Management expenses	600	
Preliminary expenses	5,000	
Ordinary dividend paid		
($3\frac{1}{2}\% \times £374,400$)	13,104	
		18,704
		82,696

(5) *Share premium account*

Share premium (working 2)	117,600
Less: Preliminary expenses written off in accordance with s. 130 CA 1985	(5,000)
	112,600

Notes:
(i) No provision has been made for bank interest payable in the period ending 31 Dec. 19–9.
(ii) No election has been made to pay group dividends without related ACT.

ANSWER G3. POOH LTD

(a) *Statement showing the number of shares to be issued*

Acquisitions of net assets:

	Tiger Ltd £	Kanga & Roo £
Freehold premises at valuation	60,000	25,000
Other fixed assets at valuation	33,000	21,000
Stocks	18,000	10,000
Debtor	41,500	
Balance at bank	12,000	
Goodwill (see working 1)	24,500	8,000
	189,000	
Creditors	52,000	
Net assets acquired	137,000	64,000
No. of ordinary shares of £1 each to be issued:		
4/5ths × £137,000 & 4/5ths × £64,000 (the 1/5th in each case representing share premium)	109,600	51,200
Share premium	27,400	12,800

Financial Accounting — 193

(b) Balance sheet as at 1 Jan. 19–0

	Tiger Ltd £	Kanga & Roo £
Fixed assets		
Intangible assets		
Goodwill £(24,500 × 8,000) (working 1)		32,500
Tangible assets:		
Freehold premises at cost	50,000	
Freehold premises, at valuation £(60,000 + 25,000)	85,000	
Other fixed assets, at cost less depreciation	158,000	
Other fixed assets, at valuation £(33,000 + 21,000)	54,000	
		347,000
		379,500
Current assets:		
Stocks, at cost less obsolete stock £(135,000 + 18,000 + 10,000)	163,000	
Debtors £(123,000 + 41,500)	164,500	
Cash at bank and in hand £(21,000 + 12,000)	33,000	
	360,500	
Less: Creditors: amounts falling due within one year £(65,000 + 52,000)	117,000	
		243,500
		623,000
Capital and reserves:		
Called up share capital		
Ordinary shares of £1 each, issued and fully paid		460,800
Share premium account £(27,400 + 12,800)	40,200	
Profit and loss account	122,000	
		162,200
		623,000

Financial Accounting

Workings
1. Goodwill

	Tiger Ltd £	Kanga & Roo £
Profits		
Y/E 31 Dec. –7	9,000	9,000
31 Dec. –8	12,106	6,500
31 Dec. –9	13,100	9,500
	34,206	25,000
Adjustments		
Directors remuneration 3 × 2,500	7,500	
Partners salaries 3 × 5,000		(15,000)
Depreciation (working 2)	(4,956)	
Exceptional item		2,000
TOTAL ADJUSTED PROFITS FOR 3 years	36,750	12,000
Average per year	12,250	4,000
Goodwill (= 2 × average)	24,500	8,000

2. Depreciation—Tiger Ltd

	Y/E 31/12/–7 £	31/12/–8 £	31/12/–9 £
Other fixed assets at cost held during year	60,000	70,000	62,000
Depreciation at 10%	6,000	7,000	6,000
Actually provided	(5,250)	(4,458)	(4,336)
Extra provision required	750	2,542	1,664
TOTAL for 3 years		4,956	

ANSWER H1. CUMBRIA LTD AND EASEDALE LTD

Cumbria Group consolidated balance sheet at 30 Jun. 19–5

				£
Fixed assets:				
Tangible assets	Cost	*Aggregate depreciation*	Net	
Land and buildings	219,000	—	219,000	
Plant and machinery	93,900	30,400	63,500	
	312,900	30,400	282,500	282,500
Current assets:				
Stocks			102,010	
Debtors			47,570	
Cash at bank and in hand			31,820	
			181,400	
Creditors: amounts falling due within one year				
Trade creditors			28,550	
Other creditors (36,000 + 4,060)			40,060	
			68,610	
Net current assets				112,790
Total assets less current liabilities				395,290
Minority interest in subsidiary:				
In ordinary share capital and reserves			25,500	
In preference share capital			32,000	
				57,500
				337,790
Capital and reserves:				
Called up share capital (ordinary shares of £1 each)				240,000
Consolidated profit and loss reserves				97,790
				337,790

Notes: Provision has been made for the whole of the unrealised profit on stock. Some accountants would eliminate the group's share only. Goodwill on consolidation has been deducted from reserves.

Financial Accounting

Workings

(1) Adjustment account

	£		£
Cost of ordinary shares	101,300	Nominal value of ordinary shares	60,000
Cost of preference shares	16,200	Nominal value of preference shares	16,000
		Reserves—Easedale	20,880
		Balance—goodwill on consolidation to CRR	20,620
	117,500		117,500

(2) Easedale—revenue reserves

	£		£
Adjustment account 80% × £26,100	20,880	Balance b/d	52,500
Minority shareholders 20% × £52,500	10,500		
Consolidated revenue reserves account 80% × £(52,500 − 26,100)	21,120		
	52,500		52,500

(3) Minority shareholders' account

	£		£
Balances c/d:		Nominal value of ordinary shares	15,000
OSC + reserves	25,500	Reserves—Easedale	10,500
Preference share capital	32,000	Nominal value of preference shares	32,000
	57,500		57,500

(4) Dividends payable account—Easedale

	£		£
CRR: 80% × £7,500	6,000	Ordinary dividend	
MI: 20% × £7,500		payable	7,500
Balance c/d	1,500	Preference dividend	
CRR: $\frac{1}{3}$ × £3,840	1,280	payable	3,840
MI: $\frac{2}{3}$ × £3,840			
Balance c/d	2,560		
	11,340		11,340

(5) Consolidated revenue reserves account (CRR)

	£		£
Stock adjustment		Cumbria reserves	98,450
working (6))	8,440	Easedale reserves	21,120
Goodwill	20,620	Preference dividend	1,280
Balance c/d	97,790	Ordinary dividend	6,000
	126,850		126,850

(6) Consolidated stock account

	£		£
Cumbria	68,350	Consolidated revenue	
Easedale stock	42,100	reserves:	
		$\frac{25}{125}$ × £42,200	8,440
		Balance sheet	102,010
	110,450		110,450

Financial Accounting

ANSWER H2. SUN, SEA AND SKY

Sun Group consolidated balance sheet at 1 Oct. 19–8

	£	£
Fixed assets		
Tangible assets (note 1)		245,330
Current assets		
Stock	214,220	
Debtors (working 3)	167,691	
Cash at bank and in hand	249,010	
	630,921	
Creditors: amounts falling due within one year (note 2)	(399,464)	
Net current assets		231,457
Total assets less current liabilities		476,787
Minority interest (note 5)		70,575
		406,212
Capital and reserves		
Called up share capital (note 3)		250,000
Share premium account		40,000
Other reserves—reserves on consolidation (note 4)		13,750
Consolidated profit and loss account reserve (note 6)		102,462
		406,212

Notes to the accounts

(1) *Fixed assets*

	£
Equipment and fittings, at cost	446,410
Less: Aggregate depreciation	201,080
	245,330

(2) *Creditors* (amounts falling due within one year)

	£
Creditors	117,959
Corporation tax	135,105
Bills payable (see working (2))	2,400
Proposed dividends (see working (4))	144,000
	399,464

(3) *Ordinary share capital*
Authorised and issued ordinary shares of £1 each, fully paid.

(4) *Goodwill*
Negative goodwill arising on consolidation is credited to a separate reserve. Positive goodwill arising on consolidation is deducted from the separate reserve. If positive goodwill exceeds negative goodwill the excess is deducted from reserves.

(5) *Minority interests*

	£
Minority shareholders of Sea Ltd	23,403
Minority shareholders of Sky Ltd	47,172
	70,575

(6) *Reserves*
Revenue reserves include £12,000 which is regarded as non-distributable.

(7) *Contingent liability*
There is a contingent liability of £2,500 for bills receivable discounted (see working (2)).

Consolidation schedules

Share capital

	Sea Ltd £	Sky Ltd £		Sea Ltd £	Sky Ltd £
Adjustment account	85,000	160,000	Balance b/f	100,000	150,000
Minority interest	15,000	40,000	Revenue reserves —bonus issue	—	50,000
	100,000	200,000		100,000	200,000

Revenue reserves

	Sea Ltd £	Sky Ltd £		Sea Ltd £	Sky Ltd £
Share capital—bonus issue	—	50,000	Balance b/f	56,020	85,860
Adjustment account:			Adjustment account		
(25% × £45,000)	11,250	—	(60% × £20,000)	12,000	—
(80% × £(65,000 − 50,000))	—	12,000			
Minority interests:					
(15% × £56,020)	8,403	—			
(20% × £(85,860 − 50,000))	—	7,172			
Consolidated revenue reserves	48,367	16,688			
	68,020	85,860		68,020	85,860

Adjustment account

	Sea Ltd £	Sky Ltd £		Sea Ltd £	Sky Ltd £
Cost of investment	67,500	175,000	Share capital	85,000	160,000
Revenue reserves	12,000	—	Revenue reserves	11,250	12,000
Negative goodwill	16,750	—	Goodwill		3,000
	96,250	175,000		96,250	175,000

Minority interests

	Sea Ltd £	Sky Ltd £		Sea Ltd £	Sky Ltd £
Balance c/f	23,403	47,172	Share capital	15,000	40,000
			Revenue reserves	8,403	7,172
	23,403	47,172		23,403	47,172

Consolidated revenue reserves

	£	£		£	£
Balance c/f		102,462	Balance c/f		37,407
			Revenue reserves:		
			Sea Ltd		48,367
			Sky Ltd		16,688
		102,462			102,462

Workings

(1) *Shareholdings in Sea Ltd and Sky Ltd on 1 Oct. 19–8*

	Sea Ltd	Sky Ltd
	%	%
Group	85	80
Minority	15	20
	100	100

(2) *Bills receivable and payable*

	Receivable	Payable	Contingent
	£	£	£
As per balance sheets	14,600	3,900	3,000
Less: Inter-company	1,500	1,500	500
Consolidated balance sheet	13,100	2,400	2,500

In respect of the bill payable by Sea Ltd and discounted by Sun Ltd, £500 is not an inter-company liability as it is owed to the finance house.

(3) *Debtors*

	£
Sun Ltd—per balance sheet	101,558
Less: Inter-company proposed dividends (see working (4))	91,000
Revised Sun Ltd balance	10,558
Sea Ltd—per balance sheet	64,275
Sky Ltd—per balance sheet	79,758
	154,591
Add: Bills receivable (working (2))	13,100
	167,691

Financial Accounting

(4) *Proposed dividends*

	Sea Ltd £	Sky Ltd £
Per balance sheet	60,000	50,000
Less: Due to Sun Ltd	51,000	40,000
(Sea: 85% × £60,000; Sky: (80% × £50,000)		
Minority interest	9,000	10,000

Summary:

	£
Sun Ltd	125,000
Sea Ltd	9,000
Sky Ltd	10,000
	144,000

(5) It is assumed that the bonus issue has been made out of pre-acquisition profits.

(6) Non-distributable reserves:

60% × £20,000 Dr. = £12,000.

ANSWER H3. H, SA, SB, SC

Consolidated balance sheet as at 31 Dec. 19–9

	£	£
Fixed assets		
Tangible assets:		
Freehold land and property		378,000
Plant and machinery at net book value		230,700
Vehicles at net book value		32,300
		641,000
Current assets		
Stocks	229,750	
Debtors	106,130	
Cash at bank and in hand £(15,750 + 2,450)	18,200	
	354,080	
Less: Creditors: amounts falling due within one year	224,500	
Net current assets		129,580
Total assets less current liabilities		770,580
Minority interest		78,320
		692,260
Share capital and reserves		
Called up share capital		
Ordinary shares of £1 each, issued and fully paid		550,000
Consolidated profit and loss account reserves		142,260
		692,260

```
           1 Dec. 19–1   30 Jun. 19–2   30 Jan. 19–3   30 Jan. 19–4   31 Dec. 19–9
H Ltd  ────────────────────┬──────────────┬──────────────┬──────────────
                    │ 3/5         │           │ [9/25]      │ [1/5]
SA Ltd ─────────────┘           ╲           │            │
                                 ╲          │ 3/5        │
SB Ltd ──────────────────────────┘          │            ╲
                                       │ 1/3             │ 1/3
SC Ltd ────────────────────────────────┘                 ┘
```

Since the question tells us that all pre-acquisition reserves had been paid out by the respective companies before 31 Dec. 19–9, only post-acquisition reserves remain in the balance sheets of the subsidiaries.

Workings

Reserves of SA Ltd

	£		£
Minority interests ($\frac{2}{5}$)	2,112	Balance b/d	5,280
CRR ($\frac{3}{5}$)	3,168		
	5,280		5,280

Reserves of SB Ltd

	£		£
Minority interests $\frac{16}{25}$	7,680	Balance b/d	12,000
CRR ($\frac{9}{25}$)	4,320		
	12,000		12,000

Reserves of SC Ltd

	£		£
Minority interests ($\frac{7}{15}$)	1,680	Balance b/d	3,600
CRR ($\frac{8}{15}$)	1,920		
	3,600		3,600

Adjustment account (see note)

	£		£
Cost of investments:		Nominal value of shares:	
H Ltd in SA Ltd	90,000	H Ltd in SA Ltd	75,000
H Ltd in SC Ltd	8,000	H Ltd in SC Ltd	5,000
SA Ltd in SB Ltd		SA Ltd in SB Ltd	
($\frac{3}{5} \times$ £42,000)	25,200	($\frac{9}{25} \times$ £50,000)	18,000
SA Ltd in SC Ltd		SA Ltd in SC Ltd	
($\frac{3}{5} \times$ £10,500)	6,300	($\frac{1}{5} \times$ £15,000)	3,000
		Plant and machinery	
		in SB Ltd	
		($\frac{9}{25} \times$ £1,500)	540
		Goodwill to CRR	27,960
	129,500		129,500

Minority interests account

	£		£
Share of cost of investments:		Nominal value of shares:	
SA Ltd in SB Ltd		SA Ltd ($\frac{2}{5} \times$ £125,000)	50,000
($\frac{2}{5} \times$ £42,000)	16,800	SB Ltd ($\frac{16}{25} \times$ £50,000)	32,000
SA Ltd in SC Ltd		SC Ltd ($\frac{7}{15} \times$ £15,000)	7,000
($\frac{2}{5} \times$ £10,500)	4,200	Reserves:	
Additional depreciation		SA Ltd	2,112
in SB Ltd charged to		SB Ltd	7,680
minorities		SC Ltd	1,680
($\frac{16}{25} \times$ £3,300)	2,112	Plant and machinery in	
Balance c/d	78,320	SB Ltd ($\frac{16}{25} \times$ £1,500)	960
	101,432		101,432

Consolidated revenue reserves (CRR)

	£		£
Additional depreciation		H Ltd	170,000
in SB Ltd charged to		SA Ltd	3,168
group ($\frac{9}{25} \times$ £3,300)	1,188	SB Ltd	4,320
Unrealised profit in		SC Ltd	1,920
stock	8,000		
Goodwill	27,960		
Balance c/d	142,260		
	179,408		179,408

Plant and machinery in SB Ltd

	£		£
Balance b/d	9,000	Additional depreciation	
Revaluation at date of		in post-acquisition	
Acquisition:		period:	
Minority share (minority		Minority share (minority	
interest account)	960	interest account)	2,112
Group share (adjustment		Group share (CRR)	1,188
account)	540	Balance c/d	7,200
	10,500		10,500

Current account reconciliations

	H Ltd £	SA Ltd £	SB Ltd £	SC Ltd £
As given	10,250	(4,950)	(3,250)	400
Cheques in transit:				
SC Ltd to H Ltd	(350)			
SC Ltd to SA Ltd		(400)		
SB Ltd to H Ltd	(1,000)			
SA Ltd to SC Ltd				(700)
	8,900	(5,350)	(3,250)	(300)

$$\text{Cash in transit} = £(350 + 400 + 1{,}000 + 700)$$
$$= £2{,}450$$

Note:
The correct accounting treatment in the books of a holding company for the receipt of dividends from pre-acquisition reserves is to reduce the cost of the investment in the relevant subsidiary by the amount of the dividend received. In this case since all the pre-acquisition reserves were paid out in dividend the 'cost of investment' in each case must have been reduced by the holding company's shares of pre-acquisition reserves; thus no credit entry in the adjustment account is needed for these reserves since they have already been settled from the cost of investment.

ANSWER J1. GROUP ACCOUNTS

(a) The relationship between a holding company and a subsidiary is basically one of control: the holding company controls the subsidiary. The legal definition in *s. 736 CA 1985* is that a company shall be deemed to be a subsidiary of another if
(A) that other either
  (i) is a member of it and controls the composition of its board of directors; or
  (ii) holds more than half in normal value of its equity share capital; or
(B) The first mentioned company is a subsidiary of any company which is that other's subsidiary.

Equity share capital is defined as issued share capital of a company excluding any part thereof which, neither as respects dividends nor as respects capital, carries any right to participate beyond a specified amount in a distribution.

(b) Group accounts are simply financial statements of a group of companies. Consolidated accounts are one form of group accounts which present the information contained in the separate financial statements of a holding company and its subsidiaries as if they were the financial statements of a single entity.
(c) A holding company need not prepare group accounts when it is itself a wholly owned subsidiary of another body incorporated in Great Britain (*s. 229 CA 1985*). In addition, the *CA 85* allows a holding company to omit a subsidiary from the group accounts in certain situations. If these applied to all the subsidiaries no group accounts would be needed although certain information regarding the subsidiaries may still be required to be disclosed by law. In addition, *SSAP 14* would require certain information to be disclosed.
(d) The general principle in consolidated accounts is that all intra-group items are eliminated so that the consolidated statements reflect transactions between the group and parties outside the group.

1. *Intra group sales*
   These are eliminated from the consolidated profit and loss account by a contra with the appropriate purchases in the accounts of the buying company.
2. *Intra-group charges*
   Similarly, management charges on one group company would be eliminated by a contra against the credit in the books of the company making the charge.
3. *Unrealised intra-group profit*
   It is right and proper for a group company to make a profit when supplying goods or services to another group company. Indeed, not to make a profit may prejudice the minority shareholders of the supplying company. If the goods involved have not been sold before the end of the accounting year such a profit remains unrealised from the point of the group as a whole.

   The problem then arises as to what extent and in what way this unrealised profit should be eliminated. As an example, suppose a holding company sells goods to its 75% owned subsidiary, making a profit of £10,000.

   Several approaches may be adopted:

   (i) To make provision for the whole of the unrealised profit of £10,000 against the group reserves. The arguments for doing this are that since the group is being treated as a single economic activity, it realises no profit until the goods are sold to someone else. It is a prudent method of accounting. It recognises that in practical terms, the minority shareholders cannot be charged with any profit being made on such a transaction.
   (ii) To make provision for the whole of the unrealised profit of £10,000 but to charge 25% of that provision against minority interests. This method is prudent but reflects the fact that if the subsidiary company bears a higher cost this must be borne

indirectly by its shareholders. It is a method more likely to be applied to a sale made by the subsidiary to the holding company (an 'upstream' transaction) than the situation in this example (a 'downstream' transaction).

(iii) To make provision for only the group proportion (75%) of the unrealised profit. This treats the intra-group sale as being partially realised to the extent of the minority proportion. It is less prudent and ignores the fact that the holding company usually dictates the amount and price of goods being bought and sold within the group.

The entity convention and the doctrine of prudence both require method **(iii)** to be cast aside. The argument for method **(i)** in the case of an 'upstream' transaction is that some profits are 'realised' in the minds of the minority but the group still has an asset which is over-valued and so an adjustment should be made to group distributable profits. In the case of a 'downstream' transaction the profit has been 'made' by the holding company but from the point of view of the group it is unrealised and so should be deducted from group reserves. Hence method **(i)** is the preferred technique.

ANSWER J2. HSA

Consolidated balance sheet at 31 Dec. 19–5

Notes		£	£
	Fixed assets:		
(2)	Investments—associated companies	42,500	
(3)	—other investments	12,000	
			54,500
	Other net assets		1,546,000
	Total assets *less* current liabilities:		1,600,500
	Minority interest		35,600
			1,564,900
	Capital and reserves:		
(1)	Called up share capital		700,000
	Consolidated profit and loss account		864,900
			1,564,900

Consolidated profit and loss account for the year ending 31 Dec. 19–5

Notes		£
	Turnover	x
	Cost of sales	x
	Gross profit	x
	Distribution costs	(x)
	Administrative expenses	(x)
	Other operating income	x
(4)	Group trading profit	561,571
	Share of profits of associate	7,500
	Group profit on ordinary activities	569,071
(5)	Taxation on profit on ordinary activities	(295,971)
	Profit on ordinary activities after taxation	273,100
	Minority shareholders interests	(5,600)
	Profit attributable to the group (of which £249,850 is dealt with in the accounts of H Ltd)	267,500
(6)	Dividends	75,000
	Retained profits	192,500

	£
Retained in H Ltd	174,850
S Ltd	14,400
A Ltd	3,250
	192,500

| (7) | Earnings per share | 38.2p |

Statement of retained earnings

	£
Balance at 1 Jan. 19–5	677,400
Retained for year	192,500
Balance at 31 Dec. 19–5	869,900

Financial Accounting

Notes to the accounts

£

(1) *Share capital*
Ordinary shares of £1 each authorised, issued
and fully paid 700,000

(2) *Associated company*
Group share of net tangible assets 34,500
Premium on acquisition 8,000
                                                              42,500

(3) *Investments*
Quoted at book value (mid-market price £...) 12,000

(4) *Group trading profit*
Trading profit is stated after crediting:
    Income from quoted investments 1,100
    and after charging
        Depreciation x
        Hire charges x
    Directors of holding company:
        Fees x
        Compensation x
        Other emoluments x
    Auditors' remuneration including expenses x

(5) *Taxation*
Taxation on the profits of the group:
    UK corporation tax @ 50% 292,000
    Tax credits on dividends received 471
    Corporation tax on the group's share of
        profits of associated company 3,500
                                                          295,971

(6) *Dividends*
Dividends paid were:
    Ordinary of 15p per share 75,000

(7) *Earnings per share*

Calculated by dividing profit after taxation of £267,500 by the 700,000 ordinary shares in issue and ranking for dividend.

Financial Accounting

Workings

(a) *Consolidation of balance sheet*

Adjustment account

	£		£
H Ltd—cost of investment	118,600	S Ltd—shares: 80% × £100,000	80,000
		Pre-acquisition: 80% × £42,000	33,600
		Goodwill to CRR	5,000
	118,600		118,600

Minority interest account

	£		£
Balance c/d	35,600	S Ltd: Shares 20% × £100,000	20,000
		Reserves 20% × £78,000	15,600
	35,600		35,600

Consolidated revenue reserves (CRR)

	£		£
Goodwill	5,000	H Ltd	836,100
Balance c/d	864,900	S Ltd: 80% × £(78,000 − 42,000)	28,800
		A Ltd: 25% × £(58,000 − 38,000)	5,000
	869,900		869,900

(b) *Consolidation of profit and loss account*

	£
Trading profit (H Ltd + S Ltd)	560,000
Add: Income from trade investments (£1,100 + tax credit @ 3/7ths)	1,571
	561,571

Financial Accounting

(c) *Minority interest in profit of subsidiary for the year*

	£	£
Profit after tax of subsidiary		28,000
Minority share (20%)	5,600	
Group share—all post-acquisition (80%)	22,400	
	28,000	

(d) *Profit retained for year*

	£
In H Ltd—as given in question	174,850
In S Ltd—80% × £18,000	14,400
In A Ltd—25% × £13,000	3,250
	192,500

(e) *Unappropriated profits brought forward*

	£
In H Ltd	661,250
In S Ltd—80% × £(60,000 − 42,000)	14,400
In A Ltd—25% × £(45,000 − 38,000)	1,750
	677,400

(f) *Investment in associated company*

		£
Group share of net tangible assets:		
25% × £138,000		34,500
Premium on acquisition:		
Cost of investment		37,500
Group share at acquisition of:		
Share capital (25%)	20,000	
Reserves (25%)	9,500	
		29,500
		8,000

ANSWER J3. APRICOT LTD AND ITS SUBSIDIARY COMPANIES

Consolidated profit and loss account for year ended 30 Jun. 19–4

	£	£	Notes to the accounts
Group trading profit		78,150	(1)
Interest and dividends received		4,643	
Profit before taxation		82,793	
UK corporation tax		35,593	(2)
Profit after taxation		47,200	
Minority shareholders' interest in subsidiaries		4,900	
Profit after taxation attributable to Apricot Ltd (of which £39,000 is dealt with in the separate accounts of Apricot Ltd)		42,300	
Dividends paid and proposed		30,000	(3)
Profit for year retained		12,300	(4)
In accounts of Apricot Ltd	7,150		
In accounts of subsidiary companies	5,150		
	12,300		

Notes to the accounts

(1) *Accounting policies—basis of consolidation*
   (a) Where subsidiary companies are acquired during the year, their results and turnover are included from the date of acquisition.
   (b) All unrealised internal profits are eliminated on consolidation, without charge to the minority.

(2) UK corporation tax

	£
UK corporation tas has been provided on the profits of the year at a rate of x%	34,200
Tax credits on dividends received	1,393
	35,593

(3) Dividends paid and proposed

Dividend proposed on ordinary shares of Apricot Ltd = £30,000

(4) Statement of retained revenue reserves

	£
Retained reserves at 1 Jul. 19–3	87,250
Retained profit for year	12,300
Retained reserves at 30 Jun. 19–4	99,550

Workings

(a) Group trading profit

	£
Apricot Ltd	42,000
Banana Ltd	24,000
Cherry Ltd ($\frac{6}{12} \times$ £28,000)	14,000
	80,000
Less: Provision for unrealised profit	1,850
	78,150

(b) Interest and dividends received

	£
Apricot Ltd—preference dividend received (quoted company)	2,500
Banana Ltd	750
	3,250
Add: Tax credits @ $\frac{3}{7}$	1,393
	4,643

(c) *Minority shareholders' interest in subsidiaries*

	£
Banana Ltd: 20% × £14,750	2,950
Cherry Ltd: 25% × £15,600 × $\frac{6}{12}$	1,950
	4,900

(d) *Corporation tax*

	£
Apricot Ltd	18,000
Banana Ltd	10,000
Cherry Ltd ($\frac{1}{2}$ × £12,400)	6,200
	34,200

(e) *Retained reserves at 1 Jul. 19–3*

	£	£
Apricot Ltd		84,250
Banana Ltd—retained profit		
£(20,000 − 7,500 − 7,500)	5,000	
80% × $\frac{9}{12}$ × £5,000		3,000
		87,250

(f) *Profit for the year retained*

	£
Apricot Ltd:	
Per accounts	10,500
Pre-acquisition dividend:	
(75% × £8,000) − ($\frac{1}{2}$ × 75% × £12,000)	(1,500)
Unrealised inter-company profit	(1,850)
	7,150
Banana Ltd—80% × £4,750	3,800
Cherry Ltd—75% × $\frac{6}{12}$ × £3,600	1,350
	12,300

ANSWER J4. ATLANTIC AND CROSSING

(a) *Consolidated balance sheet at 31 Jan. 19–6*

	£
Fixed assets	810,000
Net current assets	520,000
Total assets *less* current liabilities	1,330,000
Creditors: Amounts falling due after more than one year; 8% debenture stock	(120,000)
	1,210,000
Capital and reserves:	
Called up share capital: Ordinary shares of £1	500,000
Share premium account	200,000
Other reserves	510,000
	1,210,000

(b) *Consolidated profit and loss account for year ended 31 Jan. 19–6*

	£
Profit on ordinary activities after taxation	110,000
Minority interest	1,000
	109,000
Extraordinary income: Gain on disposal	24,000
Profit for the financial year: Retained	133,000
Balance b/f at 1 Feb. 19–5	377,000
Balance c/f at 31 Jan. 19–6	510,000

Workings

(1) *Profit after tax (before extraordinary gain)*

	£
Atlantic £(450,000 − 350,000)	100,000
Crossing $\frac{4}{12}$ × £(240,000 − 210,000)	10,000
	110,000

(2) *Minority interest*
   $10\% \times \frac{4}{12} \times £(240,000 - 210,000)$ £1,000

(3) *Extraordinary gain on disposal*

	£	£
Sale proceeds		360,000
Cost to Atlantic		300,000
Gain to Atlantic		60,000
Less: Attributable post-acquisition reserves sold:		
B/f at 1 Feb. 19–5		
$90\% \times £(210,000 - 180,000)$	27,000	
Arising in year of disposal		
$90\% \times \frac{4}{12} \times £30,000$	9,000	
		36,000
Gain to group		24,000

(4) *Revenue reserves at 1 Feb. 19–5*

	£
Atlantic	350,000
Crossing $90\% \times £(210,000 - 180,000)$	27,000
	377,000

(5) *Revenue reserves at 31 Jan. 19–6*

	£
Per Atlantic accounts	450,000
Gain on disposal of shares	60,000
	510,000

ANSWER J5. ATLANTIC AND CROSSING—PART 2

(a) *Draft consolidation working papers*

Adjustment account

	£		£
Cost of remaining shares		Shares held	80,000
($\frac{80}{90}$ × £300,000)	266,667	Pre-acquisition reserves	
		(80% × £180,000)	144,000
		Goodwill to CRR	42,667
	266,667		266,667

Minority interest account

	£		£
Balance c/d	68,000	Shares	20,000
		Reserves	
		(20% × £240,000)	48,000
	68,000		68,000

Consolidated reserves (CRR)

	£		£
Goodwill	42,667	Atlantic Ltd	450,000
Balance c/d	462,000	Crossing Ltd	
		(80% × £(240,000	
		− 180,000))	48,000
		Share disposal account	6,667
	504,667		504,667

Share disposal account

	£		£
Cost ($\frac{10}{90}$ × £300,000)	33,333	Proceeds	40,000
Reserves	6,667		
	40,000		40,000

(b) *Consolidated balance sheet at 31 Jan. 19–6*

	£	£
Fixed assets:		
Tangible assets		1,100,000
Net current assets		250,000
Total assets *less* current liabilities		1,350,000
Creditors: Amounts falling due after more than one year:		
8% debenture stock	120,000	
Minority interest	68,000	
		188,000
		1,162,000
Capital and reserves:		
Called up share capital—ordinary shares of £1 each		500,000
Share premium account		200,000
Consolidated revenue reserves		462,000
		1,162,000

(c) *Calculation of gain on disposal of shares*

	Holding company	Group	
	£	£	£
Proceeds of sale	40,000		40,000
Cost ($\frac{1}{9} \times$ £300,000)	33,333	33,333	
Attributable post-acquisition profits:			

	£000	£000		
Reserves at acquisition		180		
Reserves at disposal:				
At 1 Feb. 19–5	210			
1 Feb. 19–5 to 1 Jun. 19–5 ($\frac{4}{12} \times$ £(240 − 210))	10			
		220		
		40		

Attributable to disposal	10%		4,000	
				37,333
Extraordinary gain		6,667		2,667

Financial Accounting

Calculation of minority interest

	Total £	Minority interest £
1 Feb.–31 May 19–5: 10% ×	10,000 (4m)	1,000
1 Jun.–31 Jan. 19–6: 20% ×	20,000 (8m)	4,000
	30,000	5,000

Reserves at 1 Feb. 19–5

	£
Atlantic	350,000
Crossing 90% × £(210,000 − 180,000)	27,000
	377,000

Retained profit for the year

	£	£
Retained by Crossing (80% × £30,000)		24,000
Atlantic		
As given	100,000	
Extraordinary item	2,667	
Earned by Crossing relating to shares sold (10% × £10,000)	1,000	
		103,667
		127,667

(d) *Consolidated profit and loss account for year ended 31 Jan. 19–6*

	£
Profit on ordinary activities after taxation	130,000
Minority shareholders' interest	5,000
	125,000
Extraordinary income: Gain on disposal	2,667
Profit for the financial year: Retained	127,667

Statement of retained profit

	£
Balance at 1 Feb. 19–5	377,000
Retained for year	127,667
Balance at 31 Jan. 19–6	504,667

Alternative calculation of group disposal surplus

	£	£	£
Proceeds of sale			40,000
Net assets disposed:			
OSC		100,000	
Reserves at 31 Jan. 19–5		210,000	
Profit to 1 Jun. 19–5			
($\frac{4}{12} \times £30,000$)		10,000	
		320,000	
Sold 10% of shares			32,000
			8,000
Goodwill sold:			
Cost		300,000	
OSC	100,000		
Pre-acquisition reserves	180,000		
	280,000		
Purchased 90%		252,000	
Goodwill acquired		48,000	
Sold 10% of 90%: £48,000 ÷ 9 =			5,333
Extraordinary gain			2,667

ANSWER J6. ATLANTIC AND CROSSING—PART 3

(a) *Consolidated balance sheet at 31 Jan. 19–6*

	£000
Fixed assets—tangible assets	810
Investment—associated company	177
Net current assets	400
	1,387
Creditors: amounts falling due after more than one year: Debentures	(120)
	1,267
Share capital	500
Share premium account	200
Consolidated reserves	567
	1,267

(b) *Consolidated profit and loss account for year ended 31 Jan. 19–6*

	£000	£000
Tax on profit on ordinary activities		XX
Profit on ordinary activities after taxation		119
Minority interests		1
		118
Extraordinary income: Gain on disposal		72
Consolidated profit for the financial year		190
Retained by holding company	176.5	
Retained by associate	13.5	
	190.0	

Reserves

	£000
At 1 Feb. 19–5	377
Retained for year	190
At 31 Jan. 19–6	567

Workings

Associated company

	£000		£000
Cost ($\frac{45}{90} \times £300$)	150		
Share of post-acquisition reserves			
45% × £(240 − 180)	27		
	177		

Disposal account

	£000		£000
Cost ($\frac{45}{90} \times £300$)	150	Proceeds	240
Reserves	90		
	240		240

Consolidated reserves

	£000		£000
		Atlantic Ltd	450
		Disposal	90
		Associated company	27
			567

Profit after tax

	£000
Atlantic	100
Crossing:	
As subsidiary: $\frac{4}{12} \times £30$	10
As associate: $45\% \times \frac{8}{12} \times £30$	9
	119

Minority interest

	£000
Crossing: $10\% \times \frac{4}{12} \times £30$	1

Extraordinary gain on disposal

	£000
Proceeds	240
Assets sold 45% × £320	144
	96
Goodwill sold $\frac{45}{90}$ × £48	24
	72

Retained profit for year

	£000
Associated company 45% × £30	13.5
Holding company:	
As given	100.0
Extraordinary gain	72.0
Profit of Crossing Ltd earned during year on shares sold 45% × £10	4.5
	176.5

ANSWER J7. MOORGATE PRODUCTIONS LTD AND TROPICAL ISLAND DEVELOPMENTS LTD

Consolidated balance sheet of Moorgate Productions Ltd and its subsidiary as at 31 Oct. 19–9

Ref. to workings		£000	£000	£000
	Fixed assets			371,287
	Current assets			
	Stocks		93,613	
	Debtors		115,471	
	Cash at bank and in hand		15,626	
			224,710	
(2)	Creditors (amounts falling due within one year)			
	Trade creditors	104,428		
	Dividend to MI	2,000		
	Taxation	58,363		
	Dividend	13,021	177,812	
	Net current assets			46,898
	Total assets *less* current liabilities			418,185
	Creditors (amounts falling due after more than one year)			
	Long-term loans		220,236	
(2)	Minority shareholders interest		17,046	
				237,282
				180,903
	Capital and reserves			
	Called up share capital—ordinary shares of £1 each			
	—Authorised			75,000
	—Issued and fully paid			73,000
(2)	Profit and loss account (note 1)			107,903
				180,903

Financial Accounting

Consolidated profit and loss account of Moorgate Productions Ltd and its subsidiaries for the year ended 31 Oct. 19–9

Ref. to workings		£
	Turnover	939,575
	Cost of sales	671,123
	Gross profit	268,452
	Administrative and distribution costs	172,306
	Profit on ordinary activities before taxation	96,146
	Tax on profit on ordinary activities:	49,869
	Profit on ordinary activities after taxation	46,277
(3)	Minority interests	4,201
	Profit attributable to the members of Moorgate Productions Ltd (of which £35,775 has been dealt with in the separate accounts of the holding company)	42,076
	Dividends—proposed	13,021
	Amount added to retained profit	29,055

Notes to the accounts

1. *Reserves*

	£000
At 1 Nov. 19–8 (working 6)	77,638
Profit retained for the year	29,055
Exchange adjustments (working 5)	1,210
	107,903

2. *Accounting policies*

(A statement of accounting policies, including those in the question relating to depreciation and foreign currency translation, would follow.)

Workings (all calculations to the nearest £000)

(1) Translation of final accounts of Tropical Islands Developments:

(a) Balance sheet at 31 Oct. 19–9

	N000	Rate	£000
Ordinary share capital	20,000	5	4,000
Reserves—post acq	65,230	(Bal)	38,615
Loans	200,000	2.0	100,000
Creditors	45,698	2.0	22,849
Tax	20,232	2.0	10,116
Dividends	10,000	2.0	5,000
	361,160		180,580
Fixed assets (net)	220,000	2.0	110,000
Stock	52,734	2.0	26,367
Debtors	60,596	2.0	30,298
Cash	27,830	2.0	13,915
	361,160		180,580

(b) Profit and loss account for the year ended 31 Oct. 19–9

	N000	Rate	£000
Turnover	547,634	2.05	267,139
Cost of sales	410,857	2.05	200,418
	136,777		66,721
Administration costs	95,017	2.05	46,350
Profit before tax	41,760	2.05	20,371
Taxation	20,232	2.05	9,869
	21,528		10,502
Dividends payable	10,000	2.0	5,000
Retained profit	11,528		5,502

(c) Turnover 547,634 2.05 267,139

Financial Accounting

(2) Consolidation working papers

Reserves—Tropical Islands Developments

	£000		£000
Minority interest (40% × 38,615)	15,446	Balance b/d—post acq.	38,615
Consolidated reserves (60% × 38,615)	23,169		
	38,615		38,615

Dividend payable

	£000		£000
Consolidated reserves 60% × 5,000	3,000	Balance b/d	5,000
Current liability c/d	2,000		
	5,000		5,000

Minority Interest (MI)

	£000		£000
Balance c/d	17,046	Share capital 40% × 4,000	1,600
		Reserves	15,446
	17,046		17,046

Consolidated reserves

	£000		£000
Balance c/d	107,903	Moorgate	81,734
		Inter co. dividend	3,000
		Reserves—	
		Tropical Islands	23,169
	107,903		107,903

(3) *Minority interests in the profits for the year*

	£000
40% × £10,502,000 =	4,201

(4) *Profits retained by subsidiary company*
60% × £5,502,000 =   3,301

Profits retained by holding company:
Per question   22,754
Dividend receivable from subsidiary   3,000

    25,754

(5) *Translation difference*

(i) Reconstruction and translation of opening balance sheet

	N000	Rate	£000
OSC	20,000	5	4,000
Reserves 65,230–11,528	53,702	Bal.	31,096
	73,702		35,096
Net assets	73,702	2.1	35,096

(ii) Translated opening post acq. reserves   31,096
Translated closing post acq. reserves   38,615

Increase   7,519
Less: Translated retained profit for year   5,502

Exchange gain   2,017

(iii) To reserves 60% × 2,017 =   1,210

(6) *Group reserves at 1.11.19–8*

    £000
Moorgate Productions (81,734 – 22,754)   58,980
Subsidiary
60% of translated opening reserves
(see workings) 60% × 31,096   18,658

    77,638

Tutorial note re gain arising on the disposal of the shares:
The extraordinary gain arising on the sale of the shares in 19–2 would have been 8 million shares at N50 = N4 million. This would have been included in the reserves of the holding company at the rate of exchange ruling at that date. It would not be affected by subsequent exchange rate changes. It is not possible (nor indeed necessary) to calculate the gain for the purpose of these consolidated accounts.

Financial Accounting

ANSWER J8. UK DEVELOPMENTS LTD

(a)   *Consolidated balance sheet as at 30 Apr. 19–7*

Workings   £000   £000   £000

   Fixed assets
     Plant and machinery   3,600
   Current assets
     Stock   1,386
     Debtors   700
     Cash at bank and in hand   322
                                                   2,408

   Creditors (amounts falling due within one year)

2   Creditors (300 + 40)   340
    Taxation   179
    Proposed dividends   100   619

Net current assets   1,789

Total assets *less* current liabilities   5,389
Creditors (amounts failing due after more than one year)
   Debentures   1,800
3   Minority shareholders interest   390
                                                   2,190
                                                   3,199

   Capital and reserves
   Called up share capital   1,850
   Profit and loss account   1,349
                                                   3,199

(b) *Consolidated profit before tax*

	Closing rate method £000	Temporal method £000
Working ref (4 & 5)	1,000	1,000

(c) Temporal method. Statement of group reserves for the year ended 30 Apr. 19–8

                                       £000
6   Balance 1 May 19–7   758
6   Retained profit for year   591

    Balance 30 Apr. 19–8   1,349

Workings:

(1) *Temporal method balance sheet*

	Kru 000	Rate	£000
Plant and machinery	1,600	1	1,600
Stock	200	1	200
Debtors	800	1.25	640
Cash	400	1.25	320
Creditors	(200)	1.25	(160)
Current tax	(100)	1.25	(80)
Proposed dividend	(200)	1.25	(160)
	2,500		2,360
Shares	1,000	1	1,000
Reserves	500	balance	560
Debentures	1,000	1.25	800
	2,500		2,360

Note
It is assumed that the stock was purchased before the last day of the year, and that it is recorded in the balance sheet of Emerging Country Inc at cost. Since stock is a non-monetary asset a strict application of the temporal method of translation requires the translation of stock at the historic rate of Kru 1 = £1.

(2) *Reserves of Emerging Country Inc*

	£000		£000
Consolidated reserves (75%)	420	Balance b/f	560
Minority interests (25%)	140		
	560		560

Dividend proposed by Emerging Country Inc

	£000		£000
Consolidated reserves (75%)	120	Balance b/f	160
Current liabilities	40		
	160		160

Financial Accounting

(3) Consolidated balance sheet workings

Adjustment account

	£000		£000
Cost of investment	750	Share capital	750

Consolidated reserves

	£000
UK Developments Ltd	809
Dividend receivable	120
Emerging Country Inc	420
	1,349

Minority interests

	£000
Share capital	250
Reserves	140
	390

(4) *Closing rate: profit before tax*
Under *SSAP 20* translation differences are dealt with through reserves: they do not, therefore, affect the operating profit before tax.

	Kru 000	Rate	£000
Profit of UK Developments Ltd			400
Emerging Country Inc	600	1	600
			1,000

It is assumed that the profit of UK Developments Ltd does not include any of the dividend receivable from the subsidiary.

(5) *Temporal method: profit before tax*
Under *SSAP 20* translation differences are dealt with in arriving at profit before tax. Therefore, the net translation difference must be computed.

Translation of the profit and loss account

	Kru 000	Rat	£000
Profit before tax	600	1	600
Taxation	100	1.25	80
	500		520
Dividend	200	1.25	160
	300		360

Opening translated reserves
As the exchange rate has not altered between incorporation and the opening balance sheet date the reserves of Emerging Inc. at 1.5.19–7 (200,000 Kru) would be translated at a sterling equivalent of £200,000.

(iii) *Exchange difference*

	£000
Translated post-acquisition reserves at 1.5.19–7	200
Retained for year (i) above	360
Reserves at 30.4.19–8	560

Exchange difference is Nil.

(iv) *Consolidated profit before tax*

	£000
UK Developments Ltd.	400
Emerging County Inc. (i) above	600
	1,000
Exchange difference	NIL
	1,000

(b) *Temporal method statement of reserves*
(i) Opening group reserves

	£000
UK Developments (809 − 201)	608
Emerging County inc.	
75% × £200,000 (see 5 (iii))	150
	758

(ii) Retained profit for the year
UK Developments

	£000
As given	201
Dividend receivable 75% × £160,000	120
	321
Emerging Country Inc. 75% × £360,000 (see 5 (i))	270
	591

ANSWER J9. GRIP AND HAND

Consolidated balance sheet as at 31 Dec. 19–5 (extract)

19–4 £	£		£	£
1,545		Minority interests in subsidiaries		1,135
		Capital and reserves:		
		Called up share capital		
		Authorised, issued and fully paid:		
		100,000 ordinary shares of		
100,000		£1 each		100,000
	855	Negative Goodwill	855	
	20,440	Consolidated revenue reserves	21,690	
21,295				22,545
121,295				122,545

Note: The machinery sold by Hand to Grip would be included in the Fixed assets (Tangible assets: Plant and machinery) at:

	£
Group cost	6,000
Less: Depreciation	1,200
Book value	4,800

Workings

(1) *Negative goodwill on consolidation*

	£	£	£
Original cost of investment			14,250
Less: Pre-acquisition part of dividend received from Hand (90% × £2,000 × $\frac{5}{6}$)			1,500
			12,750
Shares purchased		9,000	
Pre-acquisition reserves:			
At 31 Dec. 19–3 (90% × £3,450)	3,105		
1 Jan. 19–4 to 31 Oct. 19–4 (90% × $\frac{5}{6}$ × £2,000)	1,500		
		4,605	
			13,605
			855

(2) *Consolidated revenue reserves*

	£	£
Grip Ltd:		
At 31 Dec. 19–3		16,200
Retained year ended 31 Dec. 19–4		3,940
Hand Ltd:		
1 Nov. 19–4 to 31 Dec. 19–4 90% × $\frac{1}{6}$ × £2,000		300
At 31 Dec. 19–4		20,440
Grip Ltd:		
Year ended 31 Dec. 19–5	6,540	
Hand Ltd:		
Year ended 31 Dec. 19–5 90% × £(4,100)	(3,690)	
		2,850
		23,290
Less: Profit on sale of plant		
25% × £8,000	2,000	
Less: Depreciation thereon (20%)	400	
		1,600
		21,690

	Grip Ltd		Hand Ltd	
	£	£	£	£
Retained reserves at 31 Dec. 19–3		16,200		3,450
Year ended 31 Dec. 19–4:				
Dividends received (90% × £2,000 × ⅙)	300		—	
Profit	18,640		4,000	
Less: Dividends	15,000		2,000	
		3,940		2,000
Retained at 31 Dec. 19–4		20,140		5,450
Year ended 31 Dec. 19–5:				
Profit/(loss)	26,540		(4,100)	
Dividends	20,000		—	
		6,540		(4,100)
Retained at 31 Dec. 19–5		26,680		1,350

(3) *Minority interests in subsidiaries*

	19–4	19–5
	£	£
Share capital	1,000	1,000
Retained reserves:		
19–4 10% × £5,450	545	
19–5 10% × £1,350		135
	1,545	1,135

Notes:

(a) It is assumed that the pre-acquisition dividend received from Hand was correctly credited to the cost of the investment in the subsidiary and was not included in the profit figures given.
(b) Provision has been made for the whole of the unrealised profit in the plant. Some accountants would only provide for the group share.

	31 Dec. 19–3	31 Oct. 19–4	31 Dec. 19–4	31 Dec. 19–5
Grip Ltd	16,200		20,140	26,680
		90%		
Hand Ltd	3,450		5,450	1,350

ANSWER J10. GRIP, HOLD AND VALISE

Consolidated balance sheet as at 31 Dec. 19–6

	£	£
Fixed assets		
Intangible assets—goodwill on consolidation		9,450
Tangible assets (note 4)		435,000
		444,450
Current assets		
Stocks	164,220	
Debtors	96,370	
Cash at bank and in hand	236,025	
	496,615	
Creditors: Amounts falling due within one year:		
Trade creditors		192,344
Other creditors including taxation and social security: corporation tax		171,930
Dividends:		
—Grip Ltd shareholders	100,000	
—Minority interests	11,000	
		111,000
		475,274
Net current assets		21,341
Total assets less current liabilities		465,791
Minority interest (note 3)		60,261
		405,530
Capital and reserves		
Called up share capital (note 2)		250,000
Consolidated capital reserve		40,000
Consolidated profit and loss		115,530
		405,530

Financial Accounting

Notes to the accounts

(1) *Accounting policies*
Basis of consolidation: The results of the sub-subsidiary, Valise Ltd, have been consolidated with those of the subsidiary, Hold Ltd. The results of this sub-group have then been consolidated with those of the ultimate holding company.

(2) *Share capital*
Authorised and issued ordinary shares of £1 each, fully paid.

(3) *Minority interests*

	£
Minority shareholders of Valise Ltd	42,485
Minority shareholders of Hold Ltd	17,776
	60,261

(4) *Fixed assets—Tangible assets*

	£	£
Land and buildings at cost		275,000
Fixtures and fittings at cost	265,000	
Less: Aggregate depreciation	105,000	
		160,000
		435,000

Consolidation schedules

(a) Consolidation of the Hold Ltd group at 31 Dec. 19–6:

Adjustment account

	£		£
Shares in Valise Ltd at cost	160,000	Valise Ltd:	
		Share capital	120,000
		Capital reserve	16,000
		Revenue reserve	17,600
		Goodwill arising on consolidation	6,400
	160,000		160,000

Consolidated reserves

	Revenue £	Capital £		Revenue £	Capital £
			Hold Ltd reserves	61,420	—
			Valise Ltd reserves	8,340	8,000
				69,760	8,000

Minority interest

	£		£
		Valise Ltd:	
		Share capital	30,000
		Capital reserve	6,000
		Revenue reserve	6,485
			42,485

Valise Ltd reserves

	£		£
Adjustment account:		Balance b/f	
80% × £20,000	16,000	Capital reserve	30,000
Minority interest:			
20% × £30,000	6,000		
Consolidated reserves:			
80% × £(30,000 − 20,000)	8,000		
Adjustment account:			
80% × £22,000	17,600	Revenue reserve	32,425
Minority interest:			
20% × £32,425	6,485		
Consolidated reserves:			
80% × £(32,425 − 22,000)	8,340		
	62,425		62,425

Valise Ltd—proposed dividend

	£		£
Hold Ltd debtors (contra with dividend receivable)		Balance b/f	30,000
80% × £30,000	24,000		
Balance c/d	6,000		
	30,000		30,000

Financial Accounting

Hold Ltd Group—summary balance sheet as at 31 Dec. 19–6

	£	£
Share capital		100,000
Capital reserve		8,000
Revenue reserve		69,760
		177,760
Minority interest		42,485
		220,245
Represented by		
Fixed assets		195,000
Goodwill arising on consolidation		6,400
Current assets:		
Stocks	111,730	
Debtors £(47,640 − 24,000 + 45,430)	69,070	
Bank balances	106,575	
	287,375	
Less: Current liabilities:		
Creditors	114,020	
Corporation tax	98,510	
Proposed dividends:		
Hold Ltd	50,000	
Minority	6,000	
	268,530	
Net current assets		18,845
		220,245

(b) Consolidation of the Grip Ltd group at 31 Dec. 19–6:

Adjustment account

	£		£
Shares in Hold Ltd		Hold Ltd:	
at cost	125,000	Share capital	90,000
		Capital reserve	7,200
		Revenue reserve	24,750
		Goodwill arising on	
		consolidation	3,050
	125,000		125,000

Hold Ltd group—consolidated capital reserve

	£		£
Adjustment account:		Balance b/f	8,000
90% × £8,000	7,200		
Minority interest:			
10% × £8,000	800		
	8,000		8,000

Hold Ltd group—consolidated revenue reserve

	£		£
Adjustment account:		Balance b/f	69,760
75% × £25,000	18,750		
15% × £40,000	6,000		
Minority interest:			
10% × £69,760	6,976		
Consolidated revenue reserves—			
Grip Ltd group:			
75% × £44,760	33,570		
15% × £29,760	4,464		
	69,760		69,760

Minority interest in Hold Ltd

	£		£
		Hold Ltd:	
		Share capital	10,000
		Consolidated revenue reserves	6,976
		Consolidated capital reserves	800
			17,776

Consolidated reserves—Grip Ltd group

	Capital £	Revenue £		Capital £	Revenue £
			Grip Ltd	40,000	77,496
			Hold Ltd group	—	38,034
				40,000	115,530

ANSWER J11. LANCASHIRE, DERBYSHIRE, EAST AND COAST

(a) Consolidated balance sheet as at 31 Dec. 19–8

	£	£	£
Fixed assets			
Tangible assets			861,000
Current assets			
Stocks		184,000	
Debtors		102,000	
Cash at bank and in hand		161,000	
		447,000	
Creditors: Amounts falling due within one year:			
Creditors	330,000		
Taxation	135,000		
Dividends	52,000		
		517,000	
Net current liabilities			(70,000)
Total assets less current liabilities			791,000
Creditors: Amounts falling due after more than one year:			
Debentures		60,000	
Minority interests:			
Preference shares	45,000		
Equity capital	83,500		
		128,500	
			188,500
			602,500
Capital and reserves			
Called up share capital			
Ordinary shares of £1 each			200,000
Preference shares of £1 each			100,000
			300,000
Profit and loss account			302,500
			602,500

Workings

(1) *Structure of group*

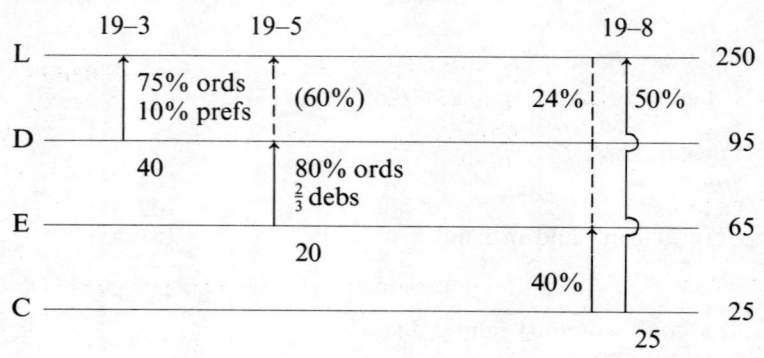

```
        19–3        19–5              19–8
L ────────┬──────────┬─────────────────┬──┬──── 250
          │75% ords  │(60%)        24% │  │50%
          │10% prefs │                 │  │
D ────────┴──────────┴─────────────────┤  ├──── 95
       40        80% ords              │  │
                 ⅔ debs                │  │
E ───────────────────┬─────────────────┴──┤──── 65
                    20                    │
                               40%        │
C ───────────────────────────────┬────────┴──── 25
                                25
```

(2) *Allocation of reserves*

Reserves of Derbyshire

	£		£
Adjustment account:		Balance b/d	95,000
75% × £40,000	30,000		
CR:			
75% × £55,000	41,250		
Minority interests:			
25% × £95,000	23,750		
	95,000		95,000

Reserves of East

	£		£
Adjustment account:		Balance b/d	65,000
60% × £20,000	12,000		
CR:			
60% × £45,000	27,000		
Minority interests:			
40% × £65,000	26,000		
	65,000		65,000

Reserves of Coast

	£		£
Adjustment account:		Balance b/d	25,000
74% × £25,000	18,500		
Minority interests:			
26% × £25,000	6,500		
	25,000		25,000

(3) *Allocation of costs of investments*

Required where costs of investment are assets in subsidiaries of Lancashire but Lancashire does not have a 100% of the share capital of that subsidiary.

(i) Cost of investments by Lancashire in Derbyshire and Coast. All to adjustment account.

(ii) Cost of investment by Derbyshire in East:

Cost of investment

	£		£
Balance b/d	87,000	Interest of Lancashire in Derbyshire:	
		75% × £87,000	65,250
		Minority interests:	
		25% × £87,000	21,750
	87,000		87,000

As part of £87,000 represents purchase of debentures in East.

East debenture account

	£		£
Inter-company elements:		Balance b/d	30,000
$\frac{2}{3} \times £30,000 = 20,000$			
of which:			
Lancashire interest is:			
Adjustment account:			
75% × £20,000	15,000		
Minority interests:			
25% × £20,000	5,000		
Balance c/d:			
$\frac{1}{3} \times £30,000$	10,000		
	30,000		30,000

(iii) Cost of investment by East in Coast:

Cost of investment

	£		£
Balance b/d	13,000	Effective interest of Lancashire in East:	
		Adjustment account:	
		60% × £13,000	7,800
		Minority interests:	
		40% × £13,000	5,200
	13,000		13,000

Financial Accounting

(4)

Dividends payable

	£		£
Lancashire debtors (75%)	22,500	Derbyshire balance b/d	30,000
Balance c/d (25%)	7,500		
	30,000		30,000
Derbyshire debtors (80%)	16,000	East balance b/d	20,000
Balance c/d (20%)	4,000		
	20,000		20,000
Lancashire debtors (50%)	2,500	Coast balance b/d	5,000
East debtors (40%)	2,000		
Balance c/d (10%)	500		
	5,000		5,000

Dividend payable = £(40,000 + 7,500 + 4,000 + 500) = 52,000

Debtors:
 As given 145,000
 Less: Dividends receivable
  £(22,500 + 16,000 + 2,500 + 2,000) = 43,000
                                        102,000

(5) *Pre-acquisition dividend*
Dividend receivable by Lancashire and East from Coast (see working (4)) should be credited to cost of investment:
  Dr. CRR account (74% × £5,000)   £3,700
   Cr. Adjustment account   £3,700

(6) *Unrealised profit in stock*

	£
Stock value in Derbyshire	12,000
Cost to East	10,000
Dr. Consolidated reserves	2,000

Note: Provision has been made for the whole of the unrealised profit in stock charged fully against group reserves.

(7)

Adjustment account

	£		£
Cost of investments:		Ordinary shares:	
L	132,000	D (75% × £80,000)	60,000
D	65,250	E (60% × £60,000)	36,000
E	7,800	C (74% × £20,000)	14,800
		Preference shares:	
		D (10% × £50,000)	5,000
		Debentures:	
		E (75% × £20,000)	15,000
		Pre-acquisition dividend	
		—C 74% × 5,000	3,700
		Reserves:	
		D 75% × 40,000	30,000
		E 60% × 20,000	12,000
		C 74% × 25,000	18,500
			195,000
		Goodwill to CRR	10,050
	205,050		205,050

(8)

Consolidated reserves

	£		£
Adjustment account— pre-acquisition dividend 74% × 5,000	3,700	Lancashire	250,000
		Derbyshire	41,250
		East	27,000
Stock	2,000		
Goodwill	10,050		
Balance c/d	302,500		
	318,250		318,250

(9)

Minority interests

	£		£
Cost of investments:		Ordinary shares:	
D (25% × £87,000)	21,750	D (25% × £80,000)	20,000
E (40% × £13,000)	5,200	E (40% × £60,000)	24,000
Balance c/d	128,500	C (26% × £20,000)	5,200
		Preference shares:	
		D (90% × £50,000)	45,000
		Debentures:	
		E (25% × £20,000)	5,000
		Reserves:	
		D (25% × £95,000)	23,750
		E (40% × £65,000)	26,000
		C (26% × £25,000)	6,500
	155,450		155,450

(b) If Lancashire held only 40% of the shares in Derbyshire, then Lancashire has no subsidiary and would not need to prepare consolidated accounts. It would appear, however, that both Derbyshire and Coast Ltd would be associated companies of Lancashire. If *SSAP 1* is followed, the profit and loss account of Lancashire would include that company's share of the profits for the year of the Derbyshire group of companies and Coast Ltd.

The balance sheet of Lancashire would include only its own reserves but would include a note of Lancashire's share of the post-acquisition reserves of Coast Ltd and the Derbyshire group. The balance sheet of Lancashire would show only the assets of that company, including the cost of investment in associated companies.

ANSWER J12. GOODWILL

(a) Goodwill on consolidation is the difference between the price paid for a subsidiary and the fair value of its net assets at the date of acquisition. Price paid includes money and money's worth.

(b) Goodwill acquired is the difference between the fair value of the assets of a business acquired and the price paid for that business (it may represent the excess of the value of the expected income stream over the market value of the assets).

Goodwill generated is the value of the customers, the name, and expertise of a business built up by that business itself. One may value it in the same way as acquired goodwill by valuing the future income stream from the business and include that figure with its net assets. Self-generated goodwill should not be shown in a company's accounts.

(c) Goodwill is an intangible asset, it is difficult to value and not easy to sell. Goodwill on consolidation is easy to calculate but its continued retention in the balance sheet is dubious. It is argued that if goodwill is acquired then over a period of time the acquired goodwill dissipates and is replaced by the goodwill generated by the acquiring concern; after a period it will be the acquiring concern's management which will run the company acquired and the expectation of future profits will be determined by the strength of that new management. On the basis of this argument acquired goodwill should be written off as it is replaced by self-generated goodwill. But should we account for generated goodwill. The writer thinks not: principally on the grounds which open the paragraph, i.e. its value is difficult to ascertain and it only has a value if the business or part of it is to be sold, in which case the going concern concept no longer applies.

(d) The EEC fourth directive deals with goodwill in the financial statements of individual companies (not groups) and provides that goodwill should be written off over 5 years or a period not exceeding the useful economic life of the asset. This was adopted in the *Companies Act 1981* (now consolidated into the *Companies Act 1985*) and for accounting periods beginning after April 1982 goodwill should be written off over the useful economic life of the asset.

SSAP 22 concerns goodwill arising on acquisition or consolidation and hence is of relevance to the implementation of the seventh directive, which is concerned with group accounts, as well as the fourth directive. *SSAP 22* requires that non-purchased goodwill should not be shown in financial statements. Purchased goodwill should normally be eliminated from the accounts immediately on acquisition or may be amortised over its useful economic life.

Thus the current position is that *SSAP 22* applies to goodwill on consolidation, and requires its immediate write-off or amortisation, while the *Companies Act 1985* does not cover goodwill on consolidation.

(e) X Ltd Group acquired a subsidiary and £100 goodwill arose on consolidation. The subsidiary was acquired 5 years ago.

Different accounting treatments with the same underlying profit and tangible assets give the following results:

	No amortisation of goodwill	Amortisation of goodwill 10% pa	Goodwill written off on acquisition	Goodwill written off this year
Profit and loss account profit	20	20	20	20
Goodwill w/o	—	(10)	—	(100)
	20	10	20	(80)
Balance sheet (extracts)				
Net tangible assets	200	200	200	200
Goodwill	100	50	—	—
	300	250	200	200
Return on capital employed $\left(\text{taken as } \frac{\text{net profit}}{\text{total assets}}\right)$	6.7%	4%	10%	(40%)

Tutorial note

The answer to this question contains an opinion. The question is a discussion question and a limited number of marks are allocated to each part. Therefore each part of the answer should set out briefly the main arguments and contrast them; reaching an opinion rounds the answer off nicely but marks are gained for clear expositions as much as for the ability to reach conclusions. Other views on goodwill and other arguments may be found in manuals and textbooks. The answer is an attempt at what might be possible in an examination.

ANSWER K1

Under *SSAP 1* a company which does not prepare consolidated accounts will show in its profit and loss account dividends received for receivable from the associate, but show in its balance sheet the investment in the associate at cost less amounts written off.

It is apparent that it is only for the purposes of consolidation that the inclusion of an associate in the balance sheet under the equity method is appropriate. In the separate balance sheet of the holding company all that need be shown is the investment at cost less amounts written off. Why this distinction? Partly because of the requirements of the *Companies Act* to show investments at cost or valuation (although these provisions are subrogated to the requirement to give a true and fair view); and partly because of the different roles of the balance sheet of the group and that of the investing or holding company. Although it seems to be very difficult to define these roles with great exactitude it can be said that the consolidated balance sheet is intended to give a picture of the distribution of the assets of an economic entity and of the performance of that entity measured *inter alia* by the return of its assets. On the other hand the balance sheet and profit and loss account for the holding company show only the way in which funds have been distributed in the past. Therefore it is inappropriate to show an equitised figure for an associate in the balance sheet of the holding company, but the nature of the consolidated statements suggest that treatment simply at cost is insufficient and inconsistent with the broad principles underlying those statements.

Now let us turn to the question: we are asked to consider whether the inability of a holding company to force the liquidation (in the form of dividends) of the retained profits of the associate should influence the balance sheet treatment of that associate. The question suggests that the equitising of profits gives rise to the presumption that they are realised profits.... But they are!—in the totality of the economic entity controlled by the holding company. Likewise the increase or diminution of assets within the entry is reflected in the growth or decline in accumulated group capital employed. Hence we reject the supposition of the question but only on the ground that we do not view the consolidated balance as an indication of value or distributability but rather as an indicator of the state of the economic entity. Whether or not this is how such financial statements are or should be viewed is open to question.

ANSWER K2

(a) An associate company is a company in which another company has an investment which satisfies various criteria. These criteria are set out in *SSAP 1* (as revised). The criteria are:
   (i) The investment in the company must not be such as to make the company invested in a subsidiary
   (ii) (a) The investing group's or company's interest is effectively that of a partner in a joint venture or consortium, and the investing group or company is in a position to exercise a significant influence over the associated company.
   or (b) The investing group or company's interest is for the long term and is substantial and having regard to the disposition of the other shareholdings, the investing group or company is in a position to exercise significant influence over the associate company. (There is a rebuttable presumption that the interest is substantial if it is above 20% of the equity voting capital and if it is below that figure then it may be proved that it is substantial against the presumption that it is not.)

(b) If a company or a group conducts a significant part of its business through the medium of associates the mere disclosure of the dividend income from those companies will not give users of the financial statements sufficient information regarding the sources of income and the manner in which funds are employed. Some method of accounting for associates must thus be devised to show the real activity of the economic entity.
(c) From what goes above we can see that disclosing just the cost of an associate is insufficient.

> 1. (a) Under *SSAP 1* before it was revised the investing company's share of the profits or losses of an associate are taken into the profit and loss account, and in the consolidated balance sheet the associate is shown at cost (less amounts written off) plus accumulated retained postacquisition profits or losses.
> (b) *SSAP 1* as revised requires that the balance sheet figure should be broken down to show the effective element of the investment.
> 2. Another possible way of accounting for the associate would be to include in each of the headings of the consolidated balance sheet the relevant share of the associate; this method is often called proportionate consolidation.
> 3. A third-way would be to consolidate the associate fully and show a full minority interest.

How then should we choose between these methods? The method selected must depend upon the nature of the investment and the degree of control exercised. If the investing group or company provides finance for the operations and assets then the writer would prefer a method involving a fairly full consolidation such as 1b, 2 or 3 above (on the other hand the use of methods 2 or 3 might suggest that the investing company or group had real control over the assets and operations, which could be misleading; therefore method 3 in particular would be used with caution).

On the other hand where the investment in the associates involves participation but not effective control by the investor the normal equity method would be more appropriate. The difficulty in permitting more than one method would be defining circumstances in which each should be used and in preventing partial consolidation methods being used to distort the financial position of a concern.

ANSWER K3. KESTREL LTD

Consolidated profit and loss account for year ended 31 Mar. 19–5

Notes		£	£
1	Operating profit of the group		457,700
	Share of profit of associated company		78,300
	Profit on ordinary activities before taxation		536,000
	Tax on profit on ordinary activities—UK corporation tax based on profits for year:		
	Group	235,000	
	Associated company	39,150	
			274,150
	Profit after taxation		261,850
	Minority shareholders' interest in subsidiaries	7,150	
2	Extraordinary charge	8,000	
			15,150
	Profit for year attributable to the members of the investing company (of which £223,500 is dealt with in the separate accounts of Kestrel Ltd)		246,700
	Appropriations:		
	Transfer to reserve	50,000	
	Proposed dividend	150,000	
			200,000
3	Profit for year retained		46,700
	By Kestrel Ltd	19,500	
	By subsidiaries	15,050	
	By associated company	12,150	
		46,700	

Notes to the accounts:
1. *Operating profit*
   Operating profit of the group is stated after charging:

	£
Depreciation	47,000
Directors' fees	40,000
Audit fees	3,300

   The whole of the unrealised profit on inter-group stock has been eliminated. Some accountants would eliminate the group share only.

Financial Accounting

2. *Extraordinary item*
   Amount written off shares in subsidiary company   £8,000

Tutorial note:
This would be reflected by a reduction of the goodwill on consolidation of Thrush Ltd by £8,000. Such an adjustment would only be made when reserves fall below their pre-acquisition level.

3. *Statement of retained reserves*

	Kestrel Ltd £	Subsidiary companies £	Associated company £	Total £
At 1 Apr. 19–4 (working (g))	45,000	24,300	—	69,300
Retained profit for year (working (e))	19,500	15,050	12,150	46,700
At 31 Apr. 19–5	64,500	39,350	12,150	116,000

Consolidation schedules

(a) *Operating profit of group*

	£	£
Kestrel		416,000
Sparrow		126,000
Thrush		10,000
		552,000
Less: Directors' fees	40,000	
Depreciation	47,000	
Audit fees	3,300	
		90,300
		461,700
Less: Unrealised profit in stock (valuation less cost, i.e. £(19,000) − 15,000))		4,000
		457,700

(b) *Share of profit of associated company*

	£	£
Osprey—trading profit		210,000
Less: Directors' fees	20,000	
Depreciation	15,000	
Audit fees	1,000	
		36,000
		174,000
Group share: 45% × £174,000		78,300

(c) *Share of corporation tax of associated company*
45% × £87,000   £39,150

(d) *Minority shareholders' interest in subsidiaries*

	Sparrow Ltd		*Thrush Ltd*	
	£	£	£	£
Trading profit		126,000		10,000
Less: Directors' fees	12,000		10,000	
Depreciation	18,000		9,000	
Audit fees	1,000		800	
Corporation tax	47,000		—	
		78,000		19,800
		48,000		(9,800)
Minority share		20%		25%
		9,600		(2,450)
i.e.			7,150	

(e) *Profit for year retained*

	£	£
By Kestrel:		
£(68,500 − 45,000) − 4,000 re stock		19,500
By subsidiaries:		
Sparrow 80% × £(58,500 − 30,500)	22,400	
Thrush 75% × £(9,800)	(7,350)	
		15,050
By associated company:		
Osprey 45% × £27,000		12,150
		46,700

Financial Accounting

(f) *Profit dealt with in the accounts of Kestrel Ltd*

	£	£
Trading profit		416,000
Add: Income from group companies		
£(16,000 + 27,000 + 6,000)		49,000
		465,000
Less:		
Directors' fees	24,000	
Depreciation	20,000	
Audit fees	1,500	
Tax	188,000	
Written off shares in Thrush	8,000	
		241,500
		223,500

(g) *Retained reserves at 1 Apr. 19–4*

	£	£
Kestrel Ltd		45,000
Subsidiary companies:		
Sparrow:		
60% × £(30,500 − (40,000))	42,300	
20% × £(30,500 − 30,500)	Nil	
Thrush:		
75% × £((20,000) − 4.000)	(18,000)	
		24,300
		69,300

ANSWER K4. SIGN LTD GROUP

Sign Ltd Group
Consolidated profit and loss account for the year ending 31 Mar. 19–8

	£	£
Turnover of group		1,500,000
Cost of sales		x
Gross profit		x
Less: Distribution cost	(x)	
Administrative expenses	(x)	
	—	(x)
Trading profit		80,000
Share of profit of associated company		1,750
Income from other fixed asset investments		3,714
Interest payable and similar charges		(x)
Profit on ordinary activities		85,464
Tax on profit on ordinary activities:		
Investing company and subsidiaries		
—UK corporation tax at 35%	34,000	
—Tax credits on dividends received	1,114	
Associated company	750	
		35,864
Profit after tax		49,600
Minority shareholders interest in profit		(6,000)
Profit before extraordinary items		43,600
Extraordinary charges—loss on sale of investments		(13,000)
Profit for the financial year attributable to members of investing company		30,600
Dividend proposed		13,000
Profit for the year retained		17,600
By the Investing company		13,250
Subsidiary company		4,100
Associated company		250
		17,600

Statement of retained profits

	£	£
Retained profits for year		17,600
Retained profits at beginning of year:		
As previously reported	80,000	
Prior year adjustment for marketing expenditure	12,000	
As restated		68,000
Retained profits at end of year		85,600

Sign Ltd group
Consolidated balance sheet as at 31 Mar. 19–8 (extracts)

	£	£
Fixed assets:		
Intangible assets: Goodwill on consolidation		x
Tangible assets		x
Investments—Investment in associate (working 8)		
Goodwill on acquisition	x	
Share of net assets	x	
		46,250
Current assets:		
Debtors—ACT recoverable	5,571	
Dividend receivable	750	
Other	x	
	x	
Creditors: Amounts falling due within one year:		
Including: Proposed dividend	13,000	
ACT on proposed dividend	5,571	
Other	x	
	x	
Net current assets		x
Total assets *less* current liabilities		x
Minority interest		x
		x
Capital and reserves:		
Called up share capital		x
Consolidated profit and loss account		85,600
		x

Workings

(1) *Turnover, operating profit and depreciation*
The results of the associated company are not included in these items.

(2) *Investment income*

	£
Dividends received	2,600
Tax credit $\frac{3}{7}$	1,114
	3,714

(3) *Profit of associated company*
25% × £7,000   £1,750

(4) *Tax of associated company*
25% × £3,000   £750

(5) *Profit for the year retained*

	£
Subsidiary company—given	4,100
Associated company £(1,750 − 750 − 750)	250
Investing company—balancing figure	13,250
	17,600

(6) *Retained profits brought forward*

	£
Holding company	60,000
Subsidiary company	18,000
Associated company 25% × £(10,000 − 2,000)	2,000
	80,000

(7) *Associated company—share of retained profits at year-end*

	£
As at 1 Apr. 19–7 (working 6)	2,000
Year ended 31 Mar. 19–8 (working 5)	250
	2,250

Financial Accounting

(8) *Associate:* Total balance sheet figure
The share of goodwill on acquisition and of net assets will be equal to cost plus share of post-acquisition retained earnings

	£
Shares at cost	44,000
Share of earnings (working 7)	2,250
	46,250

ANSWER K5. THE ROLLER GROUP LTD

Profit and loss account for year ended 31 Mar. 19–9

Notes		£	£
(1)	Trading profit		343,800
	Share of profit of associated company (45% × £176,000)		79,200
(2)	Income from other fixed asset investments		2,700
	Profit on ordinary activities before taxation		425,700
	Tax on profit on ordinary activities:		
(3)	Holding company and subsidiary £(161,000 + ($\frac{1}{2}$ + 29,000))	175,500	
	Share of tax of associated company £(45% × 89,000)	40,050	
			215,550
	Profit on ordinary activities after taxation		210,150
	Minority interests		2,925
(4)	Profit for the financial year attributable to members of Roller Ltd		207,225
	Dividends proposed		200,000
	Profit retained for year		7,225
	Retained by holding company	(5,300)	
	Retained by subsidiary company £($\frac{1}{2}$ × 75% × 1,000)	375	
	Retained by associated company £(45% × 27,000)	12,150	
		7,225	

FA–R

Movement on reserves

	Roller Ltd £	Subsidiary £	Associate £	Total £
Reserves at 1 Apr. 19–8	62,000	—	9,000	71,000
Retained for the year	(5,300)	375	12,150	7,225
	56,700	375	21,150	78,225

Notes to the accounts

(1) *Trading profit*
This is calculated after charging the following expenses:

	£
Directors' emoluments	31,000
Audit fees	3,950
Depreciation	22,500

Included in the trading profit is £28,000 relating to the new subsidiary, Grind Ltd, acquired during the accounting year.

(2) *Investment income*

This is a preference dividend received from Grind Ltd during the year before that company became a member of the Roller group.

(3) *Taxation*
UK corporation tax on the profits for the year.

(4) *Profit attributable to member of Roller Ltd*
A profit after tax of £194,700 has been dealt with in the separate accounts of Roller Ltd.

Workings

(a) *Shareholdings of Roller Ltd*

Grind Ltd: 90% preference shares
75% ordinary shares (six months post-acquisition)
Sift Ltd: 45% ordinary shares—associated company

Financial Accounting

(b) *Profit and loss accounts*

	Roller Ltd £	Grind Ltd £	Sift Ltd £
Profit as given	364,000	74,500	210,000
Directors' fees, depreciation and audit fees	48,200	18,500	34,000
Trading profit	315,800	56,000	176,000
Dividends (working (c))	39,900		
	355,700		
Tax	161,000	29,000	89,000
Profit after tax	194,700	27,000	87,000
Dividends	200,000	26,000	60,000
	(5,300)	1,000	27,000
B/f	62,000	22,000	50,000
C/f	56,700	23,000	77,000

(c) *Dividends receivable by Roller Ltd*

	£
Grind Ltd:	
Preference shares: 90% × £6,000	5,400
Ordinary:	
Receivable : 75% × £10,000 = £7,500	
Post-acquisition (max) : 75% × $\frac{1}{2}$ × £20,000 = £7,500	7,500
Sift Ltd:	
45% × £60,000	27,000
	39,900

(d) *Group trading profit*

	£
Roller Ltd	315,800
Grind Ltd ($\frac{1}{2}$ × £56,000)	28,000
	343,800

(e) *Minority interests*

	£		£
Profit of Grind Ltd (six months)	13,500		
Preference dividend (six months)	3,000	10%	300
	10,500	25%	2,625
			2,925

ANSWER L1. DEATH OF AN INSOLVENT PARTNER

Profit and loss appropriation account

Net profit for year ended 30 Sep. 1980 £2,743

Allocated as follows:

	Fozzie £	Rolf £	Zoot £	Total £
Partners' salaries	1,200	1,200	—	2,400
Share of profit	137	137	69	343
	1,337	1,337	69	2,743

Workings

	£	£
Profit as given		3,965
Less: Loss on disposal of freehold £(7,200 − 6,700)		500
		3,465
Less: Interest on loan (10% × £3,569)		357
		3,108
Less: Depreciation		
Motor vehicle	125	
Fixtures	240	
		365
		2,743

Partners' fixed capital accounts

Date	Details	Fozzie £	Rolf £	Zoot £	Date	Details	Fozzie £	Rolf £	Zoot £
19–9					19–9				
					2 Oct.	Balances b/d	3,000	3,000	600
19–0					19–0				
30 Sep.	Fozzie account	3,000							
	Loss on account of Fozzie (see working)		719	144					
	Balances c/d		2,281	456					
		3,000	3,000	600					
					1 Oct.	Balances b/d		2,281	456

Partners' current accounts

Date	Details	Fozzie £	Rolf £	Zoot £	Date	Details	Fozzie £	Rolf £	Zoot £
19-0					19-0				
30 Sep.	Drawings	5,200	1,200		30 Sep.	Share of profit	1,337	1,337	69
	Balances c/d		137	69		Fozzie account	3,863		
		5,200	1,337	69			5,200	1,337	69
					1 Oct.	Balances b/d		137	69

Working: Fozzie Account

	£
Loss on Fozzie account:	
Fixed capital	3,000 Cr.
Current account	3,863 Dr.
	863

Under the rule in *Garner v Murray* this should be apportioned in capital sharing ratio based upon the fixed capital accounts of Rolf and Zoot (£3,000:£600). In practice partners can agree to exclude the rule in *Garner v Murray* and share these losses in PSR.

Financial Accounting

The Growl Hairdressing Salon
Balance sheet as at 30 Sep. 1980

	£	£
Fixed assets:		
Fixtures and fittings		1,760
Motor van		375
		2,135
Current assets:		
Stock	100	
Prepaid items	2,560	
Cash at bank	1,117	
	3,777	
Less: Current liabilities:		
Creditors and accruals	590	
		3,187
Total assets less current liabilities		5,322
Represented by:		
Partners' fixed capital:		
Rolf	2,281	
Zoot	456	
		2,737
Partners' current accounts:		
Rolf	137	
Zoot	69	
		206
		2,943
Loan account:		
Kermit		2,379
		5,322

Workings:

	£
Cash: overdraft b/f	1,536
Capital repayment to Kermit ($\frac{1}{3} \times$ £3,569)	1,190
Interest paid to Kermit (10% $\times$ £3,569)	357
Rent paid	2,500
	5,583
Received from sale of freehold	6,700
	1,117

ANSWER L2. DISSOLUTION BY SALE TO A LIMITED COMPANY

Partners' accounts

	Rolf £	Zoot £		Rolf £	Zoot £
Realisation account—motor	1,200		Fixed capital accounts	2,281	456
Shares at valuation	2,542	2,543	Current accounts	2,010	1,783
Loan stock	2,874	126	Realisation account—profit	860	430
			Kermit—loan account	1,190	
			Cash	275	
	6,616	2,669		6,616	2,669

Realisation account

	£	£		£
Freehold		4,000	Creditors and accruals	930
Fixtures		2,400	Rolf—car taken over	1,200
Vehicles		1,500	Growl Ltd	8,085
Stock		350		
Prepaid items		90		
		8,340		
Cash—payment to Wuff Hairdressers		585		
Profit allocated in PSR:				
Rolf (⅔)	860			
Zoot (⅓)	430			
		1,290		
		10,215		10,215

Growl Ltd account

	£		£	£
Consideration to be received	8,085	Ordinary shares at valuation:		
		Rolf	2,542	
		Zoot	2,543	
				5,085
		Unsecured loan stock:		
		Rolf	2,874	
		Zoot	126	
				3,000
	8,085			8,085

Working

Cash account

	£		£
Balance b/d	310	Realisation account—	
Rolf—cash introduced to close account	275	to Wuff Hairdressers	585
	585		585

Financial Accounting

Growl Ltd

Balance sheet as at 1 Oct. 19–1

	£	£
Share capital:		
Ordinary shares of £1 each		12,000
Share premium account		8,340
		20,340
20% unsecured loan stock		13,560
		33,900
Fixed assets:		
Freehold property		25,500
Fixtures		9,000
		34,500
Current assets:		
Stock	910	
Prepaid items	220	
	1,130	
Less: Current liabilities:		
Creditors and accruals	1,730	
		(600)
		33,900

Workings:

(1) *Take-over valuations*

	Growl	Wuff
	£	£
Freehold	5,500	20,000
Fixtures	2,500	6,500
Stock	340	570
Prepaid items	90	130
	8,430	27,200
Less: Creditors and accruals	930	800
	7,500	26,400

(2) *Amount of 20% loan stock*

	Growl £	Wuff £
Required income (8%)	600	2,112
Capitalised @ 20% $\frac{100}{20}$	3,000	10,560

(3) *Apportionment of shares*

	Growl £	Wuff £
Profits for three years to 30 Sep. 19–1	12,900	38,700
Average profit per year	4,300	12,900
Shares to each partnership (43:129)	3,000	9,000

(4) *Calculation of share premium*

	£
Assets from Growl	26,400
Assets from Wuff	7,500
	33,900
Less: Loan stock at par	13,560
	20,340
Shares at nominal value	12,000
Share premium	8,340

Allocation of share premium (43:129)	£2,085 Growl	£6,255 Wuff

(5) *Calculation of cash transfer required*

	Growl £	Growl £	Wuff £	Wuff £
Valuation of net assets		7,500		26,400
Loan stock		3,000		10,560
		4,500		15,840
Shares:				
Nominal value	3,000		9,000	
Premium	2,085		6,255	
		5,085		15,255
		585		585

Cash payable by Growl to Wuff = £585.

ANSWER L3. NORTHSOUTHS

(a) *Profit and loss accounts for periods ending 31 Dec. 19–7*

	Norths		Souths		Wests	
	£	£	£	£	£	£
Fees earned		9,800		11,400		4,450
Rent and rates	600		1,550		450	
Staff salaries	4,500		7,200		2,000	
Expenses	1,150		3,250		1,190	
Depreciation:						
(i) Furniture	100		75		60 (9m)	
(ii) Cars	125		250		150 (9m)	
		6,475		12,325		3,850
Net profit/(loss)		3,325		(925)		600

= £2,400

Allocated:

	North	South	East	Dee
	£	£	£	£	£
Profit of Northsouths:					
Period 1 Jan. 19–7 to 31 Mar. 19–7:					
$\frac{3}{12} \times £2,400$		200	200	200	
Profit of:					
Northsouths		1,800			
Wests		600			
Period 1 Apr. 19–7 to 31 Dec. 19–7	2,400	600	600	600	600
		800	800	800	600
Less:					
Legal charges (£600) to be borne by each firm equally		200	100	100	200
		600	700	700	400

(b)

Capital accounts

	North £	South £	East £	Dee £		North £	South £	East £	Dee £
Goodwill	4,250	250	250		Balances b/f	1,000	2,900	2,500	
Debtors collected		525	525		Goodwill	2,500			
Balances c/d	2,500	2,825	2,425		Car	500			
					Creditors not taken over	2,750	700	700	3,500
	6,750	3,600	3,200			6,750	3,600	3,200	3,500
Drawings	1,500	1,100	1,200	1,000	Balances b/d	2,500	2,825	2,425	
Amount written off West's foodwill	250	250	250	250	Cash introduced	600			
Balances c/f	1,350	2,175	1,675	2,650	Shares of profit		700	700	400
	3,100	3,525	3,125	3,900		3,100	3,525	3,125	3,900

(c) *Balance sheets at 1 Jan. 19–8*

	Norths		Souths		Wests	
	£	£	£	£	£	£
Employment of capital:						
Fixed assets:						
Goodwill		2,500		2,500		3,000
Furniture (less depreciation)		900		675		740
Car (less depreciation)		375		750		650
		3,775		3,925		4,390
Net current assets:						
Debtors	2,900		3,150		850	
Cash at bank					350	
					1,200	
Less: Creditors:						
Expenses	(400)		(1,400)		(490)	
Legal fees	(200)		(200)		(200)	
Bank overdraft	(1.950)		(3,650)			
		350		(2,100)		510
		4,125		1,825		4,900
Amounts due by Norths to:						
Souths		(2,775)		2,025		
Wests						750
		1,350		3,850		5,650
Represented by:						
Capital accounts:						
North		1,350				
South				2,175		
East				1,675		
Dee						2,650
Loan account:						
West						3,000
		1,350		3,850		5,650

ANSWER L4. FAIRWAY LTD

(a) (i) *Computation of loan stock*

	Interest for year to 31 Dec. 19-7 £	9% unsecured loan stock required £
Par	720	$\frac{720}{9} \times 100 = 8,000$
Green	540	$\frac{540}{9} \times 100 = 6,000$
Bogey	450	$\frac{450}{9} \times 100 = 5,000$

Alternative method:
Interest on the 9% unsecured loan stock is treble the rate the partners received on their capital (3%); therefore the loan stock allocated to each partner must equal one-third of the capital account.

	Par £	Green £	Bogey £
Capital account	24,000	18,000	15,000
One-third of above	8,000	6,000	5,000

(ii) *Computation of shares*

Assets and liabilities to be taken over at valuation:

	£
Land and buildings	30,000
Plant and machinery	15,000
Stocks	22,400
Debtors	12,200
Cash	15,000
	94,600
Less: Creditors	35,600
Purchase price	59,000
Less: Discharged by issue of loan stock (see above)	19,000
Balance discharged by issue of shares	40,000

Profit sharing ratio:

	Profit share £	Proportion	Shares issued
Par	6,126	3	15,000
Green	6,126	3	15,000
Bogey	4,084	2	10,000
	16,336	8	40,000

(b) Partners' accounts

	Par £	Green £	Bogey £		Par £	Green £	Bogey £
Realisation account:				Capital account	24,000	18,000	15,000
Motor vehicles	4,900	3,500	3,600	Current account	9,860	6,420	6,470
Loss on realisation	1,500	1,500	1,000	Cash	—	1,580	—
Fairway Ltd:							
9% unsecured loan stock	8,000	6,000	5,000				
Ordinary shares	15,000	15,000	10,000				
Cash	4,460	—	1,870				
	33,860	26,000	21,470		33,860	26,000	21,470

(c) *Fairway Ltd*
Balance sheet as at 1 Jan. 19–8

	£	£
Share capital:		
Authorised 100,000 ordinary shares of £1 each		100,000
Issued and fully paid 40,000 ordinary shares of £1 each		40,000
9% unsecured loan stock		19,000
		59,000
Represented by:		
Fixed assets:		
Freehold land and buildings		30,000
Plant and machinery		15,000
		45,000
Current assets:		
Stock	22,400	
Debtors	12,200	
Cash	15,000	
	49,600	
Less: Current liabilities:		
Creditors	35,600	
Net current assets		14,000
		59,000

Workings:

(1) Realisation account

	£		£	£
Land and buildings—		Creditors		35,600
cost	26,000	Plant and machinery—		
Plant and machinery—		depreciation		22,000
cost	42,000	Motor vehicles—		
Motor vehicles—cost	19,700	depreciation		4,700
Stock	22,400	Fairway Ltd		
Debtors	12,200	purchase		
Cash	15,000	consideration		59,000
		Capital accounts:		
		Cars take over:		
		Par		4,900
		Green		3,500
		Bogey		3,600
				133,300
		Share of loss:		
		Par	1,500	
		Green	1,500	
		Bogey	1,000	
				4,000
	137,300			137,300

(2) Fairway Ltd account

	£		£	£
Realisation account:		Capital accounts:		
Purchase		9% unsecured loan		
consideration	59,000	stock:		
		Par	8,000	
		Green	6,000	
		Bogey	5,000	
				19,000
		Ordinary shares:		
		Par	15,000	
		Green	15,000	
		Bogey	10,000	
				40,000
	59,000			59,000

Financial Accounting

(3) Cash account

	£		£
Balance	19,750	Realisation account	15,000
Capital account:		Capital account:	
Green	1,580	Par	4,460
		Bogey	1,870
	21,330		21,330

ANSWER M1. DIGIT AND THUMB

(a) *Joint venture accounts*

(i) Books of Digit

Joint venture with Thumb account

Date	Details	£	Date	Details	£
1 May	cash—purchases	15,420	3 May	Cash—from Thumb	2,055
1 May	Bill payable—		3 Jun.	Bill payable—	
	purchases	4,040		paid by Thumb	4,040
30 Jun.	Commission	813	30 Jun.	Cash—sales	16,490
30 Jun.	Balance c/f	2,852	30 Jun.	Stock taken over	540
		23,125			23,125
30 Sep.	P. & L. account—		1 Jul.	Balance b/f	2,852
	share of joint		30 Sep.	Cash—sale of	
	venture profit	2,892		machine as scrap	10
			30 Sep.	Cash—special	
				bank account	30
		2,892			2,892

(ii) *Books of Thumb*

Joint venture with Digit account

Date	Details	£	Date	Details	£
3 May	Cash—carriage charges	126	30 Jun.	Cash—sales	17,250
3 May	Cash—to Digit	2,055			
10 May	Cash—purchases	7,671			
3 Jun.	Cash—settlement of bill accepted by Digit	4,040			
15 Jun.	Cash—shipping and insurance	426			
15 Jun.	Cash—carriage charges	304			
28 Jun.	Cash—special bank account	510			
30 Jun.	Balance c/f	2,118			
		17,250			17,250
30 Sep.	P & L account—share of joint venture profit	2,169	1 Jul.	Balance b/f	2,118
			30 Sep.	Cash—special bank account	51
		2,169			2,169

(b) *Memorandum joint venture account*

	£	£
Sales:		
Digit		16,490
Thumb		17,250
		33,740
Less: Purchases:		
Digit	19,460	
Thumb	7,671	
	27,131	
less: Closing stock	540	
		26,591
Gross profit		7,149
Less: Expenses:		
Carriage charges £(126 + 304)	430	
Shipping and insurance	426	
Commission	813	
Costs and damages on faulty goods	510	
		2,179
Net profit to 30 Jun.		4,970
Share of profits:		
Digit ($\frac{4}{7}$ × £4,970)	2,840	
Thumb ($\frac{3}{7}$ × £4,970)	2,130	
Add: Over-provision on faulty goods	81	
Proceeds from sale of faulty goods		
as scrap	10	
		91
Net profit to 30 Sep.		5,061
Share of profits:		
Digit ($\frac{4}{7}$ × £5,061)	2,892	
Thumb ($\frac{3}{7}$ × £5,061)	2,169	

Workings

(1) *Commission due to Digit*

	£
Export sales by:	
Digit	12,400
Thumb	4,260
	16,660
Less: Goods returned	400
Net export sales	16,260
Commission due to Digit (5% × £16,260)	813

(2) *Special bank account*

Memorandum special bank account

Date	Details	£	Date	Details	£
28 Jun.	Cash—from thumb	510	30 Sep.	Cash—to customer in France	429
			30 Sep.	Cash to:	
				Digit	30
				Thumb	51
		510			510

Financial Accounting

Estimated bank balance for joint venture

	Month 1 £	Month 2 £	Month 3 £	Month 4 £	Month 5 £	Month 6 £
Receipts:						
Paid in by partners:						
Star Ltd	10,000	531	286	102	—	—
Garter Ltd	10,000	531	286	102	—	—
	20,000	1,062	572	204	—	—
Customers for sales	—	25,000	27,500	30,250	33,275	36,602
	20,000	26,062	28,072	30,454	33,275	36,602
Payments:						
Overdraft b/f	—	23,262	25,022	27,129	29,396	32,248
Commission to agents	—	625	688	756	832	915
Wages	3,000	3,000	3,000	3,000	3,600	3,600
Overheads	600	1,200	1,200	1,150	1,100	1,100
Suppliers for purchases	39,375	22,688	24,956	27,452	30,197	33,217
	42,975	50,775	54,866	59,487	65,125	71,080
Overdraft before interest	22,975	24,713	26,794	29,033	31,850	34,478
Interest @ 1¼%	287	309	335	363	398	431
Overdraft c/f	23,262	25,022	27,129	29,396	31,850	34,909
Half of working capital (see working (1))	22,200	24,450	26,925	29,673	32,667	35,962
Reduction in overdraft, to be paid in at beginning of next month	1,062	572	204	Nil	Nil	Nil

Financial Accounting

Workings

(1) *Working capital*

	Month 1 £	Month 2 £	Month 3 £	Month 4 £	Month 5 £	Month 6 £
Stock	20,625	22,688	24,956	27,452	30,197	33,217
Debtors	25,000	27,500	30,250	33,275	36,602	40,263
Less: Commission to agents	(625)	(688)	(756)	(832)	(915)	(1,007)
Accrued overheads	(600)	(600)	(600)	(550)	(550)	(550)
	44,400	48,900	53,850	59,345	65,334	71,923
Half of working capital	22,200	24,450	26,925	29,673	32,667	35,962

(2) *Sales and purchases*

	Sales		Purchases	
Month	£	75% of sales in month(s)		£
1	25,000	1 & 2		39,375
2	27,500	3		22,688
3	30,250	4		24,956
4	33,275	5		27,452
5	36,602	6		30,197
6	40,263	7		33,217
7	44,289			

ANSWER M3. TRILBY AND BOWLER

(a) *Books of Trilby*

Joint venture with Bowler

	£		£
Purchases:		Cash from Bowler	1,000
Bank	4,000	Sales	8,000
Loan account	2,000	Purchases—stock	
Carriage	280	taken over	1,800
Insurance	600	Loan account—paid	
Commission—5% ×		direct by Bowler	2,000
£8,000	400		
Share of profit	5,040		
Balance—cash to Bowler	480		
	12,800		12,800

Books of Bowler

Joint venture with Trilby

	£		£
Loan repaid	2,000	Sales	5,000
Loan interest	30	Balance—cash from	
Rent	40	Trilby	480
Cash to Trilby	1,000		
Commission—5% ×			
£5,000	250		
Share of profit	2,160		
	5,480		5,480

Memorandum joint venture account

	£	£		£
Purchases		6,000	Sales	13,000
Carriage		280	Trilby—stock taken	
Insurance		600	over	1,800
Rent		40		
Loan interest		30		
Commission		650		
Net profit:				
Trilby ($\frac{7}{10}$)	5,040			
Bowler ($\frac{3}{10}$)	2,160			
		7,200		
		14,800		14,800

(b) *Books of Trilby*

Joint venture account

	£	£		£
Purchases			Sales	8,000
Bank		4,000	Purchases—stock	
Loan account		2,000	taken over	1,800
Carriage		280	Bowler—sales	5,000
Insurance		600		
Commission:				
Trilby		400		
Bowler		250		
Bowler:				
Interest		30		
Rent		40		
		7,600		
Balance—profit:				
Trilby ($\frac{7}{10}$)	5,040			
Bowler ($\frac{3}{10}$)	2,160			
		7,200		
		14,800		14,800

Bowler

	£		£
Joint venture account—		Loan account—repaid	2,000
sales	5,000	Joint venture account:	
Bank—cash to Bowler	480	Interest	30
		Rent	40
		Bank account—cash from	
		Bowler	1,000
		Joint venture account:	
		Commission	250
		Profit	2,160
	5,480		5,480

ANSWER N1. BERT CROOK

Second hand business

Trading, profit and loss account for year ended 31 Dec. 19–6

	£	£
Sales		15,600
Purchases	14,800	
Less: Closing stock	3,500	
		11,300
Gross profit		4,300
Provision for doubtful debt	100	
Rent	700	
Petrol	800	
Other expenses	500	
Interest on loan	200	
Depreciation on van	280	
		2,580
Net profit		1,720

Balance sheet as at 31 Dec. 19–6

	£	£	£
Ownership:			
Capital at 1 Jan. 19–6			10,000
Profit for year		1,720	
Less: Drawings		3,280	
			(1,560)
			8,440
Loan			2,000
Due on van purchase			853
			11,293
Capital employed:			
Fixed assets:			
Van at cost			1,680
Less: Depreciation			280
			1,400
Current assets:			
Stock		3,500	
Debtors *less* provision		900	
Prepayment		100	
Bank		9,800	
Cash		620	
		14,920	
Less: Current liabilities:			
Creditors	4,400		
Accruals	200		
Due on van purchase	427		
		5,027	
			9,893
			11,293

Financial Accounting

Workings and notes

(1) ### Bank account

	£		£
Cash	11,000	Van	400
Sales	11,600	Rent	800
		Purchases	8,000
		Purchases	2,400
		Drawings	1,200
		Balance c/d	9,800
	22,600		22,600

(2) ### Cash account

	£		£
Capital	10,000	Bank	11,000
Loan	2,000	Petrol	800
Sales	3,000	Expenses	500
		Drawings	2,080
		Balance c/d	620
	15,000		15,000

(3) Depreciation on the van is assumed to be straight line over six years, i.e.

$$\frac{£1,680}{6} = £280 \text{ pa.}$$

(4) Provision for doubtful debts to, say, £100 (on the £1,000 outstanding).

(5) Stock of T-shirts at estimated net realisable value (£100), being lower than the cost.

(6) Stock of jeans values at cost (1,000 @ £3) = £3,000.

(7) Stock of calculators valued at £400.

(8) Interest accrued on loan = £200.

ANSWER N2. THE POT BLACK

(a) *Income and expenditure account for the year ended 31 Dec. 19–1*

	£	£
Income:		
Subscriptions		7,150
Table charges		6,450
Surplus on bar trading (before defalcation)		3,340
		16,940
Expenditure:		
Repairs	1,020	
Depreciation	3,000	
Rent and rates	2,910	
Light and heat	1,540	
Telephone and sundries	185	
Insurance	180	
Defalcation £(45,000–30,516–10,000)	4,484	
		13,319
Surplus of income over expenditure for year		3,621
Accumulated fund b/f		12,597
Accumulated fund c/f		16,218

Bar trading account

	£	£
Sales (being $\frac{100}{80}$ × cost of goods sold)		45,000
Opening stock	3,880	
Purchases	38,110	
	41,990	
Closing stock	(5,990)	
Cost of goods sold		(36,000)
		9,000
Expenses:		
Wages	3,950	
Sundry	580	
Loss of glasses and crockery	1,130	
		5,660
Bar net profit before defalcation		3,340

(b) Balance sheet at 31 Dec. 19–1

	31 Dec. 19–1 £	31 Dec. 19–1 £	31 Dec. 19–0 £	31 Dec. 19–0 £
Accumulated fund		16,218		12,597
New building reserves		6,000		—
		22,218		12,597
Fixed assets:				
Snooker tables		9,400		9,800
Wasting assets:				
Bar glasses and crockery		1,100		1,370
Current assets:				
Bar stocks	5,990		3,880	
Insurance claim	10,000		—	
Rates prepaid	300		250	
Cash at bank	2,888		397	
	19,178		4,527	
Current liabilities:				
Bar creditors	4,660		2,860	
Snooker table	2,340		—	
Electricity accrued	310		240	
Subscriptions in advance	150		—	
	7,460		3,100	
Net current assets		11,718		1,427
		22,218		12,597

Bar purchases account

	£		£
Bank—purchases	36,310	Creditors b/d	2,860
Creditors c/d	4,660	Bar trading account	38,110
	40,970		40,970

Bar crockery and glasses

	£		£
Opening balance	1,370	Losses—bar trading account	1,130
Purchases	860	Closing balance	1,100
	2,230		2,230

Subscriptions account

	£		£
Creditors c/d	150	Cash	7,300
Income and expenditure account	7,150		
	7,300		7,300

Cash account

	£		£
Subscriptions	7,300	Bar crockery	860
Table charges	6,450	Bar wages	3,950
Bank	8,465	Bar expenses	580
Donation	6,000	Snooker repairs	1,020
Bar takings (balance) after defalcation	30,516	Bankings	52,321
	58,731		58,731

Rent and rates

	£		£
Bank	2,960	Prepayment c/d	300
Prepayment b/d	250	Income and expenditure account	2,910
	3,210		3,210

Light and heat

	£		£
Cash	1,470	Accrual b/d	240
Accrual c/d	310	Income and expenditure account	1,540
	1,780		1,780

ANSWER N3. KENSINGTON WORKING MEN'S CLUB

(a) *Bar trading account for year ended 30 Jun. 19–8*

	£	£
Takings (working 6)		33,312
Less: Opening stock	2,197	
Purchases	26,028	
	28,225	
Less: Closing stock	3,241	
		24,984
Gross profit		8,328

(b) *Income and expenditure account for year ended 30 Jun. 19–8*

	£	£	£
Bar trading account—gross profit			8,328
Subscriptions			5,440
Fruit machine rental			8,793
			22,561
Wages		2,391	
Rates		2,252	
Light and heat		1,618	
Telephone		748	
Sundries		4,416	
Machine rental		5,424	
Glasses and crockery		2,179	
Repairs and renewals		1,382	
Bank interest		42	
Depreciation	1,239		
Loss on sale	71		
		1,310	
Cash deficiency		3,045	
			24,807
Excess of expenditure over income			2,246

(c) *Balance sheet as at 30 Jun. 19–8*

	£	£
Capital employed:		
General fund:		
Balance at 1 Jul. 19–7	21,241	
Less: Excess of expenditure over income	2,246	
		18,995
Entertainment fund:		
Balance at 1 Jul. 19–7	4,261	
Add: Donations	1,360	
Interest	364	
		5,985
		24,980
Represented by:		
Fixed assets:		
Land and buildings	15,000	
Fixtures and fittings	3,717	
		18,717
Current assets:		
Stock	3,241	
Subscriptions due	100	
Prepayments	647	
Cash in hand	50	
	4,038	
Less: Current liabilities:		
Creditors	2,323	
Subscriptions in advance	60	
Bank overdraft	1,377	
	3,760	
Net current assets		278
		18,995
Entertainment fund: deposit account		5,985
		24,980

Financial Accounting

Workings

(1) *Balance sheet at 30 Jun. 19–7*

	£	£	£
Fixed assets:			
Land and buildings			15,000
Fixtures and fittings			3,643
			18,643
Current assets:			
Stocks		2,197	
Subscriptions due		40	
Prepayments		539	
Cash at bank:			
Deposit account		4,261	
Current account		2,119	
Cash in hand		50	
		9,206	
Less: Current liabilities:			
Creditors		2,347	
			6,859
			25,502
General fund (balancing figure)			21,241
Entertainment fund			4,261
			25,502

(2) *Creditors*

	19–8	*19–7*
	£	£
Telephone	152	136
Electricity	279	251
Purchases	1,405	1,537
Fruit machine	487	423
	2,323	2,347

(3)

Subscriptions account

Arrears b/f	40	In advance	—
Income and expenditure		Cash 1,360 × £4	5,440
account	5,440	Arrears c/f	100
In advance	60		
	5,540		5,540

		£
Total members	1,360 × £4	5,440
Less: Not paid	(25) × £4	(100)
Add: Paid 19–8/–9	15 × £4	60
Paid 19–6/–7	10 × £4	40
	1,360	5,440

(4)

Cash account

	£		£
Balance b/d	50	Cash to bank	40,340
Fruit machine takings	8,793	Sundry expenses	593
Subscriptions	5,440	Bar wages	2,391
Bar takings	33,312	Printing and stationery	634
Sale of fixtures	250	Bar purchases	792
		Cash difference	3,045
		Balance c/f	50
	47,845		47,845

(5)

Bar purchases account

	£		£
Cash account	792	Balance b/f	1,537
Bank account	25,368	Purchases	26,028
Balance c/f	1,405		
	27,565		27,565

(6) *Bar trading account*

	£
Opening stock	2,197
Purchases	26,028
	28,225
Closing stock	3,241
Cost of sales	24,984
Gross profit (one-third)	8,328
Takings	33,312

(7) Deposit account

	£		£
Balance at 30 Jun. 19–7	4,261		
Special fund:			
£1 levy	1,360		
Interest	364	Balance at 30 Jun. 19–8	5,985
	5,985		5,985

(8)

	Rates	Light and heat	Telephone	Sundries	Fruit machine rental	Glasses and crockery	Repairs and renewals	Wages
Opening prepayment (accrual)	539	(251)	(136)	—	(423)	—	—	—
Cash	—	—	—	593	—	—	634	2,391
Bank	2,360	1,590	732	3,823	5,360	2,179	748	—
Closing prepayment (accrual)	(647)	279	152	—	487	—	—	—
Income and expenditure account	2,252	1,618	748	4,416	5,424	2,179	1,382	2,391

ANSWER P1. X LTD

Branch stock control account

	£	£		£	£
Goods sent to branch account	21,000		Goods sent to branch account	750	
Adjustment account	7,000		Adjustment account	250	
		28,000			1,000
			Cash—sales		18,000
			Branch debtors' control account		2,000
			Adjustment account		820
			Branch closing stock, at selling price, c/d		6,180
		28,000			28,000

Branch stock adjustment account

	£		£
Branch stock control account	250	Branch stock control account	7,000
Branch stock control account	820		
Mark-up in branch closing stock c/d	1,545		
P & L account—branch gross profit	4,385		
	7,000		7,000

Goods sent to branch account

	£		£
Branch stock control account	750	Goods sent to branch account	21,000
Trading account—goods sent to branch	20,250		
	21,000		21,000

Branch debtors' control account

	£		£
Branch stock control account	2,000	Cash	1,730
		Balance c/d	270
	2,000		2,000

Purchases account

	£		£
Purchases	27,130		

Head office sales account

	£		£
		Sales	9,100

*Trading and profit and loss account
for three months ended 31 Mar. 19...*

	£	£
Head office sales		9,100
Opening stock at head office	2,900	
Purchases	27,130	
	30,030	
Less: Goods sent to branch	20,250	
	9,780	
Less: Closing stock	2,650	
		7,130
Gross profit of head office		1,970
Gross profit of branch		4,385
		6,355
Less: Expenses:		
Head office	1,200	
Branch	1,000	
		2,200
Net profit		4,155

ANSWER P2. COLTS LTD

Liverpool branch stock account

	(Memo) selling price £	£		(Memo) selling price £	£
19-3			19-4		
1 Oct. Balance—stock b/f	5,400	4,050	30 Sep. Goods returned from branch	900	675
19-4			Sales	24,800	24,800
30 Sep. Goods sent to branch	27,000	20,250	Stock shortage at branch	100	
P & L account			Balance—stock c/f	6,600	4,950
—branch gross profit		6,125			
	32,400	30,425		32,400	30,425

Goods sent to branch account

19–4	£	19–4	£
30 Sep. Liverpool branch stock account—returns	675	30 Sep. Liverpool branch stock account	20,250
Head office trading account—cost of goods sent to branch	19,575		
	20,250		20,250

Liverpool branch debtors' control account

	£		£
19–3		19–4	
1 Oct. Balance b/f	1,800	30 Sep. Cash	22,800
19–4		Discount allowed	950
30 Sep. Sales	24,800	Bad debts	300
		Balance c/f	2,550
	26,600		26,600

ANSWER P3. HECTOR AND IVOR

Trading, profit and loss and appropriation account for year ended 30 Sep. 19-8

	Guildford £	Farnham £	Whole business £	£		Guildford £	Farnham £	Whole business £
Stock at 30 Sep. 19-7	4,300	2,900		7,200	Sales	43,400	32,500	75,900
Purchases	50,200	21,600		50,200				
Goods from head office	(21,600)							
	32,900	24,500		57,400				
Stock at 30 Sep. 19-8	4,900	2,800		7,700				
Cost of goods sold	28,000	21,700		49,700				
Gross profit c/d	15,400	10,800		26,200				
	43,400	32,500		75,900		43,400	32,500	75,900
Salaries and wages	3,600	3,020		6,620	Gross profit b/d	15,400	10,800	26,200
Motor expenses	610	540		1,150				
Rent, lighting and trade expenses	1,870	1,320		3,190				
Depreciation:								
Motor vans	180	140		320				
Shop fittings	340	280		620				
Net profit c/d	8,800	5,500		14,300				
	15,400	10,800		26,200		15,400	10,800	26,200

Allocated as follows:

	Total £	Hector £	Ivor £
Commission	1,430	880	550
Interest on capital	600	360	240
Balance (7:3)	12,270	8,589	3,681
	14,300	9,829	4,471

(b) *Balance sheet as at 30 Sep. 19–8*

	Cost and depn. £	£	£
Fixed assets:			
Shop fittings	6,200	1,520	4,680
Motor vans	1,600	640	960
	7,800	2,160	5,640
Net current assets:			
Stock		7,700	
Bank balance		12,570	
Cash in transit		350	
		20,620	
Less: Sundry creditors		1,740	
			18,880
			24,520

Financed by:

	Capital £	Current £	Total £
Partners' accounts:			
Hector	6,000	12,229	18,229
Ivor	4,000	2,291	6,291
	10,000	14,520	24,520

Financial Accounting

Workings

Guildford books
(1)

Branch current account

	£		£	£
Balance b/f	5,800	Cash in transit account		350
		Goods in transit (goods sent to branch account)		300
		Balance c/d		5,150
	5,800			5,800
Balance b/d	5,150	Ivor:		
Administration charge to branch	400	Drawings	480	
		Commission (on account)	100	
Branch profit	5,500			580
		Balance c/f		10,470
	11,050			11,050

(2)

Partners' current account

	Hector £	Ivor £		Hector £	Ivor £
Balance b/f		1,600	Balance b/f	3,200	
Drawings	600	480	Share of profit	9,829	4,471
Commission (on account)	200	100			
Balances c/f	12,229	2,291			
	13,029	4,471		13,029	4,471

ANSWER P4. ROSE LTD

Trading and profit and loss account for year ended 31 Mar. 19-5

	Head office £	Head office £	Branch £	Branch £	Combined business £	Combined business £
Sales to customers		375,050		70,000		445,050
Goods lost and charged to manager at selling price (bal. fig)		—		100		100
		375,050		70,100		445,150
Cost of sales:						
Opening stock	35,600		2,400		35,600	
Purchases	360,000		58,560		362,400	
Goods from head office at cost	—					
	395,600		60,960		398,000	
Less: Closing stock	58,560		—		41,880	
	337,040		60,960		356,120	
Less: Cost of goods sent to branch	37,000		4,880			
		300,040		56,080		
Gross profit		75,010		14,020		89,030
Salaries and expenses	44,680		6,330		51,010	
Depreciation—fixtures and fittings	1,220		450		1,670	
Branch manager's commission ($\frac{10}{110} \times £(14,020 - 6,780)$)	—		658		658	
		45,900		7,438		53,338
Net profit		29,110		6,582		35,692

Balance sheet as at 31 Mar. 19–5

	£	£	£
Capital employed:			
Share capital:			
£1 ordinary shares, issued and fully paid			20,000
Reserves:			
General reserve		5,000	
Profit and loss account at 1 Apr. 19–4	5,298		
Add: Total profit for year	35,692		
		40,990	
			45,990
			65,990

Represented by

	Cost £	Depn. £	£
Fixed assets:			
Fixtures and fittings	16,700	8,470	8,230
Current assets:			
Stocks		41,880	
Debtors		15,648	
Cash at bank and in hand		30,490	
		88,018	
Less: Current liabilities:			
Creditors	29,700		
Amount owing to branch manager	558		
		30,258	
			57,760
			65,990

Workings

(1) Branch stock control account

	£	£		£
Purchases in cash at cost	2,400		Sales	70,000
Mark-up account (25% × £2,400)	600		Stock lost at selling prices (balance)—manager's account	100
		3,000	Stock in hand at selling price c/f	6,100
Purchases from head office at cost (80% × £73,200)	58,560			
Mark-up account	14,640			
		73,200		
		76,200		76,200

(2) Branch cash account

	£		£
Cash from head office	200	Stock account—purchases	2,400
Sales account—cash collected in year	69,752	Expenses paid	210
		Remittances to head office	67,052
		Balance c/f	290
	69,952		69,952

(3) Branch total sales account

	£		£
Stock account—sales for year	70,000	Cash collected	69,752
		Debtors c/f	248
	70,000		70,000

(4) *Computation of uniform mark-up*

	%	£	£
Head office sales:			
To customers			375,050
To branch			73,200
	100		448,250
Cost of sales:			
Opening stock		35,600	
Purchases		360,000	
		395,600	
Less: Closing stock		37,000	
	80		358,600
Gross profit	20		89,650

(5) Branch manager's account

	£		£
Branch stock account		Branch profit and loss	
(shortage)	100	account—commission	658
Balance c/d	558		
	658		658

ANSWER P5. COLONIA LTD

(a)

Trading and profit and loss accounts for year ended 31 Dec. 19–5

	Head office £	Branch £	Whole business £		Head office £	Branch £	Whole business £
Opening stock	64,983	24,992	89,515	Sales	659,320	275,840	935,160
Purchases	620,650	34,000	654,650	Goods sent to branch	139,280	—	—
Goods from head office	—	139,280	—				
	685,633	198,272	744,165				
Less: Closing stock	58,320	22,752	80,742				
	627,313	175,520	663,423				
Gross profit c/d	171,287	100,320	271,737				
	798,600	275,840	935,160		798,600	275,840	935,160
Salaries, etc.	62,143	56,960	119,103	Gross profit b/d	171,287	100,320	271,737
Commission	—	1,354	1,354	Provision for branch stock no longer required	130	—	—
Depreciation	5,480	1,333	6,813				
Net profit	103,794	40,673	144,467				
	171,417	100,320	271,737		171,417	100,320	271,737

Balance sheets as at 31 Dec. 19–5

	Head office £	Head office £	Branch £	Branch £	Whole business £	Whole business £
Net assets:						
Fixed assets:						
Cost		54,800		13,330		68,130
Depreciation		26,410		7,998		34,408
		28,390		5,332		33,722
Branch account		58,762		—		—
Current assets:						
Debtors	88,100		30,072		118,172	
Stock	58,320		22,752		80,742	
Cash	38,530		14,399		52,929	
		184,950		67,223		251,843
Less: Current liabilities:						
Creditors	40,354		12,439		52,793	
Manager's commission	—		1,354		1,354	
Stock provision	330		—		—	
		(40,684)		(13,793)		(54,147)
		231,418		58,762		231,418
Capital employed:						
Ordinary £1 shares		80,000		—		80,000
Head office account		—		58,762		—
Reserves		151,418		—		151,418
		231,418		58,762		231,418

Workings

(1) *Commission to branch manager*

	£
Debtors at start of year	25,000
Sales during year	275,840
	300,840
Less: Debtors at end of year	30,072
Cash collected	270,768
$\frac{1}{2}\% \times £270,768$	1,354

(2) Provision for unrealised profit account

	£		£
Balance c/d:		Balance b/d (given)	460
$\frac{2}{110} \times £18,152$*	330		
P & L account of head office	130		
	460		460

	£
*Branch closing stock (given)	22,752
Local purchases therein (given)	4,600
Head office purchases therein	18,152

(3) *Stocks*

	Opening £	*Closing* £
Head office	64,983	58,320
Branch	24,992	22,752
	89,975	81,072
Less: Provision	460	330
	89,515	80,742

ANSWER R1. LORRY LTD

(a)

Motor vehicles account

	£		£
19–3		19–3	
31 May Hire purchase: Company account: Cash price:		31 Dec. Balance c/d	4,200
NOL 862B	1,800		
NOM 760C	2,400		
	4,200		4,200
19–4		19–4	
1 Jan. Balance b/d	4,200	1 Sep. Motor vehicle disposals: Cash price of lorry NOL 862B	1,800
		31 Dec. Balance c/f: NOM 760C	2,400
	4,200		4,200

(b)

Depreciation of motor vehicles account

	£		£
19–3		19–3	
31 Dec. Balance c/d	290	31 Dec. P & L account: NOL 862B—20% for 7 months on £1,800	210
		NOM 760C—20% for 2 months on £2,400	80
	290		290
19–4		19–4	
1 Sep. Motor vehicle disposals— depreciation re NOL 862B £(210 + 240)	450	1 Jan. Balance b/d	290
		1 Sep. P & L account: NOL 862B—20% for 8 months on £1,800	240
31 Dec. Balance c/f	560	NOM 760C—20% for year on £2,400	480
	1,010		1,010

(c) Motor vehicles disposals account

	£		£
19–4		19–4	
1 Sep. Motor vehicles account:		1 Sep. Depreciation account NOL 862B	450
Cash price: NOL 862B	1,800	20 Sep. Cash—proceeds from insurance company	1,250
		31 Dec. P & L account—under-provision for depreciation	100
	1,800		1,800

(d) Hire purchase company account

	NOL 862B £	NOM 760C £		NOL 862B £	NOM 760C £
19–3			19–3		
31 May Cash book deposit	312		Motor vehicles account:		
Cash book deposit		480	31 May Cash price	1,800	
31 Oct. Cash instalments:			31 Dec. Cash price		2,400
7 × £70	490		P & L account: HP interest:		
2 × £90		180	7 × £8	56	
Balance c/d	1,054	1,760	2 × £10		20
	1,856	2,420		1,856	2,420
19–4			19–4		
31 Aug. Cash instalments to date:			1 Jan. Balance b/d	1,054	1,760
8 × £70	560		20 Sep. P & L account: *HP interest arising on final settlement	106	
20 Sep. Cash in settlement	600				
31 Dec. Cash instalments:			31 Dec. 12 × £10		120
12 × £90		1,080			
Balance c/f		800			
	1,160	1,880		1,160	1,880

* Some accountants would prefer to show H.P. interest of 8 × £8 = £64 and to show £42 (= £106 − 64) as an extra cost arising on termination of the agreement.

Financial Accounting

Workings

	NOL 862B £	NOM 760C £
Cash price	1,800	2,400
Less: Deposit	312	480
	1,488	1,920
Add: Interest	192	240
	1,680	2,160

Repayable by 24 monthly instalments representing:

	£	£
Capital	62	80
Interest	8	10
	70	90

ANSWER R2. EASY PAYMENTS LTD

(a) *Trading and profit and loss account for year ended 31 Dec. 19–6*

	£	£
Sales		94,650 (150%)
Opening stock	6,600	
Purchases	60,600	
	67,200	
Less: Closing stock	4,100	
		63,100 (100%)
		31,550 (50%)
Less:		
Loss on goods repossessed	800	
Unearned profit on hire purchase sales	3,875	
		4,675
Gross profit		26,875
General expenses	16,150	
Depreciation	1,000	
		17,150
Net profit for year		9,725

(b) Balance sheet as at 31 Dec. 19–6

	£	£
Share capital		35,000
Reserves:		
At 1 Jan. 19–6	5,115	
Retained for year	9,725	
		14,840
		49,840
Fixed assets:		
Cost		10,000
Depreciation		2,000
		8,000
Current assets:		
Stock	4,100	
Hire purchase debtors	36,100	
Cash at bank	6,500	
	46,700	
Less: Current liabilities:		
Creditors	4,860	
		41,840
		49,840

Hire purchase debtors' account

19–6	£	19–6	£
1 Jan. Balances b/d	42,525	31 Dec. Cash	80,625
31 Dec. Sales	94,650	Repossessions	2,400
		Balance c/d	54,150
	137,175		137,175

Workings
Provision for unrealised profit

	£		£
Balance c/d		Balance b/d	14,175
($\frac{1}{3}$ × £54,150)	18,050	Trading account	3,875
	18,050		18,050

Repossessions account

	£		£
Hire purchase debtors	2,400	Purchases	1,600
		Loss on repossession	800
	2,400		2,400

Jan. 19–6

			£
Gross debtors	= £28,350 × $\frac{3}{2}$	=	42,525
Provision	= £42,525 × $\frac{1}{3}$	=	14,175
			28,350

ANSWER R3. SMITH

(a) *Trading and profit and loss account for year ended 31 Dec. 19–0*

	£	£
Sales:		
Cash		10,528
Hire purchase		5,712
By agent		4,480
		20,720
Purchases	18,000	
Less: Closing stock	3,200	
		14,800
		5,920
Add: Hire charges		800
HP interest earned		117
		6,837
Less:		
Loss on reposession	10	
Agent's commission	560	
Depreciation	400	
Expenses	2,500	
		3,470
Net profit		3,367

Notes:

(1) Interest on hire purchase sales has been taken in proportion to the cash collected.
(2) Tools on hire have been capitalised and depreciated over their expected useful lives. Hire charges have been credited as income when accounts have been settled.
(3) Tools in the hands of the agent have been included in closing stock since the agent is entitled to return these.

Financial Accounting

(b) Balance sheet as at 31 Dec. 19–0

	£	£	£
Fixed assets:			
Equipment held for hire:			
Cost		2,060	
Less: Depreciation		400	
			1,660
Current assets:			
Stock		3,200	
HP debtors	4,110		
Less: Interest not yet earned	685		
		3,425	
Debtor (agent)		392	
Bank balance		11,050	
		18,067	
Less: Creditors (amount due within one year)			
Deposits from hirers		360	
			17,707
			19,367
Capital account:			
Capital introduced			20,000
Add: Net profit			3,367
			23,367
Less: Drawings			4,000
			19,367

Workings

(1) *Hire purchase sales*

HP debtors' control account

	£		£
HP sales (£56 × 102)	5,712	Cash received	
Interest suspense		£(2,290 + 44)	2,334
(£8 × 102)	816	Repossessions account—	
		outstanding instalments	
		on repossessed goods	
		(£6 × 14)	84
		Balance c/d	4,110
	6,528		6,528

Repossessions account

	£		£
HP debtors account	84	H.P. Interest written off	14
		Tools for hire (£30 × 2)	60
		P & L account—loss on repossession	10
	84		84

HP interest account

	£		£
Profit and loss account (117 instalments paid × £1)	117	HP debtors' control account	816
Repossessions account (2 × 7 × £1 interest in unpaid instalments)	14		
Balance c/d (685 × £1)	685		
	816		816

(2) *Sales by agent*
80 × £56 = £4,480.

(3) *Commission due to agent*
$12\frac{1}{2}\% \times £4{,}480 = £560$.

(4) *Depreciation on tools for hire*
Expected useful life 40 days per tool
∴ For 50 tools, total life 2,000 days
Actual days on hire in year   400
Total cost of tools on hire: 50 × £40   £2,000

Depreciation charge: $\dfrac{400}{2{,}000} \times £2{,}000$ £400

(5) Bank balance

Bank account

	£		£
Capital introduced	20,000	Tools purchased	
Receipts (per question)	17,550	(500 × £40)	20,000
		Expenses	2,500
		Drawings	4,000
		Balance c/d	11,050
	37,550		37,550

ANSWER R4. MAYDAY LTD

(a) (i)

CBA Ltd account

	£		£
19–1		19–1	
1 Jul. Cash (deposit)	800	1 Jul. Machinery	8,000
31 Dec. Cash	2,052		
19–2		19–2	
30 Jun. Cash	2,052	30 Jun. HP interest	504
Balance c/d	3,600		
	8,504		8,504
		1 Jul. Balance b/d	3,600

Machinery account

	£		£
19–1		19–1	
1 Jul. CBA Ltd	8,000		

HP interest account

	£		£
10–2		19–2	
30 Jun. CBA Ltd	504	30 Jun. P & L account	504

(ii)

Royalties account

	£		£
19–2		19–2	
30 Jun. FED Ltd	2,000	30 Jun. P & L account	3,750
Shortworkings c/d	1,750		
	3,750		3,750
		1 Jul. Balance b/d	1,750

FED Ltd account

	£		£
19–1			
31 Dec. Cash (1,000 × 50p)	500		
19–2		19–2	
31 Mar. Cash (1,200 × 50p)	600	30 Jun. Royalties account	2,000
31 Jun. Cash (1,800 × 50p)	900		
	2,000		2,000

(iii)

IHG Ltd account (consignor account)

	£		£
19–2		19–2	
May Cash	120	Jun. Cash	3,600
30 Jun. Commission	180		
Cash	3,300		
	3,600		3,600

Commission received account

	£		£
10–2		10–2	
30 Jun. P & L account	180	30 Jun. IHG Ltd account	180

(b) (i)

	£
Cash price of machinery	8,000
Total payable	9,008
Therefore, interest	1,008

The total interest payable must be debited to profit and loss account over the life of the agreement. The question requires the relatively simple straight line approach, i.e. the interest is spread evenly over the life of the agreement. Since half the instalments have been paid, half the interest has been debited to profit and loss account.

A better approach would be a method that recognises that the amount of interest charges falls over the life of the agreement as the amount outstanding reduces.

The sum of digits method recognises this. Using this method the interest would be calculated as follows:

$$\text{Sum of digits of no. of instalments} = 4 + 3 + 2 + 1 = 10$$

	£
1st instalment $\frac{4}{10} \times £1,008$	= 403
2nd instalment $\frac{3}{10} \times £1,008$	= 302
Total 19–1/–2	705

The outstanding liability to the HP company is shown by the balance on the CBA account of £3,600. However, this is only the capital outstanding. No provision is made for the interest but this would be shown as a note to the accounts.

(ii) Many royalty agreements are based on a minimum rent payable each year with the right to recover shortworkings on future years. Shortworkings arise when the actual royalties payable on items sold are less than the minimum payment. In future years, when the royalties exceed the minimum payment, the shortworkings may be recovered. In such cases, the charge to profit and loss account each year should be the actual royalties based on sales made, i.e. excluding the effect on shortworkings.

In this case, the shortworkings are not recoverable and, therefore, they should be written off to profit and loss account. The answer has been based on charging three-quarters of the minimum payment to profit and loss account since three-quarters of the royalty agreement falls in the year.

An alternative view would be:

	£
Projected total royalties for year ended 30 Sep. 19–2 ($6,400 \times 50p$)	3,200
Minimum royalty payment	5,000
Projected total shortworkings	1,800
Charges for nine months to 30 Jun. 19–2: $\frac{9}{12} \times £1,800$ =	1,350
Total profit and loss account charge for year ended 30 Jun. 10–2 £(2,000 + 1,350) =	3,350

The answer takes the more conservative approach.

ANSWER R5. H PRICE

(a) *Trading and profit and loss account for year ended 31 Dec. 19–6*

	£	£
Sales:		
Hire purchase		60,000
Cash		14,250
		74,250
Cost of goods sold:		
Opening stock	11,000	
Purchases	42,400	
	53,400	
Less: Closing stock	14,100	
		39,300
Gross profit		34,950
Expenses:		
General trade expenses	10,600	
Provision for unrealised profit on HP sales	19,400	
Loss on repossessions	1,150	
		31,150
Net profit		3,800

Financial Accounting

(b) *Balance sheet as at 31 Dec. 19–6*

	£	£
Capital account:		
Balance at 1 Jan. 19–6		22,000
Net profit for year		3,800
		25,800
Drawings		2,000
		23,800

	£	£
Represented by:		
Current assets:		
Stock		14,100
Debtors	39,200	
Less: provision	19,400	
		19,800
Cash at bank		1,200
		35,100
Less: Current liabilities:		
Creditors		11,300
		23,800

Workings

(1) *Gross profit percentage on HP sales*

    Either: (a) *Consider all sales as HP sales*

	£	£
HP sales made		60,000
Cash sales made	14,250	
Less: Repossession resold	1,050	
	13,200	
HP mark-up (25% × £13,200)	3,300	
		16,500
All sales as HP sales		76,500

Cost of goods sold:
  Opening stock ... 11,000
  Purchases ... 40,750
  ... 51,750

Closing stock ... 14,600
  Less: Repossession unsold ... 1,100
  ... 13,500

Cost of goods sold ... 38,250

Gross profit percentage on HP sales:

$$\frac{£(76,500 - 38,250)}{£76,500} \times 100 = \underline{50\%}$$

Or: (b) *Consider all sales as cash sales*

	£	£
Cash sales made		14,250
Less: Repossession resold		1,050
		13,200
HP sales made	60,000	
HP mark-up		
$\frac{25}{125} \times £60,000$	12,000	
		48,000
All sales as cash sales		61,200
Cost of goods sold (above)		38,250

Gross profit percentage on cash sales:

$$\frac{£(61,200 - 38,250)}{£61,200} \times 100 = \underline{37\tfrac{1}{2}\%}$$

Therefore:

	%
Cost of goods	$62\tfrac{1}{2}$
Gross profit on cash sales	$37\tfrac{1}{2}$
Cash sale price	100
HP mark-up	25
HP sale price	125

Gross profit percentage on HP sales:

$$\frac{62\frac{1}{2}}{125} \times 100 = \underline{50\%}$$

(2) Repossessions account

	£		£
HP debtors' account	2,800	Cash sales	1,050
		Stock	600
		P & L account—loss on repossession	1,150
	2,800		2,800

(3) HP debtors' account

	£		£
Balance b/d:		Repossessions account	2,800
Pre-19–6 sales	4,000	Balance c/d	39,200
19–6 sales	38,000		
	42,000		42,000

(4) Provision for unrealised profit account

	£		£
Balance c/d:		P & L account	19,400
45% × £4,000	1,800		
50% × £(38,000 − 2,800)	17,600		
	19,400		19,400

(5) *Closing stock*

	£
Per question	14,600
Repossession unsold—wrongly valued	(1,100)
	13,500
Repossession unsold—correctly valued	600
	14,100

ANSWER S1. HOLMES LTD

Royalties payable account

	£		L
19–9 Landlord 1,600 @ £5	8,000	19–9 Trading account	8,000
19–10 Landlord: 1,900 @ £5	9,500	19–10 Trading account	9,500
19–11 Landlord: 2,640 @ £5	12,300	19–11 Trading account	12,300
19–12 Landlord: 1,840 @ £5	9,200	19–12 Trading account	9,200
19–13 Landlord: 2,720 @ £5	13,600	19–13 Trading account	13,600

Landlord's account—Watson Ltd

	£		£
19–9 Bank—minimum rent	10,000	19–9 Royalties payable account	8,000
		Shortworkings recoverable account	2,000
	10,000		10,000
19–10 Bank—minimum rent	10,000	19–10 Royalties payable account	9,500
		Shortworkings recoverable account	500
	10,000		10,000
19–11 Bank—minimum rent	10,000	19–11 Royalties payable account	12,300
Shortworkings recoverable account	2,300		
	12,300		12,300

Financial Accounting

Landlords account—continued

		£			£
19–12	Bank—minimum rent	10,000	19–12	Royalties payable account	9,200
				Shortworkings recoverable account	800
		10,000			10,000
19–13	Shortworkings recoverable account	800	19–13	Royalties payable account	13,600
	Bank	12,800			
		13,600			13,600

Shortworkings recoverable account

		£			£
19–9	Landlord	2,000	19–9	Balance c/d	2,000
10–10	Balance b/d	2,000	19–10	Balance c/d	2,500
	Landlord	500			
		2,500			2,500
19–11	Balance b/d	2,500	19–11	Landlord	2,300
				P & L account—shortworkings no longer recoverable	200
		2,500			2,500
19–12	Landlord	800	19–12	Balance c/d	800
19–13	Balance b/d	800	19–13	Landlord	800

ANSWER S2. FELL

Consignment account

	Bicycles	£		Bicycles	£
Purchases (£27)	90	2,430	Goods returned	10	270
Insurance and freight		162	Offe—sales	60	3,240
Offe:			Balance c/d at 30 Jun. 19–8		
Return freight		30	(see working)	20	588
Warehouse charges		48			
Carriage on sales		45			
Commission		324			
Discounting charges		9			
P & L account—net profit to 30 Jun. 19–8		1,050			
	90	4,098		90	4,098
Stock b/d	20	588	Offe—sales	20	960
Offe:					
Expenses		24			
Commission		96			
Discounting charges		6			
P & L account—net profit to 30 Sep. 19–8		246			
	20	960		20	960

Financial Accounting

Consignee's account—Offe

	£		£
Sales (60)	3,240	Return freight	30
		Warehouse charges	48
		Carriage on sales	45
		Commission 10% × £3,240	324
		Bills receivable	2,793
	3,240		3,240
Sales	960	Expenses	24
		Commission 10% × £960	96
		Bills receivable	840
	960		960

Workings

(1)

Bills receivable account

	£		£
Offe	2,793	Bank	2,784
		Discounting charges	9
	2,793		2,793
Offe	840	Bank	834
		Discounting charges	6
	840		840

(2) *Stock at 30 Jun. 19–8*

	£
Basic cost of 20 bicycles @ £27	540
Add: Cost of bringing stock to existing location and condition:	
(i) Consignor's costs:	
Insurance and freight $\frac{20}{90}$ × £162	36
(i) Consignee's costs:	
Warehouse charges $\frac{20}{80}$ × £48	12
	588

ANSWER S3. BOTTLES & CO

Flasks stock account (all @ 20p)

	No.	£		No.	£
Stocks b/f:			Flasks P & L		
In hand	15,200	3,040	account:		
With customers	7,000	1,400	Breakages	1,950	390
New Flasks	3,600	720	Shortages of stock	50	10
			Retained by customers	3,000	600
			Stock c/f:		
			With customers	9,000	1,800
			In hand (bal. fig.)	11,800	2,360
	25,800	5,160		25,800	5,160

Flasks suspense account (all @ 40p)

	No.	£		No.	£
Customers returns	35,000	14,000	Balance b/f		
Sold (retained)	3,000	1,200	returnable flasks	7,000	2,800
Balance c/f— returnable (bal. fig.)	9,000	3,600	Invoiced to customers	40,000	16,000
	47,000	18,800		47,000	18,800

Flasks profit and loss account

	£		£
Depreciation of new flasks (3,600 @ 5p)	180	Profit on hire (40,000 @ 10p)	4,000
Flasks broken	390	Return price of flasks sold	1,200
Stock shortage	10		
Value of flasks sold	600		
P & L account—profit on flasks	4,020		
	5,200		5,200

ANSWER T1. BIRKDALE ENTERPRISES LTD

Statement of source and application of funds for year ended 31 Dec. 19–8

	£	£
Source of funds		
Profit before tax		56,200
Adjustment for items not involving the movement of funds:		
Depreciation		10,000
Total generated from operations		66,200
Funds from other sources:		
Issue of shares for cash	60,000	
Sale of plant and machinery	8,000	
Issue of loan stock	14,700	
		82,700
		148,900
Application of funds		
Dividends paid:		
Preference	3,000	
Ordinary	26,000	
Purchase of plant	25,200	
Redemption of preference shares	52,500	
Purchase of freehold land	31,400	
		138,100
		10,800
Increase/decrease in working capital		
Increase in stocks	1,500	
Increase in debtors	4,400	
(Increase)/decrease in creditors (excluding proposed dividends)	(3,600)	
Movement in net liquid funds:		
Increase in cash balance	8,500	
		10,800

Workings

(1) *Reconcile key accounts*

Plant and machinery account (cost)

	£		£
Balance b/f	47,800	Disposals account	12,000
Additions (bal. fig.)	25,200	Balance c/f	61,000
	73,000		73,000

Plant and machinery account (aggregate depreciation)

	£		£
Disposals account (bal. fig.)	3,500	Balance b/f	13,200
Balance c/f	19,200	Depreciation provided—P & L account	9,500
	22,700		22,700

Plant and machinery—disposals account

	£		£
Cost of plant	12,000	Depreciation	3,500
		Proceeds	8,000
		P & L account—depreciation under provided	500
	12,000		12,000

Share premium account

	£		£
Redemption of preference shares	2,500	Balance b/f	7,000
Balance c/f	14,500	Issue of ordinary shares	10,000
	17,000		17,000

Loan stock account

	£		£
Balance c/f (nominal value)	15,000	Cash received on issue £15,000 @ 98	14,700
		P & L account—discount written off	300
	15,000		15,000

Dividends account

	£		£
Cash paid (bal. fig.) £(15,000 + 11,000 + 3,000)	29,000	Balance b/d	15,000
		P & L account: Ordinary shares £(11,000 + 25,000)	36,000
Balance c/d	25,000	Preference shares	3,000
	54,000		54,000

(2) *Profit before taxation*

	£
Increase in revenue reserves	16,900
Dividends	39,000
Discount on debentures	300
	56,200

ANSWER T2. BAFFLE LTD

*Consolidated statement of source and
application of funds for year ended 31 Jul. 19–7*

	£000	£000
Group profit before tax		850
Add: Depreciation		1,950
Sources generated from operations		2,800
Other sources:		
Issue of shares	1,750	
Minority interest at date of acquisition	600	
Increase in debenture stock	500	
		2,850
		5,650
Applications:		
Additions to fixed assets	5,920	
Dividends paid:		
Baffle Ltd	450	
Minority shareholders	50	
Purchase of goodwill	200	
		6,620
		970
Decrease in working capital:		
Increase in stock	400	
Increase in debtors	800	
Increase in creditors	(1,300)	
		100
Decrease in net liquid assets		870
Decrease in cash balances		600
Increase in bank overdraft		270
		870

Financial Accounting

Summary of the effects of acquisition of New Ltd

	£000
Purchase of fixed assets	2,500
Goodwill	200
Stock	300
Debtors	400
Cash	500
Debentures	(500)
Creditors	(800)
	2,600
Less: Minority interest	600
	2,000
Financed by:	
Issue of shares	1,750
Cash	250
	2,000

Workings

(1) *Profit before taxation*

	£000	£000
Increase in group reserves £(4,700 − 3,400)		1,300
Less: Share premium £(1,750 − 700)		1,050
Increase in revenue reserves		250
Add: Dividends—holding company		450
		700
Add: Minority interests:		
At 31 Jul. 19–7	700	
At acquisition:		
Assets 3,700		
Liabilities 1,300		
2,400 × 25%	600	
Increase in post-acquisition period	100	
Add: Share of dividend (25% × £200)	50	
		150
		850
Taxation		—
		850

(2) *Fixed assets*

	£000
Increase in WDV £(9,070 − 5,100)	3,970
Add: Depreciation	1,950
Additions	5,920

ANSWER T3. SPIXWORTH PLC

(a) *Statement of value added for year ended 30 Jun. 19–8*

	£000	£000	%
Turnover		31,311	
Bought-in materials and services		12,818	
Value added		18,493	
Dividends received from associated company		40	
		18,533	
Applied as follows			
To pay employees' wages, salaries and pensions		12,123	65.4
To pay providers of capital:			
Interest on loans	120		
Dividends to shareholders	900		
Dividends to minority interests	13		
		1,033	5.6
To pay government:			
Corporation tax £(2,600 − 100)		2,500	13.5
To provide for maintenance and expansion:			
Depreciation	1,056		
Transfer to replacement reserve	300		
Retained profits	1,521		
		2,877	15.5
		18,533	100.0

Workings

(1) *Bought-in materials, etc.*

	£000
Purchases	7,192
Direct overheads	3,520
Indirect overheads	2,106
	12,818

(2) *To pay employees*

	£000
Wages	8,306
Salaries	2,941
Pension contributions	840
Directors' remuneration	36
	12,123

(3) *Dividends to minority interests*

	£000
Preferential dividends 70% × £10,000	7
Ordinary dividends 40% × £15,000	6
	13

(4) *Retained profits*

	£000
Group retained	1,657
Less: Group share of retained profit of associate 40% × £35,000	140
	1,517
Add: Minority interests' share in retained profit 40% × £10,000	4
	1,521

(b) The making of profit has been and always will be a very important element in the objectives of any organisation in a capitalistic economy. Although profit making may not be the most important aim of business enterprises and will certainly not be the only aim, it is difficult to see business enterprises continuing in existence in the long term unless profits are made.

Published reports of business enterprises certainly lay great stress on the profit figure and it is without doubt the keynote figure in the profit and loss account. The idea that profit is the sole aim of business enterprises also tends to be supported by articles in the financial press and indeed the media as a whole.

Despite this, published reports are tending to become more comprehensive than previously, although a downturn in the economy may force companies to reduce the volume and hence the cost of their reports. Thus, a modern report deals not merely with a profit and loss account but also with such matters as:

(i) a balance sheet giving the financial position of the company at a particular date;
(ii) a statement of source and application of funds showing how the liquidity of the company has changed;
(iii) a directors' report giving details required by statute, little of which relates directly to profitability;
(iv) a chairman's report dealing with the general progress of the firm and possibly with future prospects.

Additional objectives of business enterprises include the following:

(1) *To create wealth for different groups in a stable manner over the long term*

   The corporate report could, therefore, give details of a value added statement, showing how the wealth of the organisation has been allocated among the various groups within the concern over a ten year period.

(2) *To create stable employment*

   The report could contain an employment report dealing with the number of employees during the year, how this has changed, and the distribution as regards sex, age, locality, etc.

(3) *Continued existence*

   In some cases a company may have done well merely to survive. This might be outlined in a chairman's report (and often will be if profits are very low!).

Financial Accounting

ANSWER T4. SUNLIGHT PLC

(a) **(i)** Primary ratio $= \dfrac{\text{Profit before tax and interest}}{\text{Book value of total assets}}$

$= \dfrac{220{,}000 \times 100}{1{,}600{,}000}$

$= 13.7\%$

(ii) Secondary ratio $= \dfrac{\text{Profit before tax and interest}}{\text{Sales}}$

$= \dfrac{220{,}000 \times 100}{2{,}000{,}000}$

$= 11\%$

(iii) Secondary ratio $= \dfrac{\text{Sales}}{\text{Book value of total assets}}$

$= \dfrac{2{,}000{,}000}{1{,}600{,}000}$

$= 1.25 \text{ times}$

(iv) Current ratio = Current assets:Current liabilities
= 760,000:700,000
= 1.08 to 1

(v) Liquid ratio = Liquid assets:Current liabilities
= 260,000:700,000
= 0.37 to 1

or = Liquid assets:Current liabilities excluding bank overdraft
= 260,000:260,800
= 0.99 to 1

(vi) Debtors' ratio $= \dfrac{\text{Debtors} \times 365}{\text{Sales}}$

$= \dfrac{200{,}000 \times 365}{2{,}000{,}000}$

$= 36.5 \text{ days}$

(vii) Proprietary ratio = Shareholders' funds:Total assets
= 700,000:1,600,000
= 43.8%

(viii) Stock turnover ratio $= \dfrac{\text{Cost of sales}}{\text{Average stock}}$

$= \dfrac{1{,}500{,}000}{\frac{1}{2} \times (500{,}000 + 920{,}000^*)}$

$= 2.1$ times

	£
* Opening stock (bal. fig.)	920,000
Purchases	1,080,000
	2,000,000
Closing stock	500,000
Cost of sales	1,500,000

Note: The 'stock' of a manufacturing company comprises materials, work-in-progress and finished goods. The stock turnover ratio should be related to the latter.

(ix) Dividend yield $= \dfrac{\text{Dividend}}{\text{Market value ordinary share}}$

$= \dfrac{53{,}600 \times 100}{800{,}000}$

$= 6.7\%$

With income tax at 30%, the gross dividend yield is 9.6%. i.e.

$\dfrac{6.7\%}{70\%} \times 100$

(x) Price earnings ratio $= 800{,}000 : 112{,}000$
$= 7.1$ to 1

or

Earnings per share $= \dfrac{£112{,}000}{200{,}000}$
$= 56\text{p per share}$
$= \text{price:earnings of } £4:56\text{p}$
$= 7.1$ to 1

Reciprocal of price earnings ratio is the earnings yield $= 1:7.1$
$= 14.1\%$

(b) The company is experiencing liquidity problems. The current ratio of 1.08 to 1 is low and the liquid ratio of 0.37 to 1 suggest that great problems with short-term finance may be experienced. If the bank overdraft is excluded from the liabilities the liquid ratio becomes 0.99 to 1 which is more respectable; however, this highlights the dependence of the company on the bank as a source of working capital. The bank overdraft is secured by a floating charge which makes the position of the other creditors less secure. The payment of a dividend will cause the liquidity position to deteriorate.

The proprietary ratio shows that only 43.8% of the book value of the assets is funded by the ordinary shareholders. This highlights the dependence of the company on long- and short-term loan capital. It would be advisable if the company could obtain further long-term capital.

Liquidity should be monitored by the comparison of actual and budgeted cash flow and the long-term trend can be examined through previous and budgeted liquidity ratios. Sometimes comparisons may be made with enterprises in the same industry through the figures available from the Centre for Inter-firm Comparisons.

(c) To: The Managing Director
From: The Chief Accountant
Date: 31 July 19–9
Subject: Goodwill

Goodwill may be adopted as the difference between the value of the business and the book value of its assets. The value of a business may be considered as the present value of the future income stream from that business. Such a value may only be exactly determined when a business is sold or acquired. When such an acquisition takes place the value of goodwill is termed the 'goodwill on acquisition' or 'purchased goodwill'. If the ownership of the business does not change, the value of the business is difficult to ascertain exactly.

It is normal accountancy practice only to show acquired goodwill in published accounts. This practice arises from the accountant's dislike of uncertain figures: acquired goodwill is easily ascertained; internal goodwill is only subjectively determined. The company has not purchased any goodwill so none appears in the account.

Internal goodwill is generated by the way in which the business is run: its location, staff, and more of operation. Such goodwill is normally termed 'self-generated goodwill'. It exists only if the business is capable of generating profits the value of which is in excess of the book value of its assets. The value of these profits depends on the costs attached to investment in the business.

The Stock Exchange places a value of £4 on our shares. This may be compared with a book value of £3.50. This difference is probably due to the value of our properties which when taken into account at full value gives a value per share of £4.50 ((70,000 + 200,000) ÷ 200,000). Thus, the underlying asset value of our shares exceeds the market value. This suggests that the market considers that the value of our future economy is less than the value of our assets. We could hardly construe this as indicating the market considered the company to have self-generated goodwill.

Because it is not possible to place an accurate value on our self-generated goodwill (if we have any) and because external observers clearly do not believe we have such goodwill, it is inadvisable to include it in our financial statements.

Acquired goodwill is gradually replaced following an acquisition by internally generated goodwill. For this reason, current accounting practice requires that goodwill is not left permanently in the balance sheet but is written off immediately on acquisition or over its estimated useful life.

ANSWER T5. HENRY

(a) *Cash budget for 19-3*

	Jan. £	Feb. £	Mar. £	Apr. £	May £	Jun. £	Jul. £	Aug. £	Sep. £	Oct. £	Nov. £	Dec. £	Total £
Receipts:													
Barley								4,500					4,500
Fatstock				700									700
Hay						100							100
				700		100		4,500					5,300
Payments:													
Wages and expenses	200	200	200	200	200	200	200	200	200	200	200	200	2,400
Seeds				600									600
Harvesting								200					200
Rent			100			100			100			100	400
Farm buildings											1,800		1,800
Tax	200						200						400
Drawings	100	100	100	100	100	100	100	100	100	100	100	100	1,200
Holiday		200						500					200
	500	500	400	900	300	400	500	500	400	300	2,100	400	7,200

Balance at bank at 1 Jan. 19-3 750

Monthly:
Balance 250 250 650 850 1,150 1,450 1,950 2,050 1,650 1,350 750 1,150
Overdraft

(b) *Budgeted profit and loss account for 19–3*

	£	£
Sales:		
Barley		4,500
Fatstock		700
Hay		100
		5,300
Expenditure:		
Wages and expenses £(2,400 + 125)	2,525	
Seeds	600	
Harvesting	200	
Rent	400	
Depreciation	200	
		3,925
Budgeted net profit		1,375

Notes:
(1) It is assumed that there will be no variation in the opening and closing valuations of live and dead stocks.
(2) The budgeted net profit is before charging bank overdraft interest.

The figure of net profit can be reconciled by means of a source and application of funds statement as follows:

	£
Sources:	
Profit for year	1,375
Add: Depreciation	200
	1,575
Decrease in bank balance	1,900
Increase in creditors	125
	3,600
Applications	
Drawings, including holiday	1,400
Tax	400
	1,800
Farm buildings	1,800
	3,600

Financial Accounting 347

ANSWER T6. EXPLOITATION ASSOCIATES INC

(a)   *Report to the Board of Directors*

Purpose: Additional financial requirements of Exploitation Associates Inc

(i) *Introduction*

The request for financial assistance from the American company was supported by financial statements for the years 19–2 and 19–3.

Your attention is now directed to the points set out below.

(ii) *Sales and operating profit*

The accounts for 19–3 show an increase of 47% in money turnover. It is not known to what extent this is due to increased selling prices as opposed to increased sales volume.

The additional sales turnover has been achieved with some reduction of gross margin (see Schedule A(a) **(i)**), but operating profit as a percentage of net sales was down by only 1.1% as compared with 19–2.

With a net operating margin of 9.3% the company can offer reasonable cover for future interest payments.

The company's earnings before tax give a return on capital employed (net worth) of 56.7% for 19–3. This rate is no doubt deceptive as it is based on a total which includes fixed assets presumably stated at historical cost and apparently bought some years ago (total depreciation is approximately 75% of cost). It would perhaps be more significant to express the earnings as a percentage of gross asset values (ignoring accumulated depreciation).

However, despite the limitations of this profitability ratio, the fact remains that at 56.7% it represents an increase of 9% over 19–2 (see Schedule A(a) **(ii)**).

(iii) *Working capital*

A movement of funds statement is attached (Schedule B). This shows that expenditure on fixed assets has been approximately covered by depreciation retentions for the year, and that retained profit after dividends has been largely absorbed into working capital.

Current and liquidity ratios are low (see Schedule A(b) **(i)** and (b) **(ii)**)) but have improved during 19–3 due to profit retentions.

During 19–3 the company may have achieved a slightly higher rate of stock turnover, but a valid calculation cannot be made without knowing the finished stock figures (see Schedule A(b) **(iii)**)).

Debtors appear to be taking a longer period of credit (see Schedule A(b) **(iv)**), but again this cannot be conclusively determined without knowing the trend of sales over 19–3.

The company is clearly taking longer credit from trade suppliers, which at $78,000 for 19–3 have more than doubled from 19–2. During 19–3, however, the company had to meet $40,000 of bills payable.

(iv) Conclusion

No conclusive advice can be given without a great deal more information (see (b) below). In general, however, it would seem that the company is in a satisfactory trading position. Expansion of sales has been achieved without substantial reduction in margins and without disproportionate inflation of stock and debtor inventories.

It seems clear that substantial replacement of fixed assets must be necessary, and for this purpose the company has a reserve of $65,000 in addition to its accumulated depreciation. Quite apart from capital expenditure requirements, the company is in a difficult liquid position. It is not known to what extent creditors are pressing for payment. Moreover, with dividends covered nearly four times by available earnings, shareholders may be dissatisfied.

Schedule A: Interpretation of accounts

(a) *Sales and operating profit*
    (i) *Trading position*

	19–2 $000	19–2 %	19–3 $000	19–3 %	Change %
Net sales	1,070.00	100.0	1,565.00	100.00	+47
Gross margin	260.50	24.3	340.00	21.7	−2.6
Selling and administrative costs	149.43	13.9	194.31	12.4	−1.5
	111.07	10.4	145.69	9.3	−1.1

(ii) *Return on capital*

Operating profit plus/(minus) other income/(expenses) as a percentage of total capital employed—net worth plus fixed asset replacement reserve:

$$\frac{19\text{–}2}{} \quad \frac{\$91{,}070}{191{,}000} \times 100 = 47.7\% \quad \frac{19\text{–}3}{} \quad \frac{\$151{,}365}{266{,}251} \times 100 = 56.7\% \quad \text{Change } +9\%$$

(b) *Working capital*

   (i) *Current ratio*
   Current assets:current liabilities, bills and provisions

19–2	19–3	Change
0.85:1	1.3:1	+0.45x

(ii) *Liquidity ratio*
Current assets excluding inventories:current liabilities, bills and provisions

19–2	19–3	Change
0.40:1	0.71:1	+0.31x

(iii) *Stock turnover ratio*

$$\frac{\text{Cost of sales}}{\text{Average of opening/closing inventory}}$$

	19–2	19–3	Change
No. of times turned over	14.02	14.40	+0.38x

(This may be extremely misleading, as no information is given of the extent to which raw material and partly finished stocks enter into the total inventories.)

(iv) Debtors to sales, expressed as number of weeks sales:

19–2	19–3	Change
$\frac{\$52{,}500}{1{,}070{,}000} \times 52$	$\frac{\$95{,}000}{1{,}565{,}000} \times 52$	
= 2.5 weeks	= 3.15 weeks	0.65 week

Schedule B: Source and application of funds statement

	£	£
Source of funds		
Profit before tax		151,365
Adjustments for item not involving movement of funds—depreciation		60,000
Total generated from operations		211,365
Other sources:		
Sale of assets (see note)	10,000	
Issue of shares	2,000	
		12,000
		223,365
Application of funds		
Purchase of fixed assets	59,000	
Dividends paid re:		
19–2	2,000	
19–3	12,000	
Tax paid	63,115	
		136,115
		87,250
Increase in working capital		
Increase in:		
Stocks	40,000	
Debtors and prepayments	44,500	
Creditors	(43,000)	
Accrued expenses	(20,750)	
Decrease in bills of exchange	40,000	
Movement in net liquid funds:		
Increase in cash balance	26,500	
		87,250

(b)   *Schedule of additional statements required*

Statement	Reasons
(i) Accounts covering the two years 19–0 and 19–1.	So that the trend of results and of cash flows can be examined.
(ii) Sales analyses for the past five years showing units as well as turnover.	In order to examine changes in the mix of products and selling prices, and changes in sales outlets.

(iii)	Analyses of stock and debtors.	To determine stock categories and the ageing of debtors.
(iv)	Number of customers and suppliers.	To ensure that the company has an adequate range of sales outlets and sources of supply.
(v)	Cost breakdown for the last two years.	To examine changes in cost structure. It is noticeable that in 19–3 as opposed to 19–2 there have been the following increases: Raw materials 30% (subject to stock adjustments); Direct labour 64%; Factory overhead 83%. These figures indicate that there may have been material changes in manufacturing processes or in the nature of products manufactured.
(vi)	Statement from the board of Exploitation Associates Inc setting out clearly the purposes for which finance required, supported by forward budgets, with particular reference to: (1) sales budget and market research reports; (2) cash budgets, including detailed capital expenditure budget; (3) working capital budgets; (4) profit forecasts.	To ensure that management are competent and forward-looking, and to assess the feasibility of the proposition.
(vii)	Statement of proposed security of gurantees (if any) for finance raised.	To estimate the risk involved.
(viii)	Statement from management of any known present or anticipated future difficulties.	To ensure that the forward budgets are realistic.

(ix) Auditors' long reports to the members of the company.	These compare with letters of weakness, and are written by Certified Public Accountants to the members of American companies.
(x) Summaries showing the rights of shareholders and the borrowing powers of the company. Also a distribution summary of shares issued.	Information of this nature must be considered before steps are taken either to purchase shares or to make loans. Major shareholdings must also be identified.

ANSWER U1. UPPINGHAM LTD

(a) *Historical cost accounts*

	£	£
Sales 31 Jan.		2,000
38 Feb.		1,000
31 Mar.		1,100
		4,100
Cost of sales		
31 Jan. ($\frac{4}{5} \times 750$)	600	
28 Feb. ($\frac{1}{5} \times 750$)	150	
($\frac{1}{4} \times 1,400$)	350	
31 Mar. ($\frac{2}{4} \times 1,400$)	700	
		1,800
		2,300

(b) *Current purchasing power accounting*

		£
Sales		
31 Jan. 2,000 × $\frac{240}{220}$		2,182
28 Feb. 1,000 × $\frac{240}{230}$		1,043
31 Mar.		1,100
		4,325

Cost of sales

	HC £	Adj. to year end RPI	CPP £
Purchased 1 Jan.	750 ×	$\frac{240}{200}$	900
31 Jan.	1,050 ×	$\frac{240}{220}$	1,145
			2,045
	1,800		
			2,280

Financial Accounting

(c) *Current cost accounting*

	£	£
Sales (as for historical cost)		4,100
Cost of sales		
31 Jan.	1,400	
28 Feb. ($\frac{200}{50} \times 200$)	800	
31 Mar. ($\frac{200}{100} \times 500$)	1,000	3,200
		900

ANSWER U2. SOUTHPORT MANUFACTURING CO LTD

Current cost profit and loss account for the year ended 31 Dec. 19–8

	£000	£000
Turnover		800,000
Profit before interest and taxation as in the historical cost accounts		121,500
Less:		
Current cost adjustments		
Cost of sales	11,664	
Depreciation	5,739	
Monetary working capital	21,239	
		38,642
Current cost operating profit		82,858
Gearing adjustment	17,019	
Interest payable	(15,300)	
		1,719
Current cost profit before taxation		84,577
Taxation		51,000
Current cost profit attributable to shareholders		33,577
Dividends		30,000
Current cost profit retained		3,577

Current cost earnings per share 22.4p

Current cost balance sheet at 31 Dec.

	19–7			19–8	
£000	£000		£000	£000
		Assets employed		
	350,476	Fixed assets (note 3)		413,251
		Net current assets:		
53,857		Stock	76,235	
106,500		Monetary working capital	95,200	
160,357		Total working capital	171,435	
(15,000)		Proposed dividends	(20,000)	
(33,000)		Other current liabilities (net)	(49,500)	
	112,357			101,935
	462,833			515,186
		Financed by:		
		Share capital and reserves		
150,000		Share capital	150,000	
32,333		Current cost reserves (note 2)	81,109	
80,500		Retained profit	84,077	
	262,833			315,186
	200,000	5% debenture stock		200,000
	462,833			515,186

Workings

1. *Cost of sales adjustment*

	HC		CC	Difference
	£000	Index adjustment	£000	£000
Opening stock	52,000	$\times \frac{160}{140}$	59,428	7,428
Closing stock	72,000	$\times \frac{160}{170}$	67,764	4,236
				11,664

Financial Accounting

2. *Depreciation adjustment*

	HC £000	Index adjustment	CC £000	Difference £000
Charge for year:				
—on assets owned all year	40,000	$\times \frac{120}{105}$	45,714	5,714
—on purchased during year	2,000	$\times \frac{(122 + 125) \div 2}{122}$	2,025	25
	42,000		47,739	5,739

3. *Monetary working capital adjustment*

	HC £000	Index adjustment	CC £000	Difference £000
Opening debtors Less: Creditors	106,500	$\times \frac{160}{(140 + 145) \div 2}$	119,579	13,079
Closing debtors Less: Creditors	95,200	$\times \frac{160}{(170 + 180) \div 2}$	87,040	8,160
				21,239

4. *Gearing adjustment*

   (a) *Shareholders' interest at current cost*

	19–7 £000	19–7 £000	19–8 £000	19–8 £000
Per HC accounts				
—Share capital		150,000		150,000
—General revenue reserve		80,500		105,700
—Proposed dividend		15,000		20,000
		245,500		275,700

Add: Increases in year end value of non-monetary assets when restated from HC to CC

—Stock
—HC   52,000   72,000
—CC $\times \frac{145}{140}$ 53,857 $\times \frac{180}{170}$ 76,235
                          1,857   4,235

—Fixed assets (NBV)
  Bought 1.1.–6
—HC   320,000   280,000
—CC $\times \frac{115}{105}$ 350,476 $\times \frac{125}{105}$ 333,333
                          30,476   53,333

Bought 30.9.–8
—HC   —   78,000
—CC   — $\times \frac{125}{122}$ 79,918
                                —   1,918

                               277,833   335,186

Average $\dfrac{277,833 + 335,186}{2}$ = £306,510 (K)

(b) *Net borrowings*

	19–7 £000	19–8 £000
Debentures	200,000	200,000
Corporation tax	41,000	51,000
	241,000	251,000
Less: Cash	8,000	1,500
	233,000	249,500

Average   £241,250 (K)

Financial Accounting

(c) *Gearing adjustment*

$$\frac{241{,}250}{241{,}250 + 306{,}510} \times (11{,}664 + 5{,}739 + 21{,}239) = £17{,}019 \text{ (K)}$$

5. *Current cost EPS*

$$\frac{33{,}577{,}000}{150{,}000{,}000} = 22.4\text{p}$$

6. *Current cost reserve*

	19–7 £000	19–8 £000	Increase/ (decrease) £000
Unrealised surpluses on non-monetary assets held at year end			
—Stock	1,857	4,235	2,378
—Fixed assets	30,476	55,251	24,775
CC P + L adjustments to date			
—cost of sales	—	11,664	11,664
—depreciation		5,739	5,739
—monetary working capital		21,239	21,239
—gearing adjustment		(17,019)	(17,019)
	32,333	81,109	48,776

7. *Retained profit*

	19–7 £000	19–8 £000
Per HC accounts	80,500	105,700
Less: CC P + L adjustments to date		
—cost of sales	—	(11,664)
—depreciation	—	(5,739)
—monetary working capital	—	(21,239)
—gearing	—	17,019
	80,500	84,077

8. *Gross value of fixed assets at 31.12.–8*

	HC £000	Index adjustment	CC £000
Bought 1.1–6	400,000	× $\frac{125}{105}$	476,190
Bought 30.9.–8	80,000	× $\frac{125}{122}$	81,967
	480,000		558,157

Notes to current cost accounts

Note 1

A. *General description of current cost accounts*

The current cost accounts have been prepared in compliance with SSAP *16*. The current cost system, whilst not a system of accounting for general inflation, allows for price changes specific to the business when reporting assets employed and profits thereon.

The *current cost operating profit* is the surplus (before interest and taxation) arising from the ordinary activities of the business in the period. It is determined after allowing for the impact of price changes on the funds needed to maintain the productive assets of the business (the net operating assets) but does not take into account the way in which these assets are financed.

This result is achieved by making adjustments to trading profit before interest calculated on the historical cost basis. These adjustments are described in sections B and C below.

The *current cost profit attributable to shareholders* is the surplus allowing for the impact of price changes on the funds needed to maintain only their proportion of the net operating assets. It is shown after interest, taxation and the gearing adjustment described in section D below.

In the *balance sheet* fixed assets and stocks are included at their current cost (net of depreciation on fixed assets).

Corresponding amounts for previous period are shown in values relating to last year, without further adjustment. This is the first year for which the company has prepared current cost accounts and corresponding figures are not shown in the profit and loss account since they are not readily available.

B. *Fixed assets and depreciation*

The gross current cost of fixed assets has been derived as follows:

Plant and specialized buildings have been restated using appropriate government indices applied to the historical costs.

Asset lives have been reviewed upon the introduction of current cost accounting and the existing asset lives were found to be adequate.

Total depreciation charged in the CC profit and loss account represents the average current cost of the proportion of fixed assets consumed in the period. The depreciation adjustment is the difference between the depreciation charge in the HC and CC accounts.

C. *Working capital*

This includes stocks (including work-in-progress) and trade debtors less trade creditors.

In order to allow for the impact of price changes on working capital, two adjustments are made to the operatings costs calculated on the historical cost basis, one on stock and the other on monetary working capital. The adjustments are based on movements in price indices issued by the Government Statistical Service. These indices reflect closely the changes in input prices experienced by the company.

D. *The gearing adjustment*

A proportion, called the gearing proportion, of the net operating assets of the business is financed by borrowing. As the obligation to repay borrowing is fixed in monetary amounts, irrespective of price changes on the proportion of assets so financed, it is unnessary to provide for the impact of price changes on these assets when determining the current cost profit attributable to shareholders. Thus, the gearing adjustment has been applied which abates the current cost operating adjustments by the average gearing proportion in the year.

E. *Other accounting policies*

Except as set out above the policies used in the current cost accounts are the same as those used in the historical cost accounts.

Note 2

	£000	£000	£000
Current cost reserve			
Balance at 1 Jan. 19–8			32,333
Revaluation surpluses reflecting price changes			
—Plant and machinery (24,775 + 5,739)		30,514	
—Stocks and work-in-progress (2,378 + 11,664)		14,042	
		44,556	
—Monetary working capital adjustment		21,239	
—Gearing adjustment		(17,019)	
			48,776
Balance at 31 Dec. 19–8			81,109
of which = realised			21,623
unrealised (4,235 + 55,251)			59,486
			81,109

Note 3

Fixed assets

	31 Dec. 19–8			19–7
	Gross CRC £000	Depn. £000	Net CRC £000	Net CRC £000
Plant and machinery	558,157	144,906	413,251	350,476

ANSWER U3. REEFLY LTD

	Stock	Relevant index numbers
1 Jan. 19–0	300,000	120 (30.11.–9)
30 Jun.	800,000	140
31 Dec.	500,000	156 (30.11.–8)

1. COSA (1 Jan. to 30 Jun.)
   $= (800{,}000 - 300{,}000) - (800{,}000 \times \frac{133\cdot 5}{140} - 300{,}000 \times \frac{133\cdot 5}{120})$
   $= 500{,}000 - (762{,}857 - 333{,}750)$
   $= +70{,}893$

2. COSA (30 Jun. to 31 Dec.)
   $= (500{,}000 - 800{,}000) - (500{,}000 \times \frac{151}{156} - 800{,}000 \times \frac{151}{140})$
   $= -300{,}000 - (483{,}974 - 862{,}857)$
   $= -300{,}000 - (-378{,}883)$
   $= +78{,}883$

The overall cost of sales adjustment is therefore
£70,893 + £78,883 = £149,776

		£000	
MWCA Opening WC = D		150	
	C	120	
		——	30
Closing WC = D		250	
	C	228	
		——	22

$= (22 - 30) - (22 \times \frac{140}{156} - 30 \times \frac{140}{120})$
$= -8{,}000 - (19{,}743 - 35{,}000)$
$= -8{,}000 - (-15{,}257)$
$= £7{,}257$

Plant and machinery—as in
   Current cost accounts

	Gross	Acc. depn.
Adjust opening values (1.1.–0)		
1.1.–5 £300,000 $\times \frac{200}{110}$ =	545,454	272,727 ($\frac{5}{10}$)
1.1.–8 £400,000 $\times \frac{200}{150}$ =	533,333	106,666 ($\frac{2}{10}$)
	1,078,787 (A)	379,393 (B)
(A) Increase in value to mid-year		
$\times \frac{20}{200}$	107,879	
(B) Backlog depreciation		
$\times \frac{42}{200}$		79,673
	1,186,666 (C)	459,066
Purchase on 30.6.–0	400,000 (D)	
c/f	1,586,666 (E)	459,066

Financial Accounting

		Gross	Acc. depn.
	b/f	1,586,666	459,066
Year's depreciation charge			
(C) × 10%			118,667 (F)
(D) × 5%			20,000 (F)
Effect of price change			
Mid-year to year end			
(E) × $\frac{22}{220}$		158,667	
(F) × $\frac{22}{220}$			13,867
Closing balance sheet		1,745,333	611,600

Depreciation adjustments	£
CCA charge (F)	138,667
Historic cost charge	90,000
Adjustment	48,667

Adjustment opening and closing stock values	
Opening value: Historic	300,000
CCA value: 300,000 × $\frac{125}{120}$	312,500
	12,500
Closing value: Historic	500,000
CCA value: 500,000 × $\frac{160}{156}$	512,821
Adjustment	12,821

To prepare gearing adjustment

Extract from closing balance sheet (CCA)

	£
Plant and machinery	1,745,333
Less: Acc. depreciation	611,600
	1,133,733
Stock ($\frac{160}{156} \times 500$)	512,821
Debtors	250,000
Cash	50,000
	1,946,554
Liabilities	
Creditors	228,000
Taxation	112,000
Loan stock	600,000
	940,000
Shareholders' funds	1,006,554
	1,946,554

Opening balance sheet (CCA)

	£
Plant and machinery	1,078,787
Acc. depreciation	379,393
	699,394
Stock ($\frac{125}{120} \times 300$)	312,500
Debtors	150,000
Cash	200,000
	1,361,894
Creditors	120,000
Taxation	100,000
Loan stock	400,000
	620,000
Shareholders' funds	741,894
	1,361,894

Gearing adjustment

Shareholders' funds

		£
Opening		741,894
Closing		1,006,554
		1,748,448
Average for year		874,224

Net borrowings

	Opening	Closing
Taxation	100,000	112,000
Loan stock	400,000	600,000
	500,000	712,000
Less: Cash	200,000	50,000
	300,000	662,000
Average for year		481,000

Gearing ratio $\dfrac{481,000}{874,224 + 481,000} = 35.5\%$

Adjustments in profit and loss account

	£
Depreciation	48,667
Cost of sales	149,776
MWCA	7,257
	205,700

Gearing adjustment 35.5% × £205,700 = £73,023

Current cost profit and loss account for year ending 31 Dec. 19–0

	£	£
Historical cost profit (after depn.)		210,000
CCA adjustments		205,700
Current cost operating profit		4,300
Gearing adjustment	73,023	
Less: Interest	50,000	
		23,023
		27,323
Less: Tax		80,000
Current cost loss		(52,677)
Dividends		40,000
Loss to reserves		(92,677)

Current cost reserve
   Opening balance

	£	£
Plant and machinery		
CCA Gross	1,078,787	
Depreciation	379,393	
	699,394	
Less: Opening historical (net)	470,000	
		229,394
Stock		12,500
		241,894
Revaluation in Year P and M	266,546	
Depn.	93,540	
		173,006
Stock, increase in reserve		321
MWCA		7,257
Cost of sales		149,776
Gearing		(73,023)
		499,231

Financial Accounting

Current cost summarised balance sheet as at 31 Dec. 19–0

		£
Assets (as listed above)		1,946,554
Liabilities (as listed above)		940,000
		1,006,554

	£	£
Ordinary shares		300,000
Revenue reserves	300,000	
Excess of outgoings	92,677	
		207,323
Current cost reserve		499,231
		1,006,554

ANSWER U4. CHELSEA RETAILERS PLC

(a) The monetary working capital adjustment is an attempt to reflect both:
(i) The inflationary cost of maintaining the value of the monetary assets included in working capital.
(ii) The contribution to the financing of the inflationary increases in monetary and non-monetary trading assets made by monetary liabilities included in working capital.

The adjustment is best viewed as an extension of the principles and need for the cost of sales adjustment. The cost of sales adjustment is a recognition of the need to reserve historical cost profits to maintain the physical capacity of an enterprise to invest in stock. The MWCA extends this principle to other elements of working capital.

For example, a business which sells goods on credit terms will, in a period of rising costs, need to retain funds to finance a higher monetary value of both stocks and debtors in order to maintain its capacity to sell stock units to customers on credit terms. In contrast, a business which buys goods from suppliers on credit terms will be able to obtain some of the finance to purchase stock at higher prices from those suppliers who are willing to increase the amount of credit for that business.

(b) Items to be included in MWC:

Debtors
Cash (It is assumed that this represents money in tills of the retail company)
Trade creditors

It is assumed that the averaging method can be applied solely by reference to opening and closing balance sheet figures, i.e. working capital has moved steadily throughout the period.

Form of calculation

$$\left(\begin{matrix}\text{Opening}\\ \text{MWC}\end{matrix} \times \frac{\text{Representative index no. for period}}{\text{Index no. at typical transaction date}}\right) - \begin{matrix}\text{Opening}\\ \text{MWC}\end{matrix} = \text{Part of MWCA}$$

Creditors
Assume that they arise over same period as stocks (three months). Stock price index is appropriate and indices relate to price levels ruling during the month.

$$50 - \left\{50 \times \frac{132}{\left[\frac{115+117+118}{3}\right]}\right\} = (6{,}555)$$

$$\left\{60 \times \frac{132}{\left[\frac{138+140+141}{3}\right]}\right\} - 60 = (3{,}300)$$

$$\underline{(9{,}855)}$$

Debtors
Assume stock price index is appropriate.

$$\left\{40 \times \frac{132}{\left[\frac{117+118}{2}\right]}\right\} - 40 = 4{,}936$$

$$50 - \left\{50 \times \frac{132}{\left[\frac{140+141}{2}\right]}\right\} = 3{,}025$$

$$\underline{7{,}961}$$

Cash
Assume stock price index is appropriate. Balance sheet data is transaction date.

$$21 \times \left\{ \frac{132}{\left[\frac{118 + 120}{2}\right]} \right\} - 21 = 2,294$$

$$15 - \left\{ 15 \times \frac{132}{141*} \right\} = \underline{\underline{\begin{array}{c} 957 \\ \hline 3,251 \end{array}}}$$

* Index for Jan. 1981 also required but not given in the question.

$$\text{MWCA } (9,855) + 7,961 + 3,251 = \underline{\underline{1,357}}$$

$$\text{approx} = \underline{\underline{1,400}}$$

(c) There are a number of reasons why some authorities do not believe that a monetary working capital adjustment is necessary.

(i) In the view of the Sandilands Committee (*para. 537*) no gains or losses on monetary items should be recognised in CCA, since the accounts are drawn up in monetary units (pounds) not units of purchasing power. The approach in the *Sandilands Report* was to eliminate holding gains on non-monetary assets from the profit and loss account on the grounds that adjustments for stock and fixed assets alone provided a comprehensive system of accounting for inflation.

(ii) Some authorities argue that the monetary working capital adjustment confuses profitability with liquidity. The inclusion of liabilities in monetary working capital provides a CCA 'gain' not supported by a tangible asset. It may encourage too great a reliance by companies on short-term finance.

(iii) Some accept that monetary assets form an essential part of operating capability but reject the notion that creditors can reduce the company's need, except in the short term, to finance such assets from within.

(iv) Some accept the principle that liabilities reduce the need for internal financing but reject the split made in *SSAP 16* between the MWCA and the gearing adjustment. The split of monetary items between working capital and others is rejected as arbitrary in many cases.

(v) Some argue that any gain or loss on monetary items is related not to the specific cost of goods purchased and sold but instead to the fall in the value of money itself which is more accurately reflected by the use of a general index such as the RPI.

INDEX

Accounts—general
  purpose and use of accounts   A1, A4
  comparison between accounts and cash flow statements   A2
  preparation of profit under different accounting bases   B4
Accounting standards *see* SSAPs
Acquisitions and re-organisations
  acquisition of two companies by a third by means of a share issue   G1, G2
  acquisition of company and partnership by a third by means of a share issue   G3
Analysis of accounts   T6
  ratio analysis   T4

Branch accounting
  one set of books at head office   P1, P2
  one set of books with incomplete records maintained   P4
  two sets of books   P3, P5

Cash flow statements
  preparation of cash flow statement and comparison to profit statement   A9, T5
Companies Act 1985 (*see also* Statutory accounts)
  definition of distributable, non-distributable, realised and unrealised profits   C2
  capital redemption reserve—purposes and uses   C4
Consignment accounts   S2
Consolidation (*see also* SSAP 1; SSAP 14)
  preparation of consolidated balance sheet:
    preference shares, unrealised profit in stock and inter-company dividends   H1
    two subsidiaries and debit balance on reserves   H2
    mixed group   H3, J11
    loss making subsidiary   J9
    indirect consolidation required   J10
  preparation of consolidated profit and loss account:
    acquisition during year and pre-acquisition dividends   J3
    disposal of subsidiary during year   J4
    partial disposal of subsidiary during year   J5

  partial disposal of subsidiary during year with subsidiary turning into an associate   J6
  preparation of consolidated accounts of groups including associated companies   J2, K3, K4, K5
Container accounts   S3

Depreciation, *see* SSAP 12

Exit value accounting   A3

Hire purchase
  books of purchaser   R1
  books of seller   R2, R3
  hire purchase in the books of seller combined with other types of trading   R4, R5

Inflation in accounts, *see* SSAP 16
Incomplete records
  preparation of accounts from incomplete information   N1
  preparation of income and expenditure accounts from incomplete information   N2, N3

Joint venture accounts
  preparation of joint venture accounts   M1, M3
  cash flow projections for joint venture   M2

Partnership accounts
  application of rule from Garner v Murray   L1
  sale of partnership to a limited company   L2, L4
  amalgamation and dissolution of partnerships   L3

Royalty accounts   S1

Share capital and debentures
  redemption of share capital   F1
  issue and allotment of shares   F2, F4
  sinking fund accounting and debenture redemption   F3, F4
SSAP 1 (*see also* Consolidation)   K1, K2
SSAP 2   B1, E3
SSAP 3   B2
SSAP 4   E3
SSAP 5   E2

SSAP 6   C9, E5
SSAP 8   C10, E2
SSAP 9   B5, B6, E1, E4
SSAP 10   T1, T2
SSAP 12   B7, B8, E6
SSAP 13   B9
SSAP 14   (*see also* Consolidation)   J1
SSAP 15   B10, B11
SSAP 16   A6, A7, A8, U1, U2, U3, U4
SSAP 17   E7
SSAP 18   E7
SSAP 20   J7, J8
SSAP 21   E8
SSAP 22   J12
Statutory accounts
    discussion of various items appearing in accounts (reserves, fixed assets, accounting policies and extraordinary items)   B3
    definition and disclosure of liabilities, provisions and reserves   C1
    comprehensive disclosure requirements:
      directors' report   C6
      profit and loss account   C3
      whole of the accounts   C7, C8
      directors' emoluments   C5
Stock and work in progress (*see SSAP 9*)
Stock exchange
    rules governing provision of information to stock exchange   D1
    additional accounts disclosure requirements   D2
Value added statements
    discussion and preparation of a value added statement   A5
    discussion of corporate objectives and preparation of value added statement   T3

COURSES RUN BY CHART FOULKS LYNCH
Tick box for details

ORAL TUITION
Institute of Chartered Accountants in England and Wales
    Graduate Conversion Course ☐
    Professional I ☐
    Professional II ☐
Institute of Cost and Management Accountants
    Intensive revision ☐
Chartered Association of Certified Accounts
    Full-time and intensive revision ☐
Association of Accounting Technicians
    Full-time ☐
    Full-time and intensive revision ☐
Institute of Taxation – one and two week intensive revision ☐
Insolvency Practitioners Association
    Intensive Revision ☐
LL.B. External Law Degree Full-time and intensive revision ☐
G.C.E. 'A'-Levels Full-time and intensive revision ☐

CORRESPONDENCE COURSES
Institute of Chartered Accountants in England and Wales ☐
Chartered Association of Certified Accountants ☐
Institute of Cost and Management Accountants ☐
Association of Accounting Technicians ☐
Institute of Taxation ☐
Tax Update for the Accountant in Industry ☐
Institute of Bankers ☐
Institute of Chartered Secretaries and Administrators ☐
LL.B. External Law Degrees ☐
'A' Levels ☐
Insolvency Practitioners Association ☐
Association of Corporate Treasurers ☐

Please PRINT:

Name_____

Address_____

_____

POSTCODE_____ TELEPHONE_____

For details please return this form to: Chart Foulks Lynch PLC,
53 Great Sutton Street, London EC1V 0DQ,
or telephone 01-251 4981 (24 hours).

CHART FOULKS LYNCH – WHERE QUALITY COUNTS